Turkish-Azerbaijani Relations

An east-west axis of Azerbaijan and Turkey has grown into prominence within the broader structure of regional dynamics in Eurasia over the past two decades. Yet few, including among policy advisers and policymakers in either of the two states, have attempted to look deeper into the forces that lie behind the workings of this important regional nexus, a reality that resulted in a dual crisis in bilateral relations towards the end of the second decade of interaction.

This volume investigates the underlying causes that shaped the dynamics within the structure of the bilateral relationship between Azerbaijan and Turkey. It features chapters by both scholars from the region and international experts in the field, and therefore provides both in-house and outside perspectives on developments within the complex structure of the relationship. With its analysis portfolio including historical, political, economic, socio-cultural, ideological, and international underpinnings of this regional alliance, the volume offers the most systematic and broad ranged analysis of the matter available to date.

The book will serve as an important resource for students and scholars of post-Soviet Studies, Central Asia and the Caucasus, and the Middle East, while also being of interest to those of International Relations and political science disciplines.

Murad Ismayilov is PhD Researcher in Development Studies at the University of Cambridge, UK.

Norman A. Graham is Professor of International Relations at James Madison College of Public Affairs and Director of the Center for European, Russian and Eurasian Studies, Michigan State University, USA.

Routledge Advances in Central Asian Studies

1 **Oil, Transition and Security in Central Asia**
   Edited by Sally N. Cummings

2 **The European Union and Central Asia**
   Edited by Alexander Warkotsch

3 **Politics, Identity and Education in Central Asia**
   Edited by Pinar Akcali and Cennet Engin-Demir

4 **Regime Transition in Central Asia**
   Stateness, nationalism and political change in Tajikistan and Uzbekistan
   Dagikhudo Dagiev

5 **Power, Networks and Violent Conflict in Central Asia**
   A comparison of Tajikistan and Uzbekistan
   Idil Tunçer-Kılavuz

6 **From Conflict to Autonomy in the Caucasus**
   The Soviet Union and the making of Abkhazia, South Ossetia and Nagorno Karabakh
   Arsène Saparov

7 **Identity and Politics in Central Asia and the Caucasus**
   Edited by Murad Ismayilov and Mohammed Ayoob

8 **Turkish-Azerbaijani Relations**
   One nation – two states?
   Edited by Murad Ismayilov and Norman A. Graham

Turkish-Azerbaijani Relations

One nation – two states?

**Edited by
Murad Ismayilov and
Norman A. Graham**

LONDON AND NEW YORK

First published 2016
by Routledge
2 Park Square, Milton Park, Abingdon, Oxon OX14 4RN

and by Routledge
711 Third Avenue, New York, NY 10017

Routledge is an imprint of the Taylor & Francis Group, an informa business

© 2016 Murad Ismayilov and Norman A. Graham

The right of the editors to be identified as the authors of the editorial material, and of the authors for their individual chapters, has been asserted in accordance with sections 77 and 78 of the Copyright, Designs and Patents Act 1988.

All rights reserved. No part of this book may be reprinted or reproduced or utilised in any form or by any electronic, mechanical, or other means, now known or hereafter invented, including photocopying and recording, or in any information storage or retrieval system, without permission in writing from the publishers.

Trademark notice: Product or corporate names may be trademarks or registered trademarks, and are used only for identification and explanation without intent to infringe.

British Library Cataloguing in Publication Data
A catalogue record for this book is available from the British Library

Library of Congress Cataloging-in-Publication Data
Names: Ismayilov, Murad, editor of compilation. | Graham, Norman A., editor of compilation.
Title: Turkish-Azerbaijani relations : one nation—two states? / edited by Murad Ismayilov and Norman A. Graham.
Description: Abingdon, Oxon ; New York, NY : Routledge, 2016. | Series: Routledge advances in Central Asian studies ; 8 | Includes bibliographical references and index.
Identifiers: LCCN 2015048459 | ISBN 9781138650817 (hardback) | ISBN 9781315625119 (ebook)
Subjects: LCSH: Turkey—Foreign relations—Azerbaijan. | Azerbaijan—Foreign relations—Turkey. | Caucasus, South—Strategic aspects.
Classification: LCC DR479.A94 T87 2016 | DDC 327.56104754—dc23
LC record available at http://lccn.loc.gov/2015048459

ISBN: 978-1-138-65081-7 (hbk)
ISBN: 978-1-315-62511-9 (ebk)

Typeset in Times New Roman
by Apex CoVantage, LLC

Printed and bound in Great Britain by
TJ International Ltd, Padstow, Cornwall

Contents

List of tables vii
List of contributors viii
Acknowledgements xi
List of abbreviations xii

1 **Together but apart for twenty years: Azerbaijan and Turkey in pursuit of identity and survival**   1
MURAD ISMAYILOV

2 **Turkish-Azerbaijani relations: brothers in arms or brothers in the dark?**   21
ELNUR SOLTANOV

3 **Geopolitics versus ideology: Azerbaijan in Turkish views on Eurasia**   54
EMRE ERŞEN

4 **The bilateral origins of South Caucasus trilateralism**   72
MICHAEL H. CECIRE

5 **Azerbaijan–Turkey relations through the prism of economic transactions: a view from Azerbaijan**   88
ELKIN NURMAMMADOV

6 **State–business relations in Azerbaijan through the eyes of Turkish businesspeople**   113
PINAR BEDIRHANOĞLU

7 **Turkey and Azerbaijan: one religion – two states?**   127
SOFIE BEDFORD

8 **Conclusion: Azerbaijan, Turkey and the future of Eurasia**   150
   NORMAN A. GRAHAM

   Index   165

Tables

4.1	Georgian foreign trade, 2014 (USD)	79
5.1	Comparison of Turkey's trade with Azerbaijan and Georgia	90
5.2	Comparison of Azerbaijan's trade with Turkey and Russia	91
5.3	Comparison of Turkey's trade with Azerbaijan and Kazakhstan	92
5.4	Turkey's share in Azerbaijan's trade	93
5.5	Non-oil exports of Azerbaijan, 2003–2010	94
5.6	Imports of Azerbaijan, 2003–2010	94
5.7	Composition of Azerbaijani exports to Turkey	95
5.8	Composition of Turkish exports to Azerbaijan	96
5.9	Turkey's non-oil FDI in Azerbaijan	98
5.10	Selected macroeconomic indicators, 2010	104
5.11	*Doing Business* rankings for Azerbaijan, Turkey and Georgia, 2010–11	105
5.12	Trading across border rankings, 2011	106
5.13	Logistics Performance Index (LPI) for selected countries	106
5.14	World Economic Forum Competitiveness Report 2011: rankings for selected items for Azerbaijan and Turkey	108

Contributors

Sofie Bedford has a PhD in political science from Stockholm University and an MA in Peace and Conflict Research from Uppsala University. Her doctoral thesis, titled *Islamic Activism in Azerbaijan: Repression and Mobilization in a Post-Soviet Context* (Stockholm: Dept. of Political Science 2009), focused on internal, contextual and interactional aspects of the mobilization of two mosque communities in Baku. She is currently a researcher at the Uppsala Centre for Russian and Eurasian Studies at Uppsala University, where her work focuses on opposition and democracy activism across the post-Soviet sphere. She has previously been associated with the Stockholm International Peace Research Institute (SIPRI), the Swedish Defence Research Institute, the International Rescue Committee and the United Nations Development Program, and she is currently a board member of the Association for Friends of the Swedish Istanbul Institute (Föreningen svenska Istanbul institutets vänner).

Pınar Bedirhanoğlu is Associate Professor in the Department of International Relations at Middle East Technical University in Ankara, Turkey. She received her Ph.D. in international relations from the University of Sussex in Britain in 2002. She also taught at the Azerbaijan Diplomatic Academy in Baku in the 2012–13 academic year. She has published in English and Turkish on the politics of capitalist transformation in Russia, state restructuring in the neoliberal era, the political economy of corruption and anti-corruption policies, state restructuring, state-capital relations, and privatizations in Turkey and the 2008 financial crisis. Her most recent research interests include state transformation in Azerbaijan, the neoliberal transformation of states' security apparatuses and global trends in financial regulation.

Michael Hikari Cecire is Associate Scholar at the Philadelphia-based Foreign Policy Research Institute, where he primarily contributes to the Project on Democratic Transitions, which monitors and studies political development in Eurasia and worldwide. Between 2006 and 2011, he spent several years living, working and traveling throughout the South Caucasus and Black Sea region. In 2011, he was a Visiting Scholar at the Harriman Institute at Columbia University in New York conducting independent research on Turkey–Caucasus relations. His research interests include Turkey–Caucasus relations, South

Caucasus geopolitics, Georgian domestic politics and Euro-Atlantic trends. He holds an MPA from the University of Pennsylvania and is a founding member of the Georgian Institute of Politics in Tbilisi.

Emre Erşen is Assistant Professor at Marmara University's Department of Political Science and International Relations. He received his PhD at the same department. He also conducted research at the Moscow Higher School of Economics (Russia), Jagiellonian University (Poland) and the University of Kent (United Kingdom) as a visiting scholar. He has written for a number of academic publications and contributed conference papers on Turkish foreign policy, Turkish–Russian relations and politics and international relations in Eurasia.

Norman A. Graham is Professor of International Relations at James Madison College of Public Affairs, Michigan State University (MSU). He also serves as the director of the Center for European, Russian and Eurasian Studies at the university. Graham's long-term research interests include international security and economic relations, international organization, Central and Southeastern Europe, and Central and South Asia. He has taught at Columbia University and led the Yale University Summer Seminar on International Business. He has also served as a Research Associate with the United Nations, the World Health Organization, and the Futures Group. He served as Associate Dean of James Madison College in 1999–2011, and Acting Dean 1998–99 and 2006–7. His teaching at MSU focuses on international economic relations and development, the European Union and related international organizations and the foreign policies of European and Eurasian countries. He directs the Center's summer overseas study program on "International Relations in Brussels" in conjunction with the Universite Libre de Bruxelles (ULB), the European Union and NATO, alternating also as director of the summer program on "Environmental Science and Policy in the Eastern Mediterranean Basin" in collaboration with several Greek and Turkish universities and research institutes. His current research focuses on industrial and technology development in the European Union; technology transfer and defense conversion in Europe, Russia and the former Soviet Union, the future of Eurasian security, and the political economy of transition and environmental policy in Central Asia and the Caucasus. He was the recipient of an MSU Teacher-Scholar award in 1993. His published research includes eight books and numerous articles. Graham earned his BA in European and Asian History from the University of Akron, his M. Phil. in International Relations and Political Economy from Columbia University and his PhD in Political Science from Columbia University.

Murad Ismayilov is a doctoral researcher at Politics, Psychology, Sociology and International Studies (PPSIS), the University of Cambridge. He holds an MSt in International Relations from the University of Cambridge (2009) and an MA in International Relations from Baku State University (2004). In 2005, he completed a four-month NATO Senior Executive Program at the NATO Studies Centre in Bucharest (Romania). His research interests include political and social theory (with a focus on critical approaches), sociology and political economy of culture, postcolonial theory, sociology and political economy of post-Soviet transformation (with a thematic focus on social stratification and class; nationalism, identity and state-society relations), social movements, sociology and political economy of power, sociology of class, sociology of intellectuals, sociology and security of the Middle East, sociology and political economy of religion, as well as Islamic political thought. He is co-editor of *Identity and Politics in Central Asia and the Caucasus* (London: Routledge, 2015). Among his other works are "Postcolonial Hybridity, Contingency, and the Mutual Embeddedness of Identity and Politics in Post-Soviet Azerbaijan: Some Initial Thoughts" (*Caucasus Analytical Digest* 77, 2015); "Power, Knowledge, and Pipelines: Understanding the Politics of Azerbaijan's Foreign Policy" (*Caucasus Studies* 2:1–2, 2014); "State, Identity, and the Politics of Music: Eurovision and Nation-Building in Azerbaijan" (*Nationalities Papers* 40:6, 2012); and "The Impact of Energy Resources on Nation- and State-Building: The Contrasting Cases of Azerbaijan and Georgia" (Brenda Shaffer and Taleh Ziyadov, eds. *Beyond the Resource Curse*, Philadelphia: University of Pennsylvania Press, 2012).

Elkin Nurmammadov has been assistant professor of economics at ADA University since 2009. He has a BA in Business Administration from Bogazici University (2004) and a PhD in Economics from the University of Georgia (2009). At ADA, he teaches courses on Microeconomics, Macroeconomics and International Trade and Finance at both undergraduate and graduate levels, as well as various short-term economics courses to participants of the Academy's various executive education programs. His research interests lie in macroeconomics, economic growth and development and financial development. His book chapter titled "Challenges of Central Banks in Oil-Exporting Countries: The Case of Azerbaijan" came out in *Beyond Resource Curse* (2012).

Elnur Soltanov is Assistant Professor at ADA University and Dean of the School of Public and International Affairs. He holds an MA in International Relations from Middle East Technical University (2003), Turkey, and a PhD in Political Science from Texas Tech University (2009), USA. Between 2000 and 2003, Soltanov worked as Research Fellow at the Center for Eurasian Strategic Studies (ASAM) in Ankara, Turkey, where he also served as the editor of *Avrasya Haber*, a joint project with the Turkish Cooperation and Development Agency (TCDA). Prior to joining ADA, Soltanov served as Assistant Professor of Political Science at Truman State University, Missouri. He also taught at Texas Tech University, Texas, and Slippery Rock University, Pennsylvania, USA. Soltanov's teaching and research interests cover international security, political economy and energy politics.

Acknowledgements

The idea for the project that gave birth to the present volume was conceived within the walls of ADA University (then known as Azerbaijan Diplomatic Academy) a few years ago as a response to the bewilderment in which many Azerbaijanis were left by Turkey's attempted rapprochement with Armenia in 2008 and the recognition of poor knowledge of their Turkish brethren which those developments prompted in Baku at the time. The project has since benefited considerably from the generous support that ADA has made available in various forms, including the continuous backing that the university's rector, Ambassador Hafiz Pashayev, personally invested to keep it going. We also wish to extend thanks to all who have contributed their feedback to help us improve the volume at various stages of its production, particularly to the participants of the workshop on Turkey–Azerbaijan relations kindly organised by the Center for European, Russian, and Eurasian Studies (CERES) of Michigan State University on 25 August 2015. Any shortfalls that remain are our responsibility.

Murad Ismayilov and Norman A. Graham
1 November 2015

Abbreviations

ACG	Azeri-Chirag-Gunashli
AIOC	Armenian Secret Army for the Liberation of Armenia
AKP	Justice and Development Party (Adalet ve Kalkınma Partisi)
ANAP	True Path Party
ASALA	Armenian Secret Army for the Liberation of Armenia
ATIB	Azerbaijan–Turkey Business Association
BTC	Baku-Tbilisi-Ceyhan
BTE	Baku-Tbilisi-Erzurum
BTK	Baku-Tbilisi-Kars
CRRC	Caucasus Research Resource Centers
CSCE	Conference on Security and Cooperation in Europe
CSCP	Caucasus Stability and Cooperation Platform
DYP	Motherland Party
FDI	Foreign direct investment
FTA	Free trade agreement
MHP	Nationalist Action Party
NK	Nagorno-Karabakh
OBT	Obsolescing bargaining theory
OECD	Organisation for Economic Co-operation and Development
OSCE	Organization for Security and Co-operation in Europe
PKK	Kurdish Worker's Party
SCWRO	State Committee for Work with Religious Organisations
SOCAR	State Oil Company of the Azerbaijan Republic
TANAP	Trans-Anatolian Natural Gas Pipeline
TPAO	Turkish Petroleum Corporation (Türkiye Petrolleri Anonim Ortaklığı)
TRNC	Turkish Republic of Northern Cyprus
TUSIAB	Turkish Business Association in Azerbaijan
WTO	World Trade Organization

1 Together but apart for twenty years

Azerbaijan and Turkey in pursuit of identity and survival

Murad Ismayilov

Azerbaijan's relationship with Turkey, given the outwardly intimate nature of its dynamics, has often been described as a cornerstone underpinning Baku's post-independence foreign policy strategy (e.g. Soltanov 2009). Yet few, including among policy advisers and policymakers in either of the two states, have attempted to look deeper into the forces that underlay the workings of the bilateral dynamics over the first two decades of the world free of the Soviet Union and the Cold War. The result was a dual crisis in bilateral relations towards the end of the second decade of interaction (around negotiations on a bilateral gas deal and around Turkey's attempted rapprochement with Armenia) on one hand and (particularly) an overall sense of distressful surprise, most notably within the Azerbaijani political and social spectrum, by which the crisis was met on the other (Goksel 2009; Kardaş 2009; Phillips 2012; Shiriyev and Davies 2013; also Osipova and Bilgin 2013). While policymakers on both sides have now taken steps towards addressing the omissions of the past that the recent crisis served to lay bare, few if any within academia have ventured into the study of the underlying causes that shaped and conditioned the dynamics within the structure of bilateral relations between Turkey and Azerbaijan since the time of the latter's independence. It is this question that the introductory essay – and the collection of chapters that follow – is meant to address.

Several factors, many often overlooked and their interpenetrating linkages often neglected, need to be accounted for if one is to develop a clear understanding of the evolving nature of Azerbaijan–Turkey relations and the constitutive influences behind their dynamics. Perhaps most importantly, the nature of bilateral dynamics between Baku and Ankara has been subject to, and in many ways a reflection of, the two states' own evolving self-perception as to their geography and geopolitics the latter prompted, state capacity and ambitions it worked to generate and ultimately the nature of state polity and indeed its identity.

With Azerbaijan emerging from the ruins of the Soviet Union and Turkey coming out of the ashes of the Cold War, the starting phase of Azerbaijan–Turkey fraternal partnership in the early 1990s fell on the period when neither of the two states had yet to develop a clear grasp not only of the other side, but also – and even more dramatically – of its own self. Neither Ankara nor Baku had yet to advance a clear 'post' identity – a post-colonial, post-Soviet identity for

Azerbaijan and a post–Cold War identity for Turkey – and a definite foreign (and domestic) policy agenda the latter understanding would entail. As the Cold War ended, Turkey found its role as a US and NATO-backed "regional gendarme" (ICG 2010, 1) in the backyard of the Soviet Union increasingly redundant and was prompted to search for a new regional identity to embody (cf. Cowell 1990). Consequently, the quest to fill the ideational gap left by the end of the Cold War formed a motivational backbone behind Turkey's foreign policy engagement choices over the past two decades. Following independence and given territorial losses amidst which the latter emerged and the overall regional security context in which it was set to survive, Azerbaijan, in turn, was left to look to devise numerous strategies conducive to its assuming full sovereignty over the territory it was legally meant to govern, besides and in addition to the need to address the challenges associated with post-colonial state-building. In many ways, with some 16 percent of its territory left occupied by Armenian forces and Nagorno-Karabakh consequently enjoying de facto independence, reversing the consequences of the war and restoring the territorial integrity of the state has since arisen as the most powerful stimulus, and the conditioning force, behind the emerging pattern of foreign policy engagements of Azerbaijan in the early years of its independent existence.

Given the above, Azerbaijan – at the time of its post-independence encounter with Turkey – had yet to formulate a post-Soviet foreign (and indeed domestic) policy agenda beyond a mere preservation of independence and responding to the occupation of its lands, while Turkey had yet to move beyond its quest to find a new – regional and/or international – purpose to follow. It was this sense of ambivalence surrounding a new contextual setup of their existence and the first – tentative – answers thereto they tried to develop that prompted Ankara and Baku to *unconditionally* embrace each other at the initial stage of their 'post-identity' encounter: each emerged as the best or the only choice for what was the other's *passing* agenda, or – on one level – a lack thereof. For Ankara, a newly emergent sense of belonging with and assuming leadership of the rising Turkic world and a foreign policy hinged around the newfound Turkic, if post-Soviet, brethren (Azerbaijan and the four Turkic Central Asian republics) that the latter entailed came to be largely believed to provide a sought-for cornerstone to underpin the state's new post–Cold War identity. And this, in many ways, motivated Turkey's engagement in the early 1990s with Azerbaijan, which was viewed as a crucial gateway to the rest of the Turkic republics in Central Asia; a role embodied, in the first instance, by 'the Bridge of Hope' across the Araz River at Sadarak, Nakhchivan, inaugurated amidst pomp on 28 May 1992 as the first – and critical – tangible link tying Turkey to Azerbaijan and "the greater 'Turkic' world to the east" and, as such, "the first step in the dawning of the promised 'Turkic' twenty-first century" (Goltz 1999, 209). In Baku, in turn, Turkey was largely viewed as the sole friendly government amidst a largely unfriendly neighbourhood and, thus, the only potential ally in the country's efforts to successfully address the effects of Armenian aggression on one hand and the looming danger that Russian and Iranian post-imperial ambitions stood to pose on the other.

Consequently and as commendable a trajectory as Azerbaijan's early stage of relations with Turkey were (e.g. Goltz 1999, ch. 15), the particular – transitionally passing – context to which the latter owed its rise rendered the bilateral dynamics that followed contingent on the further unfolding of the parallel processes of self-reflection in which Baku and Ankara engaged and the states' individual, often divergent, pursuits of foreign and domestic policies in which these processes found their expression. While this process of self-reflection was partly (more so for Baku than for Ankara) a continuously evolving product of bilateral interaction, it was also a function of a number of other factors, including the states' individual engagements with the rest of the international community, the evolution of their individual material capacities and their perception thereof and domestic political changes of sorts. It is these latter factors – and their evolution – that need to be accounted for if one is to understand how and why the nature and structure of Azerbaijan–Turkey relations today are different from what they were two decades ago; and it is some of these contingencies to which the discussion now turns.

Georgia

Georgia has been among the key contingencies upon which bilateral relations between Azerbaijan and Turkey evolved the way they did over the past two decades. In many ways, Turkey's post–Cold War engagement with Azerbaijan had until recently (indeed until the 2008/9 crisis) never been inseparable from the dynamics within the trilateral setup among Azerbaijan, Turkey, and Georgia and emerged and unfolded across this trilateral terrain. Economic and geopolitical factors underlying the essence of bilateral relations between Baku and Ankara – including energy and pipeline politics on one hand and European and Euro-Atlantic aspirations of the two states on the other – worked simultaneously, indeed primarily, to boost and mould trilateral channels of communication and discourse, with every single item on the bilateral agenda working to prompt the need for, and feeding the dynamics within, the trilateral institutional setup with which the bilateral dynamics was tightly conjoined (and without which it was unimaginable in the form and shape it has grown to assume). Cooperation in regional transport infrastructure development in particular (including multibillion-dollar energy pipeline projects and the soon-to-be completed Kars-Baku railway) – the very lifeline of bilateral relations as it was – has evolved and unfolded on a strictly trilateral terrain and was technically inconceivable without Georgia's direct involvement.

Indeed, among the only elements within the structure of bilateral relations to have been independent of the trilateral dynamics are such practices as the engagement of Turkish businessmen in Azerbaijan and mutual student exchanges, as well as the operation of Turkish educational establishments (including numerous lyceums and the Qafqaz University) and Turkish-sponsored mosques in Azerbaijan, none of which was indeed unproblematic.[1] It is only now – with Azerbaijan's direct investments in the Turkish economy significantly augmented following the 2008/9 crisis (Socor 2013) and as a function of Baku's dramatic rise in economic power on one hand and bilateral cooperation in the military sector sizably intensified (e.g. Day.az 2013a, 2013b) on the other – that the bilateral engagement between Azerbaijan and Turkey has started to generate some notable dynamics of its own; a development still paralleled by a significant upgrade of relations within the trilateral setup as well, including as embodied in the Trabzon Declaration the three states signed in June 2012 and regularly held foreign ministerial trilateral meetings to which the declaration paved the way (Cecire 2013; Veliyev 2014).

Iran

Iran has been another regional contingency both driving the two states further together and pulling them apart. On the one hand, the continuously looming threat that Azerbaijan perceived Iran as posing to its sovereignty and indeed independence, particularly in light of Iran's rising nuclear challenge across the region, has always served as among the key factors drawing Azerbaijan closer into, and keeping it firmly within, Turkey's "orbit of gravitational attraction" (Harvey and Maus 1990, 83). Ideologically divergent from, and thus alien to, a secular vision of statehood that Ataturk's Turkey and post-Soviet Azerbaijan had come to share by the time of the latter's independent rise, Iran and its regional presence stood to engender rather negative security dynamics across the region upon which Azerbaijan's brotherly bonds with Turkey materialised into a tangible alliance and by virtue of which bilateral relations thrived (Yanarocak 2013; Zasztowt 2012). Iran's relations with Turkey had also been traditionally tense and, following a brief period of Davutoglu-inspired rapprochement in 2008–2010, were shattered again in 2011 under the weight of the Syrian crisis and Ankara's expressed commitment to hosting elements of NATO's missile defense system.

Adding to these historically conditioned negative dynamics in Iran's interaction with Azerbaijan and Turkey has been Iran's standoff with the West more broadly and the US in particular and the Western sanctions that this tension worked to generate (Vatanka 2013), an international and regional power configuration that effectively excluded Iran as a possible partner in the efforts by Baku and the West (the US) in the early-1990s to set in place an institutional infrastructure for regional cooperation, particularly in energy. Indeed, Iran's involvement with Caspian energy politics – either as a shareholder in the 1994 Contract of the Century[2] or as a transit country for 'main oil' to have flowed from Azerbaijan – was effectively blocked by the United States at the time, thus rendering Turkey as the sole transit route for Azerbaijan's regional infrastructural efforts to follow.[3] Iran's forced exclusion from regional energy politics did not, in and by itself, generate negative security dynamics in bilateral relations between Azerbaijan and Iran. These dynamics were also attributable to many other factors, not least the 'Elchibey factor' in the Azerbaijan of the early 1990s,[4] the question of Azerbaijani minorities in Iran—and Tehran's threat perception thereof—and, in large measure associated with and derived from the latter, Iran's support for Armenia in the

Nagorno-Karabakh conflict and its alleged support for Shia radicalism on the Azerbaijani proper.[5] However the perceived "imbalance between Iran's regional importance and its lack of involvement in [the] Azerbaijani oil industry" (Hemming 1998, 53) has certainly worked to sustain – and further aggravate – tension and as such has carved out a vicious circle by virtue of which Turkey's importance for Azerbaijan's energy and security agenda was only bound to rise over time.

This became all too clear in July 2001, when, in what was the most serious among Iran's disruptive efforts in the region so far, an Iranian gunboat ejected two Azerbaijani survey ships from a contested area in the southern Caspian that the ships were set to explore. At the same time, Iranian jets several times violated Azerbaijan's airspace, and it eventually took Turkey to send military jets on a "demonstrative flight over Baku" to have the crisis peacefully resolved (Aliyev 2003, 310; Cornell 2011, 330–332; Lelyveld 2001); a dramatic sequence of events that came to express the workings of the resulting tripartite dynamics in their full potential, including by laying bare the role that these dynamics play in imparting the sense of recurrent urgency and essentiality to Azerbaijan's continuously close association with Turkey. The recent efforts to institutionalise interaction within the troublesome triangle into regular, biannual discussions of the intra-regional dynamics at the foreign ministry level (primarily among the three parties directly involved)[6] have so far failed to significantly ease the tensions underlying Iran's relations with its Turkic neighbours to the north and west, thus sustaining the security conditions that had brought Azerbaijan and Turkey closer together in the first place (Zasztowt 2012, 5–6).

This being so, Iran has also, on the other hand, served as an annoying hindrance to the way towards a deeper partnership between Azerbaijan and Turkey. Thus and for a markedly long time, Azerbaijan – unlike Georgia, which has enjoyed a visa-free regime with its now strategic partner Turkey since 2009 and a passport-free regime since 2011 (Today's Zaman 2011b) – could not afford to embrace and benefit from an open border and visa-free regime with friendly Turkey, lest that prompt or indeed intensify Iranian pressure on Azerbaijan to act likewise towards its southern neighbour; an item Iran has never taken off the agenda of its engagement with Baku.[7] Indeed, following Turkey's suggestion in 2009 to introduce a visa-free regime with Azerbaijan (and Georgia), Iran allegedly went as far as to threaten "to cut off the critical supply line between Azerbaijan and the Nakhchivan Autonomous Republic if Azerbaijan lifted visa requirements for Turks but not for Iranians" (Bozkurt 2011). In early 2010, it went further and introduced unilaterally a visa-free regime for Azerbaijanis (save journalists) traveling to Iran for one month or less (many of whom, particularly from Azerbaijani regions bordering Iran, do indeed travel often to Iran, mostly for commerce, health care services, or to pay a visit to Shia pilgrimage sites like Mashad), in order to step up moral pressure on Baku to respond in kind (Eurasianet 2010). In November 2013, Baku finally moved to abolish visa requirements for "certain categories of Turkish citizens," including "scholars, athletes, businessmen, famous people, and Turkish citizens, closely related to Azerbaijan," based on a list to have been devised by the country's Ministry of Economic Development (Trend.az 2013).

Israel

Israel has been another major player with a stake in Azerbaijan–Turkey relations and, as such, with a significant role, intended or otherwise, in the unfolding of its dynamics. Indeed, its association with both states, particularly in the security (including energy security) realm, by the late 1990s had grown so intense that many, in academia and among policymakers alike, tended to describe the triangular relationship, and the nature of interaction therein, as a "trilateral axis" or indeed "entente," one often juxtaposed to a regional alignment among Russia, Iran, Armenia, and Syria (Murinson 2008, 2013). The events of 2010, when relations between Turkey and Israel hit an all-time low following the death of nine Turkish citizens (including four who were actual Turks) from an Israeli attack on the Turkish, if officially non-governmental, aid boat *Mavi Marmara* headed to the then blockaded Palestinian city of Gaza (Athanasiadis 2011; Huber and Tocci 2013; Schleifer 2010), only laid bare that individual dynamics within each of the bilateral setups constitutive of the security triangle were stronger than, if not entirely independent of, one another on one hand and the overall tripartite dynamics on the other. Back then and despite Turkey's pressures on Baku to side with it in its standoff with Israel, Azerbaijan – difficult though it was, particularly given Turkey's long-standing support for Azerbaijan's position in the conflict with Armenia over Nagorno-Karabakh – stood firm in its continued cooperation with Tel Aviv, even when at times Turkey and Israel found themselves on the brink of military confrontation (Abbasov 2011a; Shiriyev 2012a). For Israel, in turn, Azerbaijan's value as "a moderate Moslem partner" in the non-Arab Orient has grown exponentially as Turkey demonstratively let that role off its shoulders, a reality that, particularly given an allegedly continued Islamisation trend in Turkey, stood to boost Tel Aviv's interest "in Azerbaijan's independence from any Turkish influence" on one hand and Baku's growing capacity for "a positive influence in Turkey" on the other (Geifman and Course 2013; also Liphshiz 2013; Mamedov 2013).

The endurance of Azerbaijan–Israel bilateral dynamics through the crisis of shattered trilateralism should perhaps come as no surprise. Indeed and apart from other related indicators, Israel has traditionally topped the list of Azerbaijan's key trade partners over the last several years, reaching – with the bilateral trade turnover of 1,357 billion USD – the second place on the ladder (second only to Italy) as of 1 July 2012. Azerbaijan, in turn, has been a stable leader, among the Moslem and former Soviet Union states, in the list of Israel's trade partners. Azerbaijan being among Israel's key energy suppliers, indeed second only to Russia, its importance for Israel has clearly not been limited to the demands of its energy security alone, but has also been a function of Tel Aviv's active efforts to counter the perceived Iranian threat on one hand and enlist support of a friendly Moslem state amidst an unfriendly, predominantly Arab-Moslem, regional environment on the other. That being so and with Tel Aviv's alleged role as Baku's major supplier of high-tech hardware (including for Azerbaijan's energy sector) and modern military equipment[8] on one hand and the role the

American Jewish diaspora is claimed to have grown to play over the last decade in Baku's efforts to balance against the alleged sway that Armenian lobby groups hold over the US government on the other, the nature of relations the two enjoyed with each other had long evolved into one of strategic partnership independent of external shocks, including the effects of the 2010 *Mavi Marmara* incident. Indeed and as an expression of ever-growing ties, including after this crisis, it was in May 2013 that Azerbaijan's foreign minister, Elmar Mammadyarov, paid an official visit to Israel, the first time an Azerbaijani foreign minister had undertaken such a move.

The United States of America and 'the West' more broadly

Not unlike Iran, the US proved a crucial, if undeniably dubious, underlying factor in the unfolding of Azerbaijan–Turkey bilateral dynamics, both by helping – through firm political and material support it rendered for the realisation of the pipeline infrastructure projects in the region (Ismayilov 2012) – make an energy-based partnership between the two states a plausible reality in the 1990s, and – as a zealous propagator of Turkish–Armenian rapprochement as delinked from the resolution of the Nagorno-Karabakh conflict (Ismayilov 2014; Ismayilov and Tkacik 2010) – by helping bring the bilateral relationship to a near halt in the late 2000s.

The West more broadly, in turn, and Euro-Atlantic aspirations it stood to invite, served as yet another critical *variable* factoring in Azerbaijan–Turkey bilateral dynamics, serving – particularly on a perceptual level of ideas – as a post-imperial modernising force whose 'recognition' both countries sought at one point and as a neo-imperial power center whose pursuit of dominance and control and neo-orientalist ways of regional engagement were to be rejected at another.

Indeed, with Russia and Iran perceived as posing an existential threat to its statehood and with some 16 percent of its territories occupied by Armenia, Azerbaijan was born into an objectively hostile neighbourhood, Turkey (with whom the country shares only 8 kilometers of border) and Georgia being the only neighbours perceived as genuine friends. In view of the above and given the inherent weakness of its post-colonial statehood and its incapacity to pursue the country's security agenda on its own on one hand and the prevalent position 'the West' was seen to occupy in the structure of international relations in the immediate aftermath of the Cold War on the other, international – and primarily Western – recognition of its statehood emerged in the 1990s as a top priority for Azerbaijan in pursuit of security, economic development and lasting independence. With these assumptions in mind, Azerbaijan joined the CSCE/OSCE[9] in January 1992 and became a signatory to its Helsinki Final Act in July 1992 and to its Charter of Paris in December the following year; a nearly instinctively progressing sequence of moves which, combined with the extension of United Nations membership to the state in March 1992, as well as individual acts of recognition effected through different bilateral frameworks, came to amount, to use Alexander Wendt's wording, to "thin" – or juridical – recognition that Azerbaijan, and its independent statehood, was certain to secure from the West and the broader international community.[10] A deeper level of recognition from, and hence a deeper extent of legitimacy accorded by, the West (that is, to use Wendt's wording again, *thick* Western recognition) was needed, however, if Baku was to have the discursive act of Western, and international, recognition translated into actual support and if it was to have the protective shield of Western power underpin the country's pursuit of sovereignty and independence vis-à-vis Russia and Iran on one hand and its quest for territorial integrity vis-à-vis Armenia on the other. In light of the above, Baku's foreign policy – as that of many other post-Soviet states – had speedily emerged as a function of the country's struggle for 'thick' – Western – recognition, its principal objective lying in devising, and managing, the mechanisms by which 'thick' recognition could be sought and ultimately sustained. Two basic pathways have come to underlie Azerbaijan's pursuit of the struggle for thick recognition: the struggle for recognition of its cultural affinity with the West (effected through the mechanism of 'imitation')[11] and the struggle for recognition of its practical worth (effected through pipeline/energy diplomacy) (Ismayilov 2014, 2012).

Like Azerbaijan, Turkey, too, pursued its own struggle for Western recognition in the 1990s. Although a product of pre–Cold War and Cold War contextual dynamics to which its efforts at nation- and state-building trace their lineage, Turkey's struggle for recognition, too, has its roots in a triple quest for security, identity and welfare. Indeed, stripped of its Ottoman-era European and Arab land possessions by the time of independence and with the remaining territory still contested, among others, by the Armenians and the Kurds from the inside and the British and the Greeks from the outside, modern Turkey was born in 1922 into a very hostile environment (e.g. Ahmad 2003, 78–87). Consequently and with 'thin' recognition of its post-independence borders secured through the Treaty of Lausanne it signed with a group of European powers (and Japan) on 24 July 1923,[12] Turkey – still in need of deeper levels of recognition to ensure the durability of its latter achievement and more effectively address internal and external challenges to its modern-day existence, including by meeting its "desire to secure greater welfare" (Dismorr 2008, 37) – launched what was effectively a struggle for 'thick' Western recognition, one effected primarily through what came to be known as Ataturk's 'modernisation' project, an imitative set of efforts involving massive-scale top-down transformation of political, economic, social and cultural properties of Turkish statehood and officially launched with the proclamation of the Turkish Republic on 29 October 1923 and the abolition of the Caliphate on 3 March 1924.[13]

For Turkey, therefore, not unlike for Azerbaijan, "gaining Western recognition of the republic's sovereignty was key to . . . survival as an independent nation" (Fuller 2008, 28); 'westernisation,' understood in this sense, being "really a defensive process, a form of nationalism, a quest for the most efficient means to match the West's success in order to fend it off and to reduce dependency upon outsiders for national security" (Fuller 2008, 15). NATO membership Turkey acquired in February 1952 having been its most significant achievement on the path of recognition to date, it has been regarded as meeting the country's demands for security, leaving its quest for identity (a desire to be regarded as a 'European nation') and welfare largely unaddressed, the kind of gap full EU membership[14] was conceived as necessary to mend. The "project of European integration," then, has grown to signify, to Ankara, "the fulfilment of Mustafa Kemal's world vision and ultimate dreams" (Bozarslan 2006, 28), the kind of understanding that prompted Turkey to conclude the Association Agreement with the EEC in September 1963 and submit its formal application for full EC membership in April 1987. Although Turkey reached a customs union agreement with the EU in 1990 and acquired an EU candidate status in December 1999, with EU accession negotiation talks officially launched in October 2005, the country's EU membership still remains a remote, if not entirely unrealistic, possibility. One way or another, this mission grew to top the agenda of Turkish governments in the post–Cold War period until recently, particularly following the ascendance of the AKP to power in November 2002, and as such significantly shaped and conditioned the dynamics of the country's domestic and foreign policy practices over the past two decades (e.g. Ahmad 2003, 175–188; Dismorr 2008, esp. 47–97).

Consequently and in view of the above, the struggle for Western recognition – and the pursuit of cultural and geopolitical legitimation the latter entailed on one hand and a secular and modern vision for statehood in the region it shaped on the other (cf. Karademir 2012) – worked to mould a shared aspirational ground upon which post–Cold War dynamics of engagement between Azerbaijan and Turkey (and indeed Georgia), particularly in the energy and pipeline infrastructure sector but more broadly as well, emerged and further evolved. Indeed and in many ways, what drew Azerbaijan's close attention to, and closely aligned it with, Turkey in the wake of the Soviet collapse was not so much ethnic Turkic bonds which Azerbaijan also happens to share with post-Soviet states in Central Asia and not a historical embeddedness in a shared time and culture on which Azerbaijan finds itself closer to Iran,[15] but rather common values of secular, modern, national statehood embedded across a traditional milieu of indigenous culture of which Baku believed it had a model in post-Ottoman Turkey to emulate.[16]

For both countries since then, an upgrade in domestic material capital they have evolved to possess (including as a function of success of cooperative practices in which they mutually engaged)[17] on one hand and continuous 'non-recognition' their struggle would persistently face on the other, have worked to undermine the need for, and consequently the struggle for, external recognition. For both, this found expression in a dramatic diversification of their foreign policy engagements away from their regional proximities on one hand and the West on the other (Goksel 2012; Ismayilov 2014) towards embracing cultural brethren in the Middle East (and broader Eurasia) on one hand and exploring uncharted lands in Africa and Latin America on the other (e.g. Steckler and Altman 2011; also Baev 2014; Ismayilov 2014; Kramer 2010; Kucera 2013; cf. Tezcur and Grigorescu 2013). As such and given the prevalence of a bilateral framework upon which the latter pursuits have been sought and realised by each of the two states, their attempts to found and revive a Turkic Union of sorts being perhaps the only exception in this respect (Ismayilov 2012, 222), the latter shift, if still following a largely similar route and direction for both, worked to shatter the common platform their earlier, unconditional, struggle for Western recognition had served to establish and as such undermined the foundation upon which bilateral dynamics had evolved and unfolded in the early aftermath of Baku's independence.

Still, for Turkey, this shift in the recognition game, including away from an exclusively Westward orientation, has evolved in sync with – indeed was an extension of – a parallel transformation of the domestic landscape of political legitimation away from staunchly secularist and homogeneously nationalist dictates of modernity towards religiously inspired notions and understandings, a development started (following the early, if controversial, legacies of Turgut Ozal and Necmettin Erbakan [Economist 2011; Laciner 2009; Yayla 1997]) with the AKP's advent to power in 2002 (e.g. Geybulla 2014; Steckler and Altman 2011) and one set to secure a further gap with still unequivocally secular and modernising (and nationalising) Azerbaijan. In many ways, while the AKP government – no longer as secular as the Baku government was ready to accept and embrace (e.g. Bagdadi 2011; Phillips 2012) – now seems to have espoused a post-nationalist/ post-modern developmental pathway for Turkey to follow, Azerbaijan is still struggling, particularly in light of its continued quest to resolve the territorial conflict with Armenia over Nagorno-Karabakh, to stabilise the contours of its modern agenda of post-colonial nation- and state-building and, as such, has increasingly likened Ankara's growing religious dispositions to those of Tehran in terms of the potential threat they stand to pose to the homogeneously secular nature of its idealised – and culturally sterilised – society and statehood.

Energy politics, converging agendas and sectoral dependence

Energy politics proved an important structural contingency behind the dynamics of Azerbaijan's relations with Turkey over the past two decades, bringing the two states together yet monopolising the overall space of interaction in the oil era of the 1990s and setting the states apart, yet ultimately prompting them to expand the conceptual boundaries of engagement at the gas stage of cooperation in the late 2000s.

Indeed, few would question the central role that energy and pipeline politics played in carving out a structural landscape upon which Azerbaijan's relations with Turkey unfolded in the 1990s. Critical as energy-based partnership was in bringing Azerbaijan and Turkey together in the early 1990s, it quickly evolved to dominate the structure of bilateral relations, such that the space of mutual engagement between the two states was effectively confined to energy-related cooperation only, the former's success imaginable as a mere extension of success of the latter, and the engagement patterns of the former following the demands of and limited to the conceptual boundaries imposed by the latter. The dynamics within the broader realm of bilateral relations became a function of, and was effectively subordinated to, the needs and dictates the states' energy agenda stood to suggest. The energy dimension of bilateral interaction aggressively prioritised, other – alternative or additional – areas around which cooperation could potentially unfold and ultimately thrive were left utterly ignored; a reality also reflected, until recently, in gross under-institutionalisation of bilateral contact outside the demands of the energy sector.

Having embraced each other at a time of mutual weakness, however, neither Azerbaijan nor Turkey could afford to harbour ambitions beyond a mere survival or stabilisation of their statehoods at early stages of their energy-bolstered contact. As they grew in capacity (Ismayilov 2014; Kenes 2013), their concomitantly rising ambitions prompted them to claim leadership outside their national confines; ambitions they sought to pursue within the overlapping regional boundaries and leadership – vis-à-vis the broader region and vis-à-vis the West (the EU) – of which they sought legitimacy in terms of the intersecting range of capital they stood to share, whether that be richness in energy resources (Azerbaijan) or transit capacity for those riches (Azerbaijan and Turkey). The latter convergence of leadership agendas and the tension it served to engender found its ultimate expression in the negotiation crisis the two states suffered in 2009–2010 over a gas transit deal they sought to strike (an impasse tightly linked to the crisis in bilateral relations that unfolded around Turkey's attempts at rapprochement with Armenia at the time; hence its 'dual' nature): Turkey's newfound, or newly bolstered, ambition to emerge as a key energy hub for its energy-thirsty EU partners – a goal that would entail the proactive purchase, and the subsequent storage in Turkey, of Caspian (primarily Azerbaijani) gas with its subsequent re-export to Ankara's partners further afield under an exclusively Turkish brand and at a higher price – was hard to reconcile with Azerbaijan's aspiration to use its energy (now primarily gas) card in pursuit of equality and equality-based partnership with, and hence its desire to market its gas directly to, the EU (the latter otherwise critical of the country's human rights record). The nature of Azerbaijan's gas diplomacy and recognition the latter was meant to secure in the late 2000s, then, was qualitatively different from its oil diplomacy of the 1990s, when Baku's reliance on the energy card and its pursuit of Western recognition had primarily been set to achieve, through Western support and involvement, sustainable security and independence (rather than equality and equality-based partnership with the West that the gas stage of the country's energy diplomacy was meant to secure), an agenda that could have squarely reconciled with Turkish desire to emerge as a strategic energy hub in the region.[18] One way or the other, the dual crisis in Azerbaijan–Turkey relations was finally resolved with, and translated into, the Shah Deniz II agreement the two states signed in June 2010 and the broader – multifaceted – agreement on Strategic Partnership and Mutual Support they signed in December of the same year and, with the latter agreement setting the stage for the deepening of existing relations into a number of non-energy sectors (including education, health, military, and industry), ultimately helped widen the conceptual landscape and institutionalise (de-individualise) the operational setup upon which bilateral ties could further develop (Shiriyev 2012b; also Abbasov 2011b; Shiriyev and Davies 2013).

The endogenous process of interaction

Processual contingencies have also been crucial, if grossly underappreciated, in defining the nature and dynamics of interstate interaction. Although some back in the final days of Azerbaijan's Soviet existence might have argued – in good faith or otherwise – that "the Soviet Azeri people knew everything about Turkey and loved and appreciated every bit of it" (Goltz 1999, 5), to the extent the latter half of the statement was true, that would rather have been a function of euphoric ignorance than a result of total knowledge. It is only as the two states moved closer to each other in the early 1990s and immersed themselves in mutual learning through various platforms of mutual engagement that they gradually came to appreciate the extent of similarity and difference that had accrued between the two nations over some seven centuries of historical disengagement. For Azerbaijanis at least, such encounters and the many platforms upon which they happened have speedily evolved into endogenous loci of mutual learning by virtue of which the newly acquired knowledge of the other was often absorbed as part of Self on one hand and was reflected upon in a reflexive act of self-appraisal on the other. While Turkey's recognition of Azerbaijan in November 1991 generated the strongest momentum by which the latter kinds of endogenous channels were brought to bear (nearly overwhelmingly on the Azerbaijani part of the bilateral equation) – partly because Turkey was the first country to recognise Azerbaijan's independence and as such the first, and for some brief time the only, bridge linking Azerbaijan to the world beyond and to the existing patterns of practical knowledge of modernity and statehood (Goltz 1999, 106–107) – at least five platforms have gradually stabilised into continuous loci of communication and discourse to underlie the two nations' mutual engagement and cultural interpenetration over the past two decades: Turkish, if mostly non-governmental, educational establishments in Azerbaijan (Araz pre-University preparatory courses, Turkish lyceums, the Qafqaz University, and a theology department at the Baku State University) (Balci 2013); Turkey-sponsored mosques in Azerbaijan (Goksel 2011); Azerbaijani students pursuing education in Turkey (and their activities upon return to the homeland, including various kinds of publication efforts)[19] and Turkish students receiving education in Azerbaijan; Turkish businessmen in Azerbaijan and the converse; and the Turkish media operating in Azerbaijan, including Turkish television (particularly Turkish soap operas) broadcast across the country (cf. Balci 2014b).

All these joined together to mould a societal glue by which the two nations have grown to increasingly tie on to each other, such that the dominance of personalities and leaders in conditioning the dynamics of bilateral relations in the 1990s (one embodied in the intimately close personal relationship between Azerbaijan's Heydar Aliyev and Turkey's Suleiman Demirel [Aliyev 2012, 53–54]) was gradually replaced and taken over by the societal dominance in that respect, a reality shift exposed in the midst of processes that underlay Turkey's attempted, yet ultimately unsuccessful, rapprochement with Armenia in 2008/09. Indeed, that Azerbaijan managed, during the attempted rapprochement between Armenia and Turkey, to prompt the latter's AKP government to reconsider its intended actions, Baku's success in that attributed by many to its active work with, and its resultant sway over, public opinion inside Turkey, apart from and in addition to its direct involvement with the Ankara government (including through its use of the energy card) (Goksel 2009), worked all too well to bring the latter reality to light and display the obvious power 'citizen' diplomacy has evolved to play in conditioning the underlying dynamics between the two nations, particularly in light of the fact that personal chemistry between the incumbent leaders – of which there has now been allegedly little – was no longer capable of performing that role.

The above are just a few agential, structural, and processual parameters of contingency within which Azerbaijan's relations with Turkey have unfolded over the past two decades, a clear grasp of which is critical if one is to develop sound understanding of the underlying dynamics behind the workings of this important regional axis. It is some of these contingencies that are the subject of discussion in the chapters to follow.

More specifically, building on and amplifying some of the points developed above and focusing in particular on the Armenia–Azerbaijan conflict in and around Nagorno-Karabakh and the part the latter played in boosting Turkey's place in Baku's foreign policy calculations, Chapter 2 maps out a broader picture of structural dynamics that underlay the milestone shifts in Azerbaijan's engagement with Turkey over the past twenty years and as such lays bare the contextual, including historical, landscape upon which Baku's relations with Ankara developed and identifies some general stimuli to which they were bound to respond. Chapter 3 examines changing contours of Azerbaijan's place in Ankara's geopolitical calculations over the past two decades in light of Turkey's evolving – and conflicting – self-perception as a regional – Eurasian – power. Chapter 4 focuses on the past two decades of interaction among Azerbaijan, Turkey, and Georgia to demonstrate the mutually embedded nature of bilateral and trilateral dynamics within this subregional setup at the initial stage of engagement in the 1990s on one hand and the subsequent (and gradual) endogenisation of each of those individual dynamics on the other. Chapter 5 looks at the political and economic conditions that underlay the evolving patterns of mutual trade and investment between Azerbaijan and Turkey over the past twenty years, while Chapter 6 focuses specifically on the experiences of Turkish businesspeople in Azerbaijan over that period, including in the context of a broader discussion of corruption and state–business relations in post-independence Azerbaijan. Finally, Chapter 7 concludes the volume with an analysis of the ways in which Baku's post-independence engagement with Turkey interfered with the evolving contours of the religious and political landscape of post-Soviet Azerbaijan and how the perceived change in the dynamics of that influence reflected on Azerbaijan's evolving perception of Turkey, particularly in terms of the statehood model the latter has been taken to exhibit.

Notes

1 The Baku government has never been enthusiastic about the operation of Turkish-sponsored mosques across the country, for example, since, given the latter's Sunni disposition (and their lying outside the reach of state control), they have been perceived as introducing and promoting a sectarian – Sunni/Shia – divide across the largely Shia Azerbaijani social spectrum, thereby transforming the dominant cultural, indeed nationalised, representations of Islam into a more genuine – religious – understanding (and practice) of the faith (cf. Balci and Goyushov 2013); a perception that might have factored in the ruling elite's decision to close down in 2009, if for allegedly legitimate (technical) reasons, both of the two 'Turkish' mosques (sponsored/built by the Turkish Directorate for Religious Affairs, or *Diyanet*) operating in the capital (one of which was later reopened) (Muradova 2009; RFE/RL 2009; World Bulletin 2009). Also, notwithstanding an allegedly important contribution that the Baku Turkish Anadolu lyceum (so far the only high school in Baku sponsored and operated directly by the Turkish government) made to raising educational standards in Azerbaijan's secondary education provision (particularly at an initial stage of the country's independence) and despite numerous efforts on the part of the Turkish government to that effect, the Azerbaijani government has been consistently reluctant to allow for the second such Turkish government-sponsored school to open in Baku. Other Turkish (if non-governmental) educational establishments operating in the country as part of the so-called Gülen (or Hizmet) movement, of which there were at least twenty-seven (including the Qafqaz University, a private school, and twelve lyceums and at least thirteen Araz pre-university preparatory courses dispersed across the country's various regions), had been recurrently facing political and broader societal pressure and scrutiny of various kinds, given the clandestine nature of the movement's operation and its allegedly subversive longer-term political agenda, until they, save the university, were finally decreed to close down in June 2014, including as an extension of recent political developments in Turkey itself (Aliyev 2013; Balci 2013, 2014a, 2014b; Muradova 2014).
2 What has been hailed as the Contract of the Century is a production-sharing agreement that SOCAR signed with the international, mostly Western, oil consortium in September 1994.
3 While Azerbaijan's president Heydar Aliyev did discuss, in June 1994, with his Iranian counterpart Rafsanjani the possibility of Iran's inclusion in the Contract of the Century – and an agreement to that effect was signed in Baku on 12 November that year – given Washington's unconditional opposition, SOCAR was ultimately forced to disallow Iran's participation in April 1995. Ironically, Iran's National Gas Export Company was to receive, according to the November 1994 agreement, a 5 percent share in the Contract of the Century, considerably more than 1.75 percent that the Turkish State Oil Company received (Aliyev 2003, 182–183). In a similar fashion, while the Iranian route was considered by experts, including those in the AIOC, economically most feasible for the transportation of 'main oil' of the Caspian – the initial framework agreement signed on 9 March 1992 between Azerbaijan and Turkey envisaged the construction of an oil pipeline that would run from Baku through Iran and Nakhchivan to the Turkish port of Yumurtalik – the US opposition blocked this option and effectively removed it from the political agenda (Goltz 1999, 253–254; Jofi 1999; LeVine 2007, 348–349).
4 Elchibey's open criticism towards Iran's human rights performance and his active efforts to advocate the creation of Great Azerbaijan through the unification of post-Soviet Azerbaijan and the Iranian Azerbaijan provinces was an important factor in alienating Iran towards its northern neighbour (e.g. Goltz 1999, 58–64).
5 E.g. Cornell (2011, ch. 12); also Shaffer (2000, 2002, esp. ch. 1).

6 The first such discussion among foreign ministers of Azerbaijan, Turkey, and Iran was held in April 2011 in the Iranian city of Urmia (Today's Zaman 2011a); the second meeting took place in March 2012 in Azerbaijan's Nakhchivan (Zasztowt 2012, 5); the third, and latest, meeting, was held in March 2014 in Turkey's Van.
7 Azerbaijan has traditionally been resistant to opening up its borders to Iran, lest the move further spur drug trafficking from that country, which is already very intense and hard to control (Bozkurt 2011; cf. Ekici and Unlu 2013); further facilitate cross-border infiltrations therefrom, including by alleged terrorists, Islamic radicals, and spying agents (see, for example, BBC News 2012; The Telegraph 2012; Theodoulou 2012); or "trigger a huge influx of refugees" from what is seen as politically unstable Iran to Azerbaijan (Bozkurt 2011).
8 Indeed, Israeli arms supplies to Azerbaijan date back to the crucial years of the early 1990s when Baku was still involved in the active phase of its war with Armenia over Nagorno-Karabakh. For further detail on, and analysis of, the nature and evolving dynamics of relations between Azerbaijan and Israel, see, for example, Bourtman (2006); Ismayilov (2013); Murinson (2013); Perry (2012); Shiriyev (2012a). On Azerbaijan's indigenous Jewish population, see Eshman (2013).
9 At the time Azerbaijan acquired independence, the organisation was called the Conference on Security and Cooperation in Europe (CSCE). It was renamed to become the OSCE by a decision of the Budapest Summit in December 1994.
10 Alexander Wendt conceptualises "the struggle for recognition" among states and individuals as the micro-level driving force behind structural change and collective identity formation. Picking up from Georg W.F. Hegel's (1977) *Phenomenology of Spirit*, Wendt defines recognition as "a social act that invests difference with a particular meaning [in which] another actor ('the Other') is constituted as a subject with a legitimate social standing in relation to the Self." Elaborating further on the concept, Wendt differentiates between "thin" forms of recognition, which he defines as recognition of a state "as an independent subject within a community of law," and "thick" recognition, which "is about being respected for what makes [a state] special or unique" (Wendt 2003, esp. 511–512). For a conceptualisation of the struggle for recognition, also see Fukuyama (1992) and Honneth (1996).
11 "Imitation" refers to a process by which a state "tries to conform as closely as ever possible to the rules [and norms] which govern life" in the temporal and social context in which it has emerged (Ringmar 2002, 122). Conceptualising it as an evolutionary mechanism of "cultural selection," by which state identities evolve at a micro-level of interaction, Wendt (1999, 324–325) defines "imitation" as a process in which "actors adopt the self-understandings of those whom they perceive as 'successful.'" For a detailed conceptualisation of the struggle for recognition and its workings in the context of post-Soviet Azerbaijan, including the underlying tension between "imitation" and "pipeline politics" as two modalities by virtue of which Azerbaijan's struggle for recognition was effected, see Ismayilov (2012).
12 For the text of the treaty, see http://wwi.lib.byu.edu/index.php/Treaty_of_Lausanne (accessed 22 February 2014).
13 For a fine, if brief, overview of Ataturk's reforms, see, for example, Morris (2005, 35–37); Fuller (2008, 25–31); also Ahmad (2003, 85–86).
14 Before 1992, the EU was called the European Economic Community (EEC).
15 Indeed, even on the mutual intelligibility of one another's languages (particularly on the part of the Turkish population), the two states are not as close as the typological similarity between Azerbaijani and Turkish might suggest (Sagin-Simsek and Konig 2012).
16 In the same vein, Georgia's Saakashvili pointed explicitly a number of times to modern Turkey's founder Ataturk as a role model he was willing to emulate in his state-building efforts at home (e.g. Mekhuzla 2006; Mitchell 2006, 674–675; Ostrovsky 2004).

17 With billions in oil revenues flooding the Azerbaijani economy, the country has gone through what was in fact an exceptionally robust GDP outturn and, with an average annual growth rate of 21 percent registered in 2006–2010 (as opposed to a −6.3 percent average annual growth in 1990–2000), found itself among the fastest-growing economies in the world in recent years (International Monetary Fund 2012, 4). As of 2011, the overall volume of the country's economy (expressed in terms of nominal GDP) has increased 18.5 times since independence, such that it came to account for over 80 percent of the GDP of the entire South Caucasus (e.g. Bayramov 2012; Mammadyarov 2013). Turkey, in turn, had seen its economy grow some 6 percent annually and its per capita GDP tripled between 2002 and 2008, "one of the highest sustained rates of economic growth" the world saw at the time, landing the country among the world's 20 largest economies (Steckler and Altman 2011, 27, 43).

18 For a fine, if brief, analysis of the evolving nature of Azerbaijan's energy partnership with Turkey, see Kardaş (2014). Also see Kardaş (2013), Yilmaz and Kilavuz (2012).

19 As of mid-2014, six to seven thousand Azerbaijani students were pursuing their education in Turkey's universities.

References

Abbasov, Shahin. 2011a. Azerbaijan: Baku Faces Difficult Choice Between Turkey and Israel. *Eurasianet*, 26 Sep. http://goo.gl/Cr8wac.

———. 2011b. Azerbaijan-Turkey Military Pact Signals Impatience with Minsk Talks. *Eurasianet*, 18 Jan. http://goo.gl/Hkq6iE.

Ahmad, Feroz. 2003. *Turkey: The Quest for Identity*. Oxford: One World.

Aliyev, Elbay. 2012. *Azerbaijan-Turkish Relations (1992–2012): A Foreign Policy Account*. MSc thesis. Ankara: Department of International Relations, Middle East Technical University, July.

Aliyev, Fuad. 2013. The Gülen Movement in Azerbaijan. *Current Trends in Islamist Ideology* 14, Jan., 90–103. Hudson Institute: Center on Islam, Democracy, and the Future of the Muslim World.

Aliyev, Ilham. 2003. *Azerbaijan's Caspian Oil*. (In Russian.) Moscow: Izvestiya.

Athanasiadis, Iason. 2011. Turkey: Making Waves with the Mavi Marmara. *Eurasianet*, 6 Jun. http://goo.gl/NNKJRi.

Baev, Pavel K. 2014. Russia and Turkey Find a Common Cause. *Hurriyet Daily News*, 22 Mar. http://goo.gl/1eY7qb.

Bagdadi, Itir. 2011. Azerbaijan and the Revision of Turkey's Regional Policy. *Azerbaijan in the World* 4:13, 1 Jul., 3–6.

Balci, Bayram. 2013. Between Secular Education and Islamic Philosophy: The Approach and Achievements of Fethullah Gulen's Followers in Azerbaijan. *Caucasus Survey* 1:1, Oct. http://goo.gl/Rcf8ha.

———. 2014a. The Gulen Movement and Turkish Soft Power. *Carnegie Endowment for International Peace*, 4 Feb. http://goo.gl/hQqAfk.

———. 2014b. Turkey's Religious Outreach and the Turkic World. *Current Trends in Islamist Ideology* 16, Mar., 65–85. Hudson Institute: Center on Islam, Democracy, and the Future of the Muslim World.

Balci, Bayram and Altay Goyushov. 2013. Changing Islam in Post-Soviet Azerbaijan and Its Impact on the Sunni-Shia Cleavage. In: Brigitte Maréchal and Sami Zemni, eds. *The Dynamics of Sunni-Shia Relationships: Doctrine, Transnationalism, Intellectuals and the Media*. London: Hurst & Co Publishers Ltd., 193–214.

Bayramov, Vugar. 2012. Spotlight on the Azerbaijani Economy. In: Adam Hug, ed. *Spotlight on Azerbaijan*, 56–63. London: Foreign Policy Centre.
BBC News. 2012. Azerbaijan Arrests 22 Suspects in Alleged Iran Spy Plot. 14 Mar. http://goo.gl/xoliJS.
Bourtman, Ilya. 2006. Israel and Azerbaijan's Furtive Embrace. *The Middle East Quarterly* 13:3, Summer, 47–57.
Bozarslan, Hamit. 2006. Kemalism, Westernization and Anti-Liberalism. In: Hans-Lukas Kieser, ed. *Turkey Beyond Nationalism: Towards Post-Nationalist Identities*, 28–34. London & New York: I.B. Tauris.
Bozkurt, Abdullah. 2011. Azerbaijan Says Visa-Free Regime with Turkey Fell Victim to Iranian Pressure. *Today's Zaman*, 19 Jul. http://goo.gl/uRpRfr.
Cecire, Michael H. 2013. Turkey-Georgia-Azerbaijan: Trilateralism and the Future of Black Sea Regional Geopolitics. *Central Asia-Caucasus Analyst*, 16 Oct. http://goo.gl/rB8gaj.
Cornell, Svante. 2011. *Azerbaijan Since Independence*. New York & London: M.E. Sharpe.
Cowell, Alan. 1990. Upheaval in the East: Turkey; Crackdown in Azerbaijan Leaves Turks Torn Between Politics and Kinship. *The New York Times*, 24 Jan. http://goo.gl/kCDl2b.
Day.az. 2013a. Azerbaijan and Turkey Begin Military Exercises. (In Russian.) *Day.az*, 16 Jul. http://goo.gl/EJJsM7.
———. 2013b. Azerbaijan and Turkey to Form a Single Army. (In Russian.) *Day.az*, 5 Aug. http://goo.gl/K1Lb73.
Dismorr, Ann. 2008. *Turkey Decoded*. London: Saqi.
Economist. 2011. Erbakan's Legacy. 3 Mar. http://goo.gl/uF1Wgh.
Ekici, Behsat and Ali Unlu. 2013. Increased Drug Trafficking from Iran: Ankara's Challenges. *Middle East Quarterly*, Fall, 41–48.
Eshman, Rob. 2013. The Mysteries of Azerbaijan: A Shiite Nation Embraces Its Jews. *Jewish Journal*, 18 Dec. http://goo.gl/78nFAc.
Eurasianet. 2010. Azerbaijan: Iran Implements Visa-Free Travel for Azeris, Except Journalists. *Eurasianet*, 1 Feb. http://goo.gl/eo5X4t.
Fukuyama, Francis. 1992. *The End of History and the Last Man*. New York: Avon Books.
Fuller, Graham. 2008. *The New Turkish Republic: Turkey As a Pivotal State in the Muslim World*. Washington, DC: United States Institute of Peace Press.
Geifman, Anna and Dima Course. 2013. Israel and Azerbaijan: Geopolitical Reasons for Stronger Ties. *BESA Center Perspectives Paper* 208, 15 Jul. http://goo.gl/oazpuh.
Geybulla, Arzu. 2014. Turkey Under Erdogan – from Gezi to Internet Ban. *Meydan TV*, 27 Feb. https://goo.gl/eKJJ4r.
Goksel, Nigar. 2009. Starting Over? Turkey and Azerbaijan after the Protocols. *Azerbaijan in the World* 2:23, 1 Dec., 1–4. http://goo.gl/2ZKtRQ.
———. 2011. Religiously-Inspired Bonding: Changing Soft Power Elements in Turkey's Relations with Azerbaijan. *CPCEW Occasional Paper* 4:8. Bucharest: Center for Conflict Prevention and Early Warning. http://goo.gl/voo2V2.
———. 2012. Turkey and the EU: What Next? *On Turkey Series*, German Marshall Fund of the United States, 5 Dec. http://goo.gl/paCm90.
Goltz, Thomas. 1999. *Azerbaijan Diary*, paperback edition. Armonk, NY & London: M.E. Sharpe.
Harvey, Elizabeth D. and Katharine Eisaman Maus, eds. 1990. *Soliciting Interpretation: Literary Theory and Seventeenth-century English Poetry*. Chicago: University of Chicago Press.

Hegel, Georg W. F. 1977. *Phenomenology of Spirit*. Oxford: Clarendon Press.
Hemming, Jonathan. 1998. The Implications of the Revival of the Oil Industry in Azerbaijan. *CMEIS Occasional Paper* 58, Jun. Durham, UK: University of Durham, Centre for Middle Eastern and Islamic Studies.
Honneth, Axel. 1996. *The Struggle for Recognition*. Cambridge, MA: MIT Press.
Huber, Daniela and Nathalie Tocci. 2013. Behind the Scenes of the Turkish-Israeli Breakthrough. *IAI Working Papers* 13/15, Apr. http://goo.gl/W9D6m4.
ICG. 2010. Turkey and the Middle East: Ambitions and Constraints. *International Crisis Group, Europe Report* 203, 7 Apr.
International Monetary Fund. 2012. Caucasus and Central Asia Set for Solid Growth, but Global Risks Loom Large. *Regional Economic Outlook (Update): Middle East and Central Asia*, 20 Apr. Washington, DC: IMF. http://goo.gl/zj1xmX.
Ismayilov, Elnur. 2013. Israel and Azerbaijan: The Evolution of a Strategic Partnership. *Israel Journal of Foreign Affairs* 7:1, 69–76.
Ismayilov, Murad. 2012. The Impact of Energy Resources on Nation- and State-Building: The Contrasting Cases of Azerbaijan and Georgia. In: Brenda Shaffer and Taleh Ziyadov, eds. *Beyond the Resource Curse*, 203–224. Philadelphia: University of Pennsylvania Press.
———. 2014. Power, Knowledge, and Pipelines: Understanding the Politics of Azerbaijan's Foreign Policy. *Caucasus Survey* 2:1–2, Nov., 79–129.
Ismayilov, Murad and Michael Tkacik. 2010. US-Azerbaijan Relations at Risk of Failing? *Hurriyet Daily News*, 7 Apr. http://goo.gl/D4HwD7.
Jofi, Joseph. 1999. Pipeline Diplomacy: The Clinton Administration's Fight for Baku-Ceyhan. *WWS Case Study* 1/99. Princeton: Woodrow Wilson School of Public and International Affairs. http://goo.gl/RqNym2.
Karademir, Burcu S. 2012. Turkey as a 'Willing Receiver' of American Soft Power: Hollywood Movies in Turkey During the Cold War. *Turkish Studies* 13:4, 1–13.
Kardaş, Saban. 2009. Turkey Prioritizing Its Relations with Azerbaijan. *Eurasia Daily Monitor* 6:87, 6 May. http://goo.gl/a448TG.
———. 2013. Turkey and the Southern Corridor after TAP's Selection as the Main Export Route for Caspian Gas. *On Turkey Series*, German Marshall Fund of the United States, 18 Jul. http://goo.gl/CT3YEZ.
———. 2014. The Turkey-Azerbaijan Energy Partnership in the Context of the Southern Corridor. *IAI Working Papers* 14/04, Mar. http://goo.gl/7bUiYP.
Kenes, Bulent. 2013. Turkey and Azerbaijan on Converging Paths. *Today's Zaman*, 11 Apr. http://goo.gl/74k7oj.
Kramer, Heinz. 2010. AKP's 'New' Foreign Policy Between Vision and Pragmatism. *SWP Working Paper*, FG 2, 2010/01, June. Berlin: Stiftung Wissenschaft und Politik.
Kucera, Joshua. 2013. Turkey Makes It Official with SCO. *Eurasianet*, 28 Apr. http://goo.gl/UqoEAp.
Laciner, Sedat. 2009. Turgut Özal Period in Turkish Foreign Policy: Özalism. *Turkish Weekly*, 9 Mar. http://goo.gl/2wVaj7.
Lelyveld, Michael. 2001. Caspian: Tempers Flare in Iran-Azerbaijan Border Incident. *Radio Free Europe/Radio Liberty*, 25 Jul. http://goo.gl/q0ED2G.
LeVine, Steve. 2007. *The Oil and the Glory: The Pursuit of Empire and Fortune on the Caspian Sea*. London: Random House.
Liphshiz, Cnaan. 2013. Israel Forges Close Ties With Azerbaijan – Both Eye Iran. *Forward*, 17 Sep. http://goo.gl/h2zoN1.

Mamedov, Eldar. 2013. How Deep Are Azerbaijan-Israel Relations? *Eurasianet*, 18 Jan. http://goo.gl/J6LyKP.

Mammadyarov, Elmar. 2013. Foreign Minister Elmar Mammadyarov: Why Azerbaijan Can Serve as Peacemaker and Bridge-builder. *The Hill*, 1 Jul. http://goo.gl/3murZT.

Mekhuzla, Eka. 2006. Saakashvili Inspired by Ataturk Example in Georgia Unification. *TASS*, 14 Mar. http://goo.gl/3x3Hrw.

Mitchell, Lincoln. 2006. Democracy in Georgia since the Rose Revolution. *Orbis* 50:4, Autumn, 669–676.

Morris, Chris. 2005. *The New Turkey: The Quiet Revolution on the Edge of Europe*. London: Granta Books.

Muradova, Mina. 2009. Azerbaijan: Mosques Close in Baku, 'Capital of Islamic Culture.' *Eurasianet*, 26 May. http://goo.gl/oYJPnK.

———. 2014. Turkey's Gülen Controversy Spills Over to Azerbaijan. *Central Asia – Caucasus Analyst*, 2 Apr. http://goo.gl/870n0L.

Murinson, Alexander. 2008. Azerbaijan-Turkey-Israel Relations: The Energy Factor. *The Middle East Review of International Affairs (MERIA) Journal* 12:3, Sep. http://goo.gl/YcMvMZ.

———. 2013. *Turkey's Entente with Israel and Azerbaijan: State Identity and Security in the Middle East and Caucasus*. London & New York: Routledge.

Osipova, Yelena and Fevzi Bilgin. 2013. Revisiting the Armenian-Turkish Reconciliation. *Rethink Paper* 08, Jan. Washington, DC: Rethink Institute.

Ostrovsky, Arkady. 2004. How to Be a Founding Father. *Financial Times*, 9 Jul.

Perry, Mark. 2012. Israel's Secret Staging Ground. *Foreign Policy*, 28 Mar. http://goo.gl/EaKRyL.

Phillips, David L. 2012. *Diplomatic History: The Turkey-Armenia Protocols*, Mar. New York: Institute for the Study of Human Rights, Columbia University & Cambridge, MA: Belfer Center for Science and International Affairs, Harvard Kennedy School.

RFE/RL. 2009. Turkish Mosque in Baku Closed for 'Repairs'. *Radio Free Europe/Radio Liberty*, 28 Apr. http://goo.gl/lwSx29.

Ringmar, Erik. 2002. The Recognition Game: Soviet Russia Against the West, *Cooperation and Conflict* 37:2, 115–136.

Sagin-Simsek, Cigdem and Wolf Konig. 2012. Receptive Multilingualism and Language Understanding: Intelligibility of Azerbaijani to Turkish Speakers. *International Journal of Bilingualism* 16:3, Sep., 315–331.

Schleifer, Yigal. 2010. Turkey Growing More Assertive Amid Fallout from Israeli High-Seas Raid. *Eurasianet*, 1 Jun. http://goo.gl/gXrttV.

Shaffer, Brenda. 2000. The Formation of Azerbaijani Collective Identity in Iran. *Nationalities Papers* 28:3, 449–477.

———. 2002. *Borders and Brethren: Iran and the Challenge of Azerbaijani Identity*. BCSIA Studies in International Security. Cambridge, MA: MIT Press.

Shiriyev, Zaur. 2012a. Azerbaijan-Israel: Firm Alliance? *Today's Zaman*, 17 Apr. http://goo.gl/rzoYqw.

———. 2012b. Turkish-Azerbaijan Relations: Beyond Mottos. *Today's Zaman*, 11 Sep. http://goo.gl/daOnKS.

Shiriyev, Zaur and Celia Davies. 2013. The Turkey-Armenia-Azerbaijan Triangle: The Unexpected Outcomes of the Zurich Protocols. *Perceptions* 18:1, 185–206.

Socor, Vladimir. 2013. Izmir Port Project Magnifies Azerbaijan's Integrated Investments in Turkey. *Eurasia Daily Monitor* 10:55. http://t.co/0XwytjyjaM.

Soltanov, Elnur. 2009. Turkish-Armenian Soccer Diplomacy: A Direct Hit at Azerbaijan's Foreign Policy Architecture. *Hurriyet Daily News*, 30 Oct. http://goo.gl/KrgkL8.

Steckler, Jordan and Darrin Altman. 2011. Strategic Depth or Strategic Drift? Contending with Turkey's Rapprochement with Syria and the Middle East. *IMES Capstone Paper Series*, May. Washington, DC: The Institute of Middle East Studies, the Elliott School of International Affairs, the George Washington University.

The Telegraph. 2012. Azerbaijan Arrests '22 Iranian Spies'. 14 Mar. http://goo.gl/M7a8nT.

Tezcur, Gunes M. and Alexandru Grigorescu. 2013. Activism in Turkish Foreign Policy: Balancing European and Regional Interests. *International Studies Perspectives* 15:3, 257–276.

Theodoulou, Michael. 2012. Iran and Azerbaijan in Spy Feud. *The National*, 14 Feb. http://goo.gl/Y0IxWt.

Today's Zaman. 2011a. Azerbaijan, Iran, Turkey Move to Expand Regional Cooperation. 18 Apr. http://goo.gl/yTjsQs.

———. 2011b. Travel between Turkey and Georgia Now Passport-Free. 31 May. http://goo.gl/Bl6Nw3.

Trend.az. 2013. President Ilham Aliyev: Azerbaijan to Ensure Visa-Free Regime for Turkish Citizens upon List. *Trend.az*, 13 Nov. http://goo.gl/q0z38K.

Vatanka, Alex. 2013. Tangle in the Caucasus: Iran and Israel Fight for Influence in Azerbaijan. *Foreign Affairs*, 15 Jan. http://goo.gl/KgTKcZ.

Veliyev, Cavid. 2014. From Alliance to Integration: The Turkey-Azerbaijan-Georgia Triangle. *Eurasia Daily Monitor* 11:46, 11 Mar. http://goo.gl/8pPtxm.

Wendt, Alexander. 1999. *Social Theory of International Politics*. Cambridge: Cambridge University Press.

———. 2003. Why a World State Is Inevitable. *European Journal of International Relations* 9:4, 491–542.

World Bulletin. 2009. Azerbaijan Closes Turkish Mosque in Baku. 26 Apr. http://goo.gl/HTALbl.

Yanarocak, Hay E. C. 2013. Turkey and Iran: From an Ambivalent Honeymoon to Divorce? *Iran Pulse* 55, 3 Feb. http://goo.gl/ACkEqT.

Yayla, Atilla. 1997. Turkey's Leaders – Erbakan's Goals. *Middle East Quarterly*, Sep., 19–25. http://goo.gl/0CXGGl.

Yilmaz, Suhnaz and Tahir Kilavuz. 2012. Restoring Brotherly Bonds: Turkish-Azerbaijani Energy Relations. *PONARS Eurasia Policy Memo* 240, Sep.

Zasztowt, Konrad. 2012. Iran, Turkey and Azerbaijan: Heading Towards a Regional Crisis? *PISM Policy Paper* 35, Sep. Warsaw, Poland: The Polish Institute of International Affairs.

2 Turkish-Azerbaijani relations
Brothers in arms or brothers in the dark?

Elnur Soltanov

Introduction

The relationship between Azerbaijan and Turkey in the last twenty years is the story of modifications in the nature of a romanticism that can be tangibly traced back to little more than a hundred years. The modifications have been effected by the challenges posed by either changing realities or perceptions, and sometimes both. The cultural affinity between Turkey and Azerbaijan, backed by a rich ideational fraternity and pragmatic cooperation during the late nineteenth and early twentieth centuries, has been the main context where relations between the two countries began to unfold when the Soviet Union began its short and cataclysmic journey towards collapse.

The outpouring of affection and the elevation of Azerbaijani–Turkish relations to a very emotional and high level happened very swiftly during the last years of the Soviet Union. Yet already since the early months of 1993, this romanticised relationship started to be challenged and modified, a process continuing to this day. The most memorable and eye-opening blows, which brought relations to the brink of collapse, happened twice, in 1993 and 2008. This chapter aims to understand the key determinants of very close and special relations between Azerbaijan and Turkey, as well as the factors that have been challenging and modifying it.

How did it all begin? How far back in history can the basis of these relations be traced? What is the share of objective structural factors and perceptions in this relationship? And what are the lessons learned that could be applied to sustain, if not generate, a healthy relationship between Azerbaijan and Turkey?

During the last years of the Soviet Union, for the secular nationalist elite of the liberation movement of Azerbaijan, Turkey provided the most optimal alternative model in the immediate neighborhood to the past and current socialism (Larrabee and Lesse 2003, 104). It was the most progressive country in terms of political and economic institutions, closely integrated into the West, and, thus, an antidote to the potential revival of Russian imperial drive. As if overnight, Azerbaijan discovered a bigger, richer, and more powerful 'similar' to its west who spoke a language not requiring an interpreter. This is exactly what Baku felt it needed in the Western-dominated new world, to which it was planning to move from the Russian-dominated one rather swiftly.

Yet there was one concrete factor that fundamentally shaped the essence of the relationship during those fateful years in the early 1990s. The national liberation movement in Azerbaijan was born out of a response to the Armenian demands on Nagorno-Karabakh, which soon turned violent (Bolukbasi 2011, 1). From the start, Azerbaijanis looked at the world through the prism of Karabakh. And in this world, Turkey was the most important and probably the only country that seemed to care about Azerbaijan's legitimate demands and ready at least to listen to its side of the story.

One of the main arguments of this chapter is that, absent the Nagorno-Karabakh conflict, Azerbaijan's humiliating losses and the role Turkey was expected to play and the one it actually played during the early 1990s, qualitatively speaking, relations between the two states would not have been this 'special.' Relations were forged during an existential war for Azerbaijan. This is not to say that otherwise Turkey would have become 'just another country to do business with.' As indicated above, there were other important structural factors at play. But the sense of affection on the Azerbaijani side would have been different. It is also plausible to venture into an argument that without Karabakh, there might not have been enough ideological motivation and passion to push for the Baku-Ceyhan oil pipeline, the Baku-Erzurum gas pipeline and the Baku-Kars railroad.

The crucial war years since the late 1980s until 1994 conditioned bilateral relations to a large extent, including the past. Azerbaijan, especially during the Elchibey years, relied on Turkey unreservedly (Bal 2004, 275). Turkey played along somewhat reluctantly, and with the Armenian advances far beyond Nagorno-Karabakh in 1993, unrealistically exaggerated expectations and promises inevitably collapsed. Change of government in Azerbaijan in the same year and the crucial decisions Heydar Aliyev made in Nagorno-Karabakh, in consolidating his power and in the international energy policy once more proved Turkey's indispensability. Since then, more or less, relations have been riding on the wave generated by these three fateful years.

On the Turkish side, Ataturk's Turkish nationalism, the official ideology of the country, and the more general and fundamentalist versions of it that came before and after Ataturk, had already made Azerbaijan a part of Turkish ideational history (Reynolds 2011, 167–191). But the disappearance of the USSR meant much more than a chance for the fulfillment of romantic nationalistic feelings. In the early 1990s, one of the deepest concerns in Turkey was about the international identity of this nation, one that since the late 1940s had been defined in terms of an alliance with the 'free world' against communism. According to Yucel Bozdaglioglu, the political and military emphasis in the West's relations with Turkey during the Cold War resulted in the perception of Turkey as a Western/European country. With the end of the Cold War, however, the emphasis shifted to cultural factors, which suddenly started to push Turkey outwards (2003, 80).

The fear was that, in the absence of the Soviet foe, Turkey would no longer be able to benefit from the political, economic and military support of its Western allies. This was perceived almost as an existential threat. The European

Community's rejection of the Turkish membership bid in 1989 was not helping much either (Cornell 2011, 362). It would not be true to claim that the Turkish political elite have ever seriously thought of the Caucasus and Central Asia as an alternative to the West. However, in this prevailing context of the post–Cold War years, these eastern regions were generating a significant pull for Turkey as a political, economic and ideological breathing space. A junior and a relatively backward ally of the West found a place where it was looked up to as a progressive leader. At the same time, the West, and especially the US, was eyeing Turkey as the country with the biggest hard and soft power to balance Russia and Iran in the former southern Soviet Union.[1]

Turkey was also realising the promising energy potential of the region, which could turn Ankara into a crucial link to European markets with its excellent geopolitical position, besides enhancing the country's security and boosting its revenues. The combination of these roles as potential elements of a new international political identity did not sound like a bad deal for Turkey. Because of geography, culture and energy resources, there was hardly any country more important than Azerbaijan in this vision (Cornell 2011, 365).

As mentioned above, there have been several and mostly interrelated factors modifying and challenging this relationship from the start. The first and so far the biggest test has been Nagorno-Karabakh. Even by 1993, it was clear that Turkey was not to play the role most Azerbaijanis expected it to. At least the first phase of the war was lost, and Turkey as an ally was implicated in this. Though Azerbaijanis were not satisfied with the level of Turkish support, there have been significant voices in Turkey since the early years finding even this level of support too much. These voices have been very much influenced by international pressure and were definitely concerned about Turkey's overall stance vis-à-vis the Western world. In any case, Turkey gradually started to improve its relations with Armenia, culminating in an attempt at reconciliation in 2008. This created the biggest crisis in the history of relations between the two countries after the 1993 shock. Karabakh is what has made the relationship special and is also an issue with the capacity to destroy it, at least in the short run.

Another very important contextual factor has been fundamental socio-cultural and economic developments, and the concomitantly changing hegemonic discourse in Turkey. Although as an additional variable some would point to the AKP, which arose in the early 2000s, it has been only a tangible agent of these deeper trends.

The natural process of de-romanticisation is an additional element modifying relations. In time, the latter was inevitable after day-to-day contacts started to replace the affection towards a "lost brother over closed borders."[2] A structural issue exacerbating this process is the asymmetry of size, interdependence and mutual needs. Turkey is much bigger, and sometimes the perception is that losing Turkey will mean more to Azerbaijan than vice versa. Moreover, belonging to very different socio-political systems over the last several centuries, in time and particularly during bad times, the two societies would be taken aback by the lack of a common language and meaning.[3] Misperceptions abound.

It should also be noted that Turkey and Azerbaijan are not the biggest players either in the world or in their region. This means that from time to time, the pull and push of bigger actors and factors pressure these countries to act in such ways as to hurt relations with the 'brother.' The ever-closer Russo-Turkish relations can be viewed from this angle as well. For Turkey, the opportunity cost of siding with Azerbaijan on some issues to the dislike of Russia has been growing too high. Finally, as Azerbaijan nears the end regarding its hydrocarbon-related decisions, Turkey might be losing interest in the country, especially since it is perceived as the best natural destination or transit country for oil and gas resources of the wider region.

This chapter proceeds as follows. It starts with laying out the historical context of relations, mainly since the late nineteenth century. It then moves to the more concrete foundations of relations, which began to be built in the late 1980s. The next section focuses on the mutual favours that Turkey and Azerbaijan have done each other, with a particular focus on the developments around Nagorno-Karabakh and the role it played in structuring relations over the last two decades. The following three sections are devoted to the three outstanding factors shaping relations between the countries: the AKP and the larger post-modernist trend in Turkey, de-romanticisation, and the West. Then the chapter discusses the misperceptions and stereotypes in Turkey and Azerbaijan, while the penultimate part measures the pros and cons of the relations for each country. The last section concludes.

Historical context of relations: balancing idealism with reality

The very similar populations in the regions currently comprised by the Turkish and Azerbaijani republics have been present since at least the eleventh century. They became organised into sophisticated Ottoman and Iranian empires by the sixteenth century. Yet the current historical memory between Azerbaijanis of the Republic of Azerbaijan and Turks of Turkey can only be traced back to the late nineteenth and early twentieth centuries without important interruptions. Although as parts of the Iranian and Ottoman empires the two peoples were in contact and shared a lot of history (in fact, mostly as adversaries), that memory has been largely lost since the capture of the northern part of Azerbaijan from Iran by the Russian empire.[4] Consequently, the current continuous history of the Turks of Turkey and the Azerbaijanis of the Republic of Azerbaijan started in the second half of the nineteenth century.

This chapter does not aim to provide a detailed analysis of the history of the last 150 years. Rather, it tries to shed light on the last 20. Yet a more fundamental look at the causes of relations between the two nations cannot be complete without a reference to their generation under the pressure of Western ideas, arms and policies in the late nineteenth and early twentieth centuries. Indeed, the romantic-pragmatic context in which relations between the two states have been playing out since the 1990s is the outcome of this brief timeframe, especially the first two decades of the twentieth century.

For Azerbaijanis reopening their eyes under Russian control in the 1820s and trying to redefine their shaken identity, there was, at first, no hesitation that they belonged 'back' to Iran. History and religion seemed to provide good reason to believe so. But in time, as Azerbaijani intellectuals were determined to reform their people through education, and as they were looking to awaken their people as to who they 'really' were, the language and with it the ethnic identity were beginning to acquire prominence. This focus was gradually supplanting Iran's culturally Persian-dominated identity with the Ottoman empire, where the Turkish identity of the main constituent ethnic group was moving into the center-stage of their own and separate-until-that-time identity quest (Swietochowski 1996, 233).

As the Azeri intellectuals of the Russian empire were looking towards the Ottoman empire as a source of inspiration in defining their identity, they were not always satisfied with the direction and the level of sophistication of the debates in Istanbul. Eventually, their contribution to the emerging Turkish nationalism in the Ottoman lands in the early twentieth century proved unmistakably crucial. This development laid the foundation of the first serious link between Azerbaijanis and Ottoman Turks. European nationalist ideology was carried over to Turkey not through the geographically shortest route – the Balkans – but rather through the Turkic intellectuals from Russia. If the French Revolution ignited Russian nationalism, the latter inspired the Turkic one within the Russian empire. As early as the late nineteenth century, Turkic intellectuals from Russia started to visit Istanbul, giving a direction to modern Turkish nationalism, at that time in its infancy. Among the few influential Russian émigrés, Azerbaijanis such as Ahmet Agaoglu and Ali Bey Huseynzade were standing out (Altstadt 1996, 208).

The advent to power of the Union and Progress movement in Turkey in 1908 and of the Musavat in Azerbaijan in 1918 meant the coming to power of commonly shared ideas. With the involvement of the Ottoman military forces in the liberation of Azerbaijan in 1918, this ideational link manifested itself in practice and was put to the test. This was to become perhaps the most celebrated example of cooperation between the two nations. In fact, the Azerbaijani side is almost never shy to state that, more than cooperation, this was about a helping hand extended by Turks to snatch Azerbaijani independence from the jaws of the Bolshevik-Armenian yoke.[5]

This page in the history of Azerbaijan and Turkey is also an indication that relations were not based on ideas and idealism alone. Although both sides were very much inspired by Turkism, they were also pragmatic calculators. While the Ottomans were interested in expanding their empire eastwards as the lands to the west and south were being lost, and eyed Baku's oil with a keen interest, Azerbaijanis saw in the Ottomans a relatively more reliable ally in efforts to acquire and preserve their autonomy and, later on, independence. A common adversary in the Armenians was another crucial factor helping the relationship and tying the countries together (Reynolds 2011, 84).

Yet the elites of the two countries did not agree all the time, not even on strategic issues. The Ottomans did not want a completely independent Azerbaijan, to which many Azerbaijanis objected. Later on, Ataturk's close relations with Bolshevik Russia and Azerbaijan's willingness to look for British support to counter the impending threat of the Bolshevik invasion generated tensions in the relations of the two countries. One can also frequently stumble upon "who is more sophisticated" debates during those years (Oliker et al. 2003, 201).

The early 1900s, therefore, were not very different from the 1990s and 2000s. From the beginning, one of the problems between the two communities has been about balancing ideas with actions, pragmatism with idealism, and romance with reality. Then as now, being heirs to different historical processes, the elites from time to time had difficulty in communicating and treating each other as equals. Another problem, as it is now, was the asymmetry of relations, Turkey being economically, politically and demographically incomparably more powerful. This situation was aggravated by the fact that Azerbaijan needed Turkey strategically, while the same was not the case on the Turkish side. Then as now, relations between Turks and Azerbaijanis were challenged by more powerful international actors. From time to time, these structural factors would pull the two states in two different directions, while the blame would lie with the 'brother.'

The defeat of the Ottomans in the First World War, the occupation of Azerbaijan by Russia and the isolationist stance of Ataturk's Turkey pulled the countries significantly apart. But the Republic of Turkey continued to be nationalist similar to what the Committee of Union and Progress had implanted in the country, and the nationalist element was (or was allowed to be) considerably powerful in Soviet Azerbaijan until the 1930s (Hüzeyinzade 1998, 35–36). Another and more important context for continuing relations was the Turkish and Soviet stance against Western imperialism, and Russia's plans to turn Azerbaijan into a gate for Communism's march to the Middle East. The annihilation of the Azerbaijani elite during the late 1930s purges and Stalin's claims to Turkish territories after the Second World War put an end to this phase of relations (Hasanli 2011, 1). Despite these developments, the impossibility of missing the striking similarity by newer generations and the dominance of the center-right parties in Turkish politics, as well as the newly developing affection of the Turkish leftist movement towards Soviet Azerbaijan, guaranteed temporal continuity.

Therefore, all the forces occupying the Turkish political space in the 1990s, except for the politicised members of the Kurdish nationalist movement, had a share of nostalgic and romantic association with the phenomenon of Azerbaijan. Partially, it was this romantic feeling that, when the perceptions were not favourable, would keep the relationship at levels difficult to explain by political pragmatism alone. As this brief excursion into history shows, there had been considerably serious practical aspects of the relations in the early 1900s. It was the Soviet years of isolation that idealised the situation more. All in all, however, without the context of the Karabakh war, relations would not have acquired the special nature they had in the 1990s.

The Soviet collapse and early years of independence: how did it all begin?

The leaders of the resurgent national liberation movement of Azerbaijan in the late 1980s, while searching the pages of history for analogies to their situation, found the early 1900s to be a nearly perfect fit. The periods were not only similar in terms of a weakening Russia and the challenges the Armenians were posing to Azerbaijan. Just like the early 1900s, the only country that had the will and capacity to help Azerbaijan to somehow balance against Russia and Armenia was Turkey, the successor to the Ottoman empire. At the same time, the prevailing alternative discourse to the crumbling communist present was Western politico-economic models and nationalism. But western Europe and North America were far away, both geographically and culturally. Turkey, a modern moderate Moslem nation with a market economy, a working democracy and NATO membership in the immediate neighborhood was almost too good to be true.

The globally rare cultural and linguistic similarity meant that there was to be an additional dimension to the relationship lowering the transaction costs considerably. This similarity also meant that if conditions were right, a working relationship between the two countries was to have a romantic tone, augmenting the romance emanating from historical experience. There was, however, one big difference between the 1900s and 1990s: unlike the 1900s, when Russia was the only reasonable gate to the latest achievements of human civilisation, in the 1990s a more modern, a more Western and a more European alternative in Azerbaijan's neighborhood also pointed towards Turkey.

However, the criterion by which Turkey's (or any other country's) real worth in Azerbaijan's eyes was eventually measured was Ankara's stance regarding the ultimate challenge facing Azerbaijan – Nagorno-Karabakh (Cornell 1998, 60). Indeed, one thing that Turkish pundits and politicians have never been able to fully grasp is that Azerbaijan found Turkey amid the overwhelming onslaught of the Armenian demands on NK and the powerlessness it felt facing this unstoppable encroachment. In the new, unknown and hostile world, the only supporting voice came from the direction of Turkey. It entered the Azerbaijani psyche amid the existential physical threat of the Armenian aggression, which continues to be the most concrete and most important reason to this day for the unrelenting affection towards Turkey.

True, in the beginning, the Azerbaijani elite was more concerned about making Azerbaijani independence irreversible than Karabakh per se. For them, the larger and by far more important issue was about preventing Russia from coming back. In fact, NK was eventually, and not fully inadvertently, sacrificed to this bigger end, as the Elchibey government had been stubbornly pushing Russian military bases out since the day it came to power. "Striking a contrast to the protracted withdrawal of Russian troops from the Baltic states, the last Russian unit . . . withdrew from Azerbaijan in May 1993, about a year ahead of the schedule" (Suny 1996, 143). Considering that with all the Western support, Baltic states managed to get rid of the Russian troops in general only a year later, it is easy to guess what awaited Azerbaijan. Alienating the already humiliated, angry and resurgently aggressive Russia, the Elchibey government eventually brought about the loss of the huge swaths of Azerbaijani lands, as well as its own downfall.[6] In fact, it increasingly was becoming clear that if Azerbaijan was to lose its independence, it was about to unfold through Karabakh.

Although the ideational fraternity and Ottoman support in the liberation of Baku during the first experience with independence in 1918 were crucial historical factors and although Turkey also meant progress, the healthiest bridge to the West and the 'successful similar' in an alien world, in the absence of support on the NK issue, such historical memories and abstract factors would not have been unearthed with such passion and an emphasis on the positives. It was in light of this Turkish support in Karabakh that the history of Azerbaijan was rewritten.

Although there could be certain objective factors out there in history and only so much interpretation, Azerbaijan's history is too rich to lend support to only one point of view. If somehow it was Russia or Iran that took Turkey's position on NK instead, Azerbaijani history would have focused on the considerable positive moments about these countries while silencing the more negative experiences. After all, it was the Iranians who fought to the death trying to keep the Russians away from northern Azerbaijan, where they were about to suffer Armenian encroachments.

Or it would have become a historical point of emphasis that it was the Russians who brought in the message of the European Enlightenment and modern state institutions, making Azerbaijan one of the most progressive lands in the Middle East and the Moslem world in general. It should be noted that both claims are supported by counterfactuals. If Azerbaijanis perceive Iran as less than brotherly, one of the first two reasons to come to mind is their supportive stance towards Armenia.[7] Similarly, there are hardly any grudges held vis-à-vis Russia except for their (sometimes exaggerated) help for the Armenian side currently and during the war.

In the same vain, it would have become clear that the Ottoman elite who sent a military expedition to Azerbaijan in 1918 were not burning up with passion to make the country free and independent. Baku's oil was important, and more than a fully sovereign Azerbaijan, the Ottoman imperial center was looking for a suzerainty. Nuri Pasha, head of the Ottoman-established Army of Islam composed of Ottomans and Azerbaijanis, had a serious dispute with the Azerbaijani political elite in Ganja, who were not ready to settle for less than full independence.

In general, the policies under Ottoman military rule were perceived as eroding the achievements of the Russian Revolution, and its ultimate aim was seen as *Ilhaq*, some form of unification rather than federation with Turkey (Swietochowski 1995, 71).

Ataturk was not very happy with the Azerbaijanis' affection for the British as a guarantor of Baku's independence, about whom the Turks had bitter memories and who they perceived as a direct threat to their own nascent state. Ataturk did not have much hesitation in sacrificing Azerbaijan to Russia, and his deals with

Bolsheviks were among the key factors facilitating the invasion of Azerbaijan by the XI Red Army (Swietochowski 1995, 86–97). Today, Azerbaijanis emphasise the considerable amount of help in treasure and blood they extended to the Turks defending Gallipoli, but there are quite a few accounts of how brave "Caucasian Moslems" were while fighting the Ottomans since the late nineteenth century as part of the Russian imperial army (Waal 2004, 187). History can always be rewritten.

Besides Turkish support on the NK issue, the context this support culminated in, the most tangible element, the closure of the Turkish-Armenian borders, played an extremely significant role in structuring the relationship. Elchibey and the Popular Front miscalculated. Despite all the rhetoric and good intentions, Turkey was not as powerful as they thought it was; at least not to the extent of totally alienating Iran and Russia for its sake. There is no claim that Turkey encouraged such a behavior on Azerbaijan's part. To the contrary, there are reasons to believe that they were quite uncomfortable with its adventurist moves.

> Elchibey's erratic style did not align with the traditional cautiousness of Turkish foreign policy. Indeed, Elchibey was a bit too pan-Turkic even for Ankara's taste, and certainly too indiscreet a pan-Turkist.
>
> (Cornell 2011, 366)

Unlike the Popular Front leadership, the Turks had no romantic feelings about their capabilities. Turkish foreign policy in the last century has been a foreign policy acutely and pragmatically aware of the state's limitations. The Popular Front government of Azerbaijan would soon pay the price for unreasonably alienating and frightening Russia and Iran, when its successful military operations in Nagorno-Karabakh were mysteriously and swiftly stopped in the autumn of 1992.[8]

When the Armenians went beyond Nagorno-Karabakh for the second time and invaded Kalbajar province in March 1993, the limits of Turkish power finally became clear to the Azerbaijani leadership. Contrary to Azerbaijani expectations, but probably not surprisingly to an outside observer, Turkey refused to send transport helicopters to rescue stranded civilians in Kalbajar. Hundreds died fleeing Armenian occupation (Waal 2013, 225).

Armenia sided with Russia; the result was Nagorno-Karabakh plus surrounding Azerbaijani territories twice the size of Nagorno-Karabakh. The means was considerable transfer of military hardware and advice (Waal 2004, 199–205). Azerbaijan sided with Turkey; the only tangible means of support was Turkish military advisers and the only concrete act of punishment was the closure of Turkish borders with Armenia (Cornell 2011, 67–69). For the first time in the history of the Turkish Republic, there was a state completely willing to lean on Turkey for its security and well-being and the outcome was a disaster.[9] If all Turkey could do in return was close down its borders, there was no question that this was a fair trade for Turkey. Especially if you add all the affection Azerbaijan developed towards it due to this move and all the world-class projects that ensued.

As Azerbaijan and Turkey were standing together, Turkey was implicated in Azerbaijan's failure in Nagorno-Karabakh. True, the Turks never claimed to be what the Elchibey government perceived them to be, but still, "they liked their image that they saw in Azerbaijan's eyes." It was this perception that Turkey did not do enough for Azerbaijan that created additional room for romance and added to a special nature of relations. It was this sense that made Azerbaijanis think that they more than deserved a closure of borders with Armenia by Turkey. Probably, along with other factors, this attitude generated a certain sense of entitlement on the part of Azerbaijan, sometimes to the surprise and disapproval of Turkey.

Who favours whom: borders and pipelines

The border closure has cost Turkey more than any other move it made vis-à-vis Azerbaijan. Turkey added another issue to its long list of problems with the West, where Armenians have a very powerful presence. This was especially acute for a Turkey implicated in the forceful deportation of Armenians from Anatolia during the First World War. Therefore, this was the move that generated more resentment among the Turkish elite than anything else Turkey has done for Azerbaijan. At the same time, this was the biggest favour ever done to Azerbaijan in its most pressing problem by any nation. It was thus instrumental in making Turkey the friendliest nation in the eyes of Azerbaijanis. It won the hearts, minds and the biggest projects of Azerbaijan. In other words, Turkey gained from Azerbaijan more in return for this than for any other step. The interplay of these elements rendered the border issue the most important and dynamic factor shaping the relationship.[10]

The closure of Turkish borders to Armenia was probably the key factor that has fueled the 'genocide recognition' campaign of the already over-energised members of the Armenian diaspora, and since 1998, of the Republic of Armenia, with all its concomitant negative connotations in the West, both materially and discursively. True, the Armenian diaspora started its genocide recognition crusade long before the closure of 1993, and it took the change of power from Ter-Petrosyan to Karabakh Armenians in 1998 for the Republic of Armenia to become a part of the game. Still, the closure added more weight to the Armenian victimhood cry and has started to play a role in fueling the process of discrediting Turkey for the tragic events in Anatolia during the First World War.

Although not explicitly expressed, the border closure issue has been increasingly seen among the conditions Ankara has to fulfill to get the elusive EU membership (Balamir-Coskun and Demirtas-Cosgun 2009, 388). Besides this political pressure, Turkey also finds itself under the weight of the overwhelming Western cultural/intellectual discourse, which is amazed by how a 'committer of genocide' could inflict additional economic pain on its former 'victim.' Given the historical memory of the Ottoman Armenians during the late nineteenth and early twentieth centuries, Turkey will always have a weak stand in accusing Armenia, even if the latter is caught red-handed. The Turkish elite thus abhor the idea of having added one more point of difference to an already long list between Turkey and the West. The career foreign policy elite especially, who have always in their perceptions tried to narrow this cultural gap, found it difficult to put up with this situation. They had been against this move from the very beginning.

For Azerbaijan, this was the strongest tangible gesture by any single country, one that has drawn attention to the illegal and illegitimate situation created by the use of force in Azerbaijani territories. When the entire world was watching and, thanks to powerful Armenian propaganda, blaming Azerbaijan, which was losing territories and being flooded by internally displaced people, it also simply helped to keep the sanity of Azerbaijanis. This was the only biting punishment for the occupier. At the same time, Azerbaijan successfully capitalised on the strategic implications of this move. Deprived of healthy trade relations with the most dynamic major power in the region, Armenia suffered significant economic and demographic losses. Probably one of the reasons Azerbaijan relied on Turkey in almost all of its important projects (the current and planned oil and gas pipelines, the rail line) has something to do with the thinking that Turkey's gain will not be Armenia's. Besides, Azerbaijan was willing to reciprocate the favour.

Not every energy deal with Turkey could qualify as a special reward. Azerbaijan tried to satisfy all three major regional powers in its neighbourhood with shares in the development of the ACG oil and Shah Deniz gas fields. But regarding the BTC pipeline, the sense of obligation towards Turkey should have been quite instrumental. With the border move, Turkey for the first time did something that really hurt itself; truly qualifying as help. It was a sacrifice on the part of Turkey and the ball was in Azerbaijan's court. The ultimate decision to lay a major oil pipeline through Turkey was a partial sacrifice on behalf of Azerbaijan.

Turkey and certain circles in the US government unconditionally supported a pipeline going through Turkey. Russia and Iran were against it. Perhaps an even bigger challenge came from the oil companies, which calculated the cost to be too high. For the latter, shipping oil to Black Sea terminals through Georgia or even Russia made much more sense. "Despite the political support behind the BTC project and the increasing understanding of the danger of the Bosporus chokepoint, the oil companies remained reluctant" even after Turkey spent a lot of effort to defend this position (Baran 2005, 116). Azerbaijan under the Aliyev presidency was weighing its options. At the start, nothing was predetermined. Eventually Turkey was chosen despite objections by Russia and the oil companies and the very high cost of the pipeline. Turkey's stance on the NK issue, border closure being its most important ingredient, might have been a factor that tipped the balance in favour of BTC.

The counterargument would be that Turkey was still the best option for Azerbaijan. Iran and Russia aside, even getting oil to the Black Sea through Georgia was not a good idea. In this case, Turkey would be added to the list of dissatisfied neighbours because of being left out and for overcrowding the Straits. And a weaker Georgia, although unable to manipulate the pipeline against Azerbaijan, was not adding to its strategic weight either. The fact that there was a major regional power behind the pipeline, in turn supported by the sole superpower, was insurance against a likely future interference by forces unfriendly to Azerbaijan. True, in any case the Baku–Tbilisi pipeline would have the support of the United States, but having a big regional supporter also mattered (The Economist 2005).

Therefore, there were factors independent of the closure that would have pointed towards Turkey regarding the choice of the pipeline route. But absent the momentum generated by the war, there might not have been enough energy to carry out the difficult and politically and economically costly project. Another implication of the Turkish stand was the sense of trust it generated for Azerbaijanis. Reciprocating the favour, trusting Turkey, and adding to Armenia's isolation, therefore, were important elements. These foundations, coupled with the de facto success of BTC, paved the way for the BTE gas pipeline and the Baku-Akhalkalaki-Kars railroad. And now, the next pipeline to carry Shah Deniz II gas to Europe, TANAP, is being built through Turkey as well.

Another favour, according to Azerbaijanis, has been the low price of gas they started to sell to Turkey in 2007. At the start, the price was around 120 USD per thousand cubic meters, almost three times less than what Turkey paid to Russia and Iran. The agreement had in-built clauses envisioning the revision of the price the following year, in 2008. But despite this, Azerbaijan never brought up the matter, and Turkey was still buying gas at a lower price. Apparently, this was viewed by the Azerbaijani side as a favour for the border issue, for one of the first things Baku did when it was becoming clear that Turkey was serious about reopening the borders without Armenian military withdrawal was to demand to renegotiate the gas price. It was impossible to miss from the Azerbaijani rhetoric that it perceived the lower price as a quid pro quo and now there was no reason to continue it (Radikal 2009). Eventually, the sides did agree on the amount of the upward revision, and Turkey was to pay a year's worth of price difference retrospectively. But negotiations have resumed, as Azerbaijan was not satisfied with the new price either. Although Baku was not asking as much as Tehran or Moscow, it wanted the price to be still closer to theirs.

Needless to say, Turkey hardly thinks of the gas deal over Shah Deniz I as special treatment. According to a former high-level Turkish government representative, speaking on condition of anonymity, in the beginning they were planning to buy Turkmen gas and were in negotiations with Ashkhabad. It was only after the discovery of Shah Deniz that Azerbaijan began to press Turkey to buy its gas instead. Therefore, Turkey was actually helping Azerbaijan. At the same time, it was part of the deal to sell gas to Turkey for 120 USD and when Azerbaijan disagreed, the difference was paid to it anyway. It is very hard to believe that Turkey could have pulled off the trans-Caspian pipeline required to ship Turkmen gas to Turkey in the face of Russian and Iranian resistance. And whatever the reasons, buying gas for one-third of the world market price is always a good deal. Still, the Turkish claims are not baseless.

Therefore, there are two issues that qualify as favours in the eyes of one of the parties, while not totally shared by the other. Turkey thinks and feels that the closure of the borders has been a costly favour done to Azerbaijan. Azerbaijan, in turn, thinks that the closure was a natural consequence of very close relations, and probably even fell short of what a real ally should have done (Cornell 1998, 67). That is, given what Russia did for Armenia for the same issue, Turkey's help does not even count. (This issue has been tackled above.)

Similarly, Azerbaijan thinks that the oil and gas pipelines and the Shah Deniz I deal were favours extended to Turkey. The pipelines were realised at the expense of alienating Russia, as well as probably Iran, and despite the high cost and thus lower level of revenues left to Azerbaijan. A dominant view in Turkey is that for Azerbaijan, this was the best option anyway. In fact, in recent years, a dangerous and false view has been gaining uninformed consensus in Turkey that while Azerbaijan has benefited hugely from the BTC pipeline, they have been losing money on the project. On one more issue, Turkey has been underwriting Azerbaijan's national interest. A high-level US official, speaking on condition of anonymity, once indicated that Turks at one point convinced themselves that America was pushing them to accept an unfavourable deal in BTC and they had no other option but to accept it. This view apparently has become entrenched since then.

Because of the specificities of the deal with the BTC Company, the company owning the BTC pipeline, BOTAS, a state-owned company in Turkey involved in the energy deal, has been losing money with the operation of the pipeline per se. This is related to the rise in the price of fuel for the compressor stations, while the agreement takes them as constant at a much lower level. According to a high-level former BOTAS official personally involved in negotiations, so far BOTAS has lost around 90 million USD due to a missed clause in the deal (UPI 2009).

It should be noted that this deal is not between the Azerbaijani and Turkish governments, but rather between a consortium of foreign companies and Turkey. Moreover, Turkey also gets taxes and, as a result of an enriched Azerbaijan, a lot of trade, tourists and investment. Besides, a 90 million USD loss is not an issue for a country the size of Turkey. Agreements are binding, and if BOTAS is not happy with them, there are clear-cut world-class adjudication mechanisms built into them. But a brief talk with the Turkish side reveals that their expectation is that Azerbaijan should do something about it and that it could do it. However unprofessional this view is, the resentment this issue has been generating and the way it has been used to fuel skewed negative perceptions of Azerbaijan in Turkey makes it too costly for Azerbaijan to ignore. Although not much money for Turkey as a state, it is a considerable sum for BOTAS. Apparently the bad blood it generated in the company has been one of the main factors hurting relations between the countries. The problem needs to be openly discussed and addressed once and for all.

The AKP factor: part of a larger trend?

The AKP factor carries with it several elements influencing Turkey's relations with Azerbaijan. First, it signifies the reconfiguration of the entrenched Turkish political structure on which Azerbaijani–Turkish relations were erected in the early 1990s. Second, the AKP phenomenon has been more passionate in pushing its way to the EU in the early 2000s and in the process heeding pressure regarding

Armenia much more seriously than any government since the late 1980s. Third, in terms of its political identity, different from the traditional elite, in its essence the AKP phenomenon is closer to the pre-nationalist Ottoman era, when the Azerbaijani factor did not figure much. Finally and related to the third factor (and probably more important than all of the above in terms of longer-term consequences), AKP's rise to power is a by-product of a much larger and by far deeper trend: the changing social-economic conditions in Turkey and a related prevailing liberal post-materialist discourse.

AKP's coming to power has shaken most of the traditional groups in the Turkish political system, which constituted a backbone of closer relations with Azerbaijan on the Turkish side. The secular nationalistic civilian and military bureaucracy has been sidelined and eliminated considerably since AKP's ascendance in 2002, a process continuing to this day. On the other hand, what AKP represents as a party, or a political group, has been isolated from politics for decades, and at least since Azerbaijan became independent. Therefore, the Azerbaijani political elite and the AKP do not have a track record of relations with each other. The reconfiguration of the Turkish political space with the rise of the AKP creates an unfamiliar environment and results in the loss of institutional memory on the Turkish side. Therefore, regardless of its nature, the simple novelty of AKP rule in itself is one factor accounting for the cooling of relations with Azerbaijan.

Despite the expectation that the AKP could behave reluctantly vis-à-vis Europe, similar to its predecessor the Refah Party, the reality was a little paradoxical. The Justice and Development Party turned out to be an ardent supporter of integration with the EU and probably got closer to the goal than any other political party before it. Perhaps the single most important reason was the domestic political situation and the AK Party's search for international allies to consolidate its internal standing "against possible threats to them from the hyper-secularism of the established state elites and important sections of Turkish society" (Onis 2006). The EU was also a guarantee of religious freedoms.

> Hence, the prospect of European integration in a rather unexpected fashion has become a mechanism for preserving Turkey's Islamic identity and making it more compatible with a secular, democratic and pluralistic political order.
> (Onis 2006)

Focus on relations with the EU amounts to at least three things. Technically and conceptually, this means that there is not much time left for Turkey to look to the east of its borders, especially if one considers that the AKP has paid almost as much attention to the Middle Eastern countries that used to be associated with the Ottoman empire. Second, unlike the US, the European countries do not ascribe as much strategic value to Azerbaijan, while emphasising the political situation in the country very willingly. Moreover, many European countries are more inclined to the Armenian version of the story both in the context of Ottoman Turkey and in that of Azerbaijan, and therefore, the Europeans played a significant role in pushing Turkey to 'normalise' its relations with Armenia without waiting for the latter to withdraw from Azerbaijani territories.

The factor of ideology also played its role in redefining relations with Azerbaijan. According to Svante Cornell (2011), there are three basic political groups in Turkey with different attitudes vis-à-vis Azerbaijan. The first is the "thoroughly Westernised elite, which perceives itself as European." Although not having much against Azerbaijan per se, "it views the Turkic nations of the East – as much as it does the Middle East – as mere distractions from Turkey's main ambitions, to become part of the West" (361). The second group is the "secular center-right," with quite warm feelings towards Azerbaijan. This group dominated Turkish politics in the 1990s, with Suleyman Demirel as its main face, "but was pushed aside somewhat by the rise of the Islamic conservative movement" (362). The third group consists of Islamic conservatives. For them, religious identity is more important than ethnicity or nationality; their most compelling association is with the *umma* (the greater Moslem community). Azerbaijan's Soviet past and therefore its lax view of Islam, and its attitude towards alcohol and pork, as well as its Shia branch have been other factors driving a wedge in Turkish perceptions. Their main interest was about proselytising through the Gülen movement, and they were much more consumed by the Middle East. At times when Islamic conservatives have dominated Turkish politics – as during 1996–1997 and again starting in 2002 – this perspective led to a downgrading of the importance attached to Azerbaijan (Cornell 2011, 362).

This classification summarises the Turkish political establishment nicely. In the current political system, the first group is represented by the Republican People's Party and the Democratic Left Party. The second group is represented mainly by the Nationalist Movement Party today, but also yesterday's True Path Party and Motherland Party. The third group's leading party is the Justice and Development Party, and the Welfare Party of the 1990s. Although the leftist parties may not have as much affection for Azerbaijan as those on the center-right, the former are still different from the religious parties.

In general terms, the Islamic political parties are closer to pre-modern Ottoman political culture predating the ascendance of modern secular nationalism than other parties. Therefore, regarding their intellectual and spiritual foundations, they are alien to the period when the ideational links between Azerbaijan and Turkey were being forged. In fact, the late nineteenth and early twentieth centuries represent exactly the time period when the religiously inspired state idea began to be systematically marginalised. Ataturk's Turkey was the realisation of modern secular nationalist thinking, which also meant the defeat of the alternative religious nationalism: these were the forces Ataturk's Turkey was built not to represent; modern Turkey's emergence signified their defeat.

On the other hand, political Islam in Azerbaijan has never been an important force, probably given Russian/Soviet rule. Even in its marginal form, it usually leaned towards Shia Iran rather than Sunni Turkey. If one looks back to the pre-nationalist era in the Ottoman empire from a viewpoint of the Islamic parties in Turkey, then Azerbaijan is nothing more than an enemy as part of the Shia

Iranian or Christian Russian (where they forgot who they were) empires. At present, although not perceived as an enemy, Azerbaijan is definitely not a phenomenon very close to the heart of such groups. This alienation must be especially acute vis-à-vis the mainly Russian educated and staunchly secular political elite of Azerbaijan. The current political elites in power in Azerbaijan and Turkey might not have much in common to talk about beyond politics.

Thus, the AKP governance, being anti-establishment and an opposition party to the fundamental ideas of the Turkish Republic, especially given its relatively unprecedented majority rule, is gradually replacing the structure that was closer to Azerbaijan. Therefore, the role of the AKP in redefining relations between Azerbaijan and Turkey cannot be overlooked. But one important issue that scholars studying the two states often overlook is the much deeper socio-political trends that had begun to unfold in Turkey since before the emergence of the AKP. The AK Party has mainly been an agent, albeit a very important one, of this structural reconfiguration.

There is a slow, but apparently unstoppable political and social post-modernist evolution under way in Turkey (Mamedov 2011). This liberal, anti-state, anti-authority, anti-violence, anti-militant trend is partly about Turkey's generations-long drive towards Europeanisation. There are definitely structural reasons behind this liberalisation of outlook; Turkey is getting more secure and more prosperous and its population is looking beyond the traditional survival values à la Inglehart (Inglehart and Welzel 2005). There is also a conscious, subjective element in this Europeanisation. That is, sometimes people behave in 'European ways' despite the absence of a structural-material basis. Turks increasingly question everything that used to be in the political mainstream, which amounts to the country's history in the last one hundred years.

At least three reasons underlying this push should be noted: they do not agree with it, they want to dismantle the ideological base to clear their way in the landscape of the political superstructure and, finally, because it is trendy and European to do so. An increasing number of Turks feel that as the former imperial and now the main constituent nation and a 'secure and established' society, they are supposed to question their history and shoulder the responsibilities for its bloody pages, just as the Americans did regarding their treatment of the Indians during their pioneer-settler days and of Japanese Americans during the Second World War. This reexamination includes the 1915 events during the late Ottoman years and all the other sufferings that befell minority groups in Turkey.

A generational shift of dominant attitudes is under way in Turkey. The ideological paradigm in the country is becoming liberalised. There have been two main tangible agents of this trend. Not surprisingly, these are the same forces that have been marginalised in the last century after the establishment of Ataturk's Turkey. If one of those marginalised groups were the Islamists, as noted above, the other has been the leftists-turned-liberals of today. Those to the center-right and center-left, who ruled over Turkey under the vigilant eyes of the statist and secular military-civilian bureaucracy, are now on the defensive, being the marginalised groups of modern Turkish history. The political change of the last two decades has resulted in and has been realised partly by the alliance between liberal and Islamic groups (Kanira 2009, 131–154). The majority of the most powerful opinion makers in Turkey today have a liberal leaning; and without their support, AKP's current political stance might not have been as successful. But whatever the reasons, the dominant, normal and prevailing discourse in Turkey is becoming a liberal one, including accepting full responsibility for the Armenian question and sacrificing as much as possible to redeem a 'civilised Turkey.' An attempt to open up the borders with Armenia is better understood in light of this paradigmatic shift.

This brings up one of the fundamental aspects of the relationship between the two countries, of which many people, especially in Azerbaijan, do not seem to be aware. The Caucasus is to the left of Turkey (mainly the western part, where its economy and politics are concentrated) in terms of the continuum starting from "survival" and ending with "post-material" values (Inglehart and Welzel 2005). Economically less dynamic, politically inexperienced and militarily under threat, the nations in the Caucasus are more traditional in their political outlook than the Turks, at least regarding the latest trends. In this context, the language the Azerbaijanis use reminds the liberal new generation of the traditional forces represented by the statist and right-wing political parties. To speak the same language, or to hear Azerbaijanis speak the language of those espousing and behind the alleged 'deep-state' of the right-wing parties of yesterday, of the increasingly marginalised, does not help. When Azerbaijanis try to influence perceptions in that country by utilising this traditional language, they should not expect to change the situation much.

There is no difference between the Armenians and Azerbaijanis in terms of the traditional nature of the political culture and nationalism. But contact between Turks and Azerbaijanis is much more frequent than that between Turks and Armenians. Moreover, Armenians of all political creeds and everywhere, independent of any other factor, and by definition and by default, are against anything that does not blame the tragedy that befell them in the early twentieth century completely and unqualifiedly on Turkey. This automatically means being anti-Turkish-state, anti-Turkish-nationalism and anti–status quo in Turkey, which in turn automatically means a closer stand vis-à-vis the liberal intellectuals in Turkey. A governmental official in Armenia, an ASALA terrorist in the US, a Dashnak in France, and a liberal Armenian columnist in Turkey share the same views about Turkey and its past. This view is in line with the views of the new generation, of the paradigmatic shift in Turkey not because of the similar political philosophy, but because of the former's Armenian ethnic identity.

Compared with an Azerbaijan that speaks the language of the past, and Azerbaijanis in Turkey who are part and parcel of the traditionalist statist and rightist groups, there are Armenians who used to be among the most European people in Turkey (at least those living in the western parts of the country), who are living in and are revered in the West. The members of the Armenian minority in Turkey are staunch liberals and anti-establishment. Therefore, the phenomena of Azerbaijan and Armenia happen to be parts of two different socio-political trends in Turkey, and Azerbaijan's side does not seem to be the winning one.

There are several factors mitigating Azerbaijan's conundrum. To begin with, both groups dominating Turkish intellectual and political worlds still have their share of affection for Azerbaijan – the liberals because of the intellectual history of modern Turkey and their previous leftist inclinations (Azerbaijan used to be Soviet after all). As for the AKP, it could be regarded as the amalgamation of former Islamist movement members with those of the center-right. There are a substantial number of former ANAP, DYP or even MHP members within the AKP. Thus, to an extent, there are elements of traditional political and ideational forces within the AKP with which Azerbaijan shares a more similar language.

Besides, the Islamists, who are too broad a group to be gathered under one umbrella, have their power base in Anatolia, where the similarity of the identity of the two nations generates spontaneous sympathy. Therefore, the AKP phenomenon will be constrained in its policy choices vis-à-vis Azerbaijan. It should also be noted that too much emphasis on the AKP for the deterioration of relations might not be warranted. The same sort of cooling in relations could have been the case with another party in government with everything else being constant.

De-romanticisation

The process of de-romanticisation probably started as early as when the two countries began to explore each other in the first years of the 1990s. The notion of romantic relations entails at least two things. First, it is about the prevalence of altruism and disregard for rational cost-benefit calculation in the relationship; this is what sociologists term a "primary group" relationship. Second, romance implies the exaggeration of positive traits of the other and downplaying its deficiencies. For Azerbaijanis, Turkey was a developed member of the Western world with one of the best armed forces, most refined cultures, most progressive political systems and a powerful economy. For Turks, Azerbaijan was a cultured lost brother, who for years had been part of the feared and sophisticated Russian empire. In a few areas, Azerbaijan's and Turkey's interests coincided, but one factor that elevated the romance to a special level was the surprising degree of similarity between the two nations.

Disregard for cost-benefit calculation is well symbolised by Elchibey's insistence on giving a bigger share to Turkey of Azerbaijani oil resources. Elchibey proclaimed that for years the Russians exploited Azerbaijan's oil and that therefore Turks, our brothers, deserve even more.[11] The Turkish side probably was not prepared to sacrifice as much in the beginning, but this was not felt so much. Turkey was much bigger than Azerbaijan, and thus even relatively small favours from this country were big enough for Azerbaijan. Second, Azerbaijan was entering the Western world in which Turkey has had a fateful experience. Therefore, qualitatively, Turkish help was about the fundamental needs of Azerbaijan and thus carried a strategic character whatever the degree. Third, Turkish statehood was experienced enough to control the country's and its population's affection for Azerbaijan. Just the opposite applies to Azerbaijan: it was smaller; for Turkey, entering the post-Soviet space was not an existential issue; and it had no experience in interstate relations.

In any case, in time and as the relations were cooling down, both nations began to look back and claim that each had done more for the other and did not get much in return. This aspect has been tackled above; yet it needs to be reiterated that this feeling and thinking is one of the most important reasons for today's disagreements between the two nations: from gas deals to how to treat the occupied Azerbaijani lands, to Cyprus, to the PKK. Turkey and Azerbaijan are not only shifting their relations to the 'secondary group' level, but also carrying resentments from the good old days, which are not appreciated by the 'ungrateful brother.'

The degree of similarity between the nations was so high that at first differences were ignored. In fact, this first awe at the common traits was partially liable for the surprise that the eventual discovery of differences would generate.

Azerbaijan and Turkey are heirs to very different political and cultural traditions. Azerbaijan used to be part of Shia Iran, the very antithesis of the Sunni Ottoman empire. Not only are Azerbaijanis historically Shia, but also they mostly give lip service to religious practice. Since the nineteenth century, Azerbaijan had been invaded by Russia, the main nemesis of the Ottoman empire. The Russian empire was replaced by the Soviet Union, a unique political system, while Turkey became part of the other pole – the 'free world,' in the 1940s. This also meant entirely different educational backgrounds; one Russian/Soviet, the other Oriental and quasi-European. Moreover, Turkey is one of the few nations in the non-Western world that has not been colonised. The Republic of Azerbaijan was never the center of the Iranian empire and had been colonised by Russia for about two centuries.

With the increasing frequency of contact, the differences were coming ashore. One of the disappointments came when Azerbaijanis eventually realised that those who initially made their way to Baku, mostly Turkish nationalists, were not representing the majority of the political elite. Turkey was not the Nationalist Action Party. Turks, in turn, continue to evaluate Azerbaijan according to their domestic criteria. If some of them were disappointed that Azerbaijan was a foreign country composed of MHP grassroots, later on MHP people were disappointed that Azerbaijan's Turkish nationalism was something different than what they had at home.

The discovery of such differences took an interesting turn, as and when both sides started the age-old habit of comparing the self with the significant other to see who was better than whom and in what respect. Although Turkey was more developed in general, certain portions, such as the southeast, were less developed even compared with the least developed parts of Azerbaijan. And although Turkey was much closer to the West in terms of all kinds of institutions, from political to economic to educational, it struck many Azerbaijanis that Turks were simply imitating the West, unable to generate an indigenous dynamic cultural, economic and political base of its own. Different from Turkey, and as part of the Soviet Union, which was more European in many respects and which managed to develop its own original ideology of life, Azerbaijanis, especially the educated elite, felt that they were definitely not lagging behind in many respects (Cornell 2011, 361).

Turks, on the other hand, think that they have been able to build a better economic, cultural and political environment than their brethren to the east. In fact, in time, Turks started to perceive Azerbaijan as yet another eastern Anatolian province. It was not only less developed, but the language spoken in Azerbaijan is perceived as a modified version of the Turkish spoken in Anatolia. There is no question that for many Turks this is a 'sweet' and a more 'original' Turkish, but it is impossible to hide the fact that this language is also looked down on as unrefined and somewhat primitive. Although an Azerbaijani would immediately embark upon learning Turkish while in Turkey, there are very few Turks doing the same in Azerbaijan. Even the number of those trying to use Azerbaijani words in their sentences are rather rare; many Turks speak the same language in Baku as they do in Istanbul. In some cases, Turks residing in Azerbaijan have their kids taught Russian instead of Azerbaijani. On the other hand, on many occasions one can find Azerbaijanis trying to speak Turkish to Turks in Azerbaijan. It seems that on the issue of "whose language," there is already a ranking and apparently both sides agree about which one is the first choice. But such issues create resentment in Azerbaijan (Mamedov 2011).

There is a sense of 'big brotherhood' on the Turkish side, which the Turks approach in a rather innocent way. But for Azerbaijanis who just got rid of their Russian 'big brother,' this is not always welcome. Big brotherhood implies who is at the center and who is on the periphery. Especially the Turkish side, conceiving itself as the one epitomising Turkishness, finds it strange that the people of a nation (Azerbaijan) that calls itself Turkic are sometimes quite different from Turks in Istanbul or Anatolia. Thus, it is hard to say that there is an acceptance of the plurality of Turkism, rather, other 'Turks' are supposed to live up to the standards that the 'big Turk' has already achieved and established.

It would be fair to say that Azerbaijanis have a mixed feeling about this situation. Many increasingly feel that there are things to be learnt from Turkey. Especially the continuation of the occupation of the Azerbaijani lands against the background of the heroic Turkish war of independence and the attractive military culture in Turkey feeds this sense. The same similarity that has been an asset in relations could turn into a liability in this context. A more developed Russia may not generate as much resentment, since they are different in any case. But if your 'similar' is doing much better, and does not attempt to hide his successes vis-à-vis your failures, this could be a potentially explosive emotional issue. It is not impossible for Turks and Azerbaijanis to start perceiving each other as 'the opposite.' Apparently, this process has already taken off.

It is very easy to note the veiled criticism of the other if one listens to either of the sides carefully. Stereotypes regarding inferiority/superiority comparisons are in the making and when combined with the 'who favours whom' debate and 'who should be more grateful,' they acquire an unwelcome tone. The elites of the two countries are probably more different than the average Azerbaijani and Turkish person. And since the official discourse has always suppressed differences (Kardas 2009), and despite interactions, the two societies have lived in isolation (Turkish communities in Azerbaijan, for example). Such differences and inferiority/superiority perceptions have been hurting relations without being openly discussed. This trend has been accelerated following AKP's advent to power. The lack of personal chemistry between the presidents Aliyev and Erdogan has not helped much (Cagaptay 2009). It is well known that Heydar Aliyev's and Demirel's personal friendship played a great role in the development of close relations between the countries in the 1990s.[12] Apparently, similarity is not always a reason for good relations, and a good start does not have to continue the same way. One only needs to look at Russia and Ukraine, East and West Germany, or Moldova and Romania.

Prevailing discourse based on misunderstandings

The list of negative perceptions of Azerbaijan in Turkey is not short. These negative perceptions are mostly due to misperceptions. They involve the claims that Azerbaijan has taken Turkish policy towards Armenia hostage; Azerbaijan had done nothing to liberate its territories and wants Turkey to do more; it has not recognised the PKK as a terrorist organisation; it has not recognised Northern Cyprus as a state; it drags its feet on lifting the visa regime to Turkish citizens; and Azerbaijanis are stuck with the old language of nationalism and are allies of reactionary forces in Turkey.

Some circles in Turkey liken Azerbaijani–Turkish relations to US–Israeli relations (Oguz 2010). The claim could not be further away from reality. This is an indication of misinformation, disinformation and a lack of interest in trying to understand Azerbaijan in Turkey. Azerbaijani–Turkish relations are not comparable to US–Israeli relations. Unlike Israel, Azerbaijan has 16 percent of its territory occupied by Armenia. Unlike Israel, Azerbaijan witnessed the number of refugees from its regions occupied by Armenia (disregarding those expelled from Armenia) reaching 600,000 in the span of five years between 1988 and 1993. Unlike Israel, Azerbaijan is the country which has been militarily and politically powerless in the face of the Armenian onslaught. Unlike the US, Turkey has never supported a militarily powerful country and its military advances by providing it with military help changing the balance. As noted earlier, beyond advisers, Turkey never made any military move. Turkey supported an occupied country diplomatically and tangibly only by closing off its borders with the occupier.[13]

The US–Israeli analogy is used to support a widespread claim in Turkey that 'Azerbaijan has taken Turkish foreign policy hostage.' But unlike the legendarily powerful Jewish diaspora in the US, Azerbaijan has nothing comparable in Turkey. Although the total number of the Caucasian diaspora in Turkey is around 8–10 million (Cornell 2011, 365), this is not a coherent body, and regarding the Azerbaijani segment of it, they are politically marginal. The greatest support Azerbaijan has in Turkey comes from the Turkish grassroots who perceive

Azerbaijani lands as their own, which therefore becomes a matter of domestic politics. And a political party in Turkey cannot afford to overlook this perception. Hence, Azerbaijan never skillfully manipulated the intricate internal political mechanisms in Turkey. The support for Azerbaijan is a spontaneous issue. Turkish governments have been pressed into taking a more pro-Azerbaijani stand because of Turkish public opinion, which "sided heavily with Azerbaijan."[14]

Every country is restricted in its foreign policy making. A restriction may not be morally acceptable if it is the result of a fear of punishment, or of negative leverage by another entity/country. But if it is the result of mutual gain, which results in mutual restraint, there is nothing to complain about. If the deal is not beneficial, it is up to the losing country to take a different action. It is Turkey's choice to determine its policy vis-à-vis Armenia, and it is Turkey's choice to include and exclude different factors in formulating this policy. The only time Azerbaijan tried to exert an influence on Turkey was when it grumbled about the price of gas it was selling to Turkey. But it was in fact almost three times lower than the Russian and Iranian gas flowing to the country and therefore can hardly be regarded as undue pressure.

From time to time, one can hear voices from Turkey asking what Azerbaijan wants of Turkey or whether it wants too much (Birand 2010). According to this view, Azerbaijan by now should have done something to liberate its territories, and if it had not, then Turkey's attempt to try something new (like opening the borders) should not be seen as a stab in the back. Rather, this is an alternative attempt to move the situation from a dead point (Candar 2009). But if Turkey really wants to help Azerbaijan, and wonders why it has been so slow in liberating its territories, the only thing Azerbaijan wants of Turkey as an ally is to prevent Armenian ally Russia's intervention in case Azerbaijan tries to liberate the occupied territories.

Other ingredients of the misinformed rhetoric in Turkey about Azerbaijan involve complaints that Baku has not recognised the PKK as a terrorist group, has not established a visa-free regime with Turkey despite having one with Russia, and has failed to recognise Cyprus, Turkey's 'Karabakh' (Ortadogu 2011). The extent to which the latter discourse is based on misunderstanding rather than a sound assessment of reality is seen in the fact that Azerbaijan has actually several times stated, at the highest levels, that it views the PKK as a terrorist group, this stance being no less definitive than the ones Azerbaijan has taken against other terrorist groups (Milaz 2011). It goes without saying that one cannot talk of any kind of tangible support for the PKK by Azerbaijan at either the official or non-official level. The only reason the Azerbaijani government has been slow in making this legal enough to the satisfaction of Turkey stems from the cautiousness of the new state against a powerful and dangerous entity. Especially given the war with Armenia and the good relations of Armenia with Kurdish nationalists, Azerbaijan is reluctant to strengthen Armenia's hand. At the same time, because of the specific nature of the culture of governance in Azerbaijan, the political will of the top leadership is much more consequential than a legal document and there is no doubt about the existence of the former.

Regarding the visa-free regime demand by Turkey, here too it needs to be kept in mind that Azerbaijan is a country at war and such moves are viewed with caution. More specifically, it has been made clear through different channels that a visa-free regime towards Turkey will add legitimacy to the relentless Iranian pressure to open up the gates of Azerbaijan to its southern neighbor as well. Azerbaijan is already concerned with the influence of Iran through its substantial religious and intelligence network in the country; without the visa barrier, the situation could worsen.

Azerbaijan's recognition of the Turkish Republic of Northern Cyprus will not change anything in terms of the bargaining position of Turkish Cypriots or Turkey. But it will definitely result in a deepening bias vis-à-vis Azerbaijan in the West, probably bringing about the recognition of NK at least by Cyprus and Greece (Shiriyev 2012). This is too much harm for Azerbaijan and no gain for Turkey and is just the opposite of the situation around NK. In the latter, the Turkish support is almost the only thing besides Azerbaijan's position that makes a difference. And the difference it makes is at least as much as Azerbaijan's own stand. The current bargaining position of Azerbaijan, which is weak in any case, will be totally demolished if Turkey changes its position. The cost Turkey bears cannot be ignored, but neither is it backbreaking, and Turkey also reaps significant benefits as a result. The Cyprus and NK cases are not comparable.

Another view is about Azerbaijan being stuck with the old-fashioned rhetoric of traditional nationalism, and being an ally of reactionary forces in Turkey. Nationalism in Turkey and nationalism in Azerbaijan are qualitatively different. Turkey, traditionally an imperial nation, has been under the imminent pressure of Western colonialism for about two hundred years, while it has been independent under the banner of the new republic for eighty. Therefore, Turkey is almost functionally done with the mobilisational potential of traditional nationalism, with its military implications. The only exception is the Kurdish military challenge to divide the country; yet, this brings only a certain segment of society under the umbrella of traditional nationalism. In the case of Azerbaijan, the liberation movement began only twenty years ago, and the war in Nagorno-Karabakh is still on. These processes are continuing to this day. Concomitantly, Azerbaijani nationalism has been progressive, anti-imperial, pro-independence and the very tool of emancipation and enlightenment. Although the Azerbaijani elite and grassroots could have felt closer to the traditional statist establishment in Turkey, this closeness has not meant direct intervention in Turkish internal politics.

There has been much misperception on the part of Azerbaijanis as well. They failed to see that the rhetoric of the nationalist clique in Turkey is not Turkey. For years, starting with the Popular Front of Azerbaijan, Azerbaijanis viewed the Nationalist Action Party of Turkey as embodying Turkey's stance vis-à-vis their country. This attitude continues to this day in wide circles among both the elite and the population. Turkey does not have the capacity, the political will and, probably most importantly, the obligation to extend military support to Azerbaijan over the NK issue. Turkey does incur costs due to the closure of the borders, and it is frustrated because of the lack of new initiatives on NK. Turkey (and more concretely BOTAS) is losing money on the BTC pipeline, and Azerbaijan may have enough influence over the Western oil companies to mitigate the situation.

The West: a bigger factor than Turkey and Azerbaijan

The West has played its role regarding Azerbaijani–Turkish relations in three phases. During the first phase, since Azerbaijan's independence and until the AKP's ascendance to power, it largely pulled the countries together through common security concerns. In this vision, Turkey was perceived as the main bridge between the West and the Caucasus, most notably in energy projects. After the AKP's coming to power in 2002, Turkey started to push its way to the EU with unprecedented determination. It was partially related to this drive that the border issue came to the fore, risking the destruction of relations between Azerbaijan and Turkey. At this phase, Azerbaijan experienced a deterioration of relations with both Turkey and the West. The third phase started with the cooling of Turkey's relations with Israel and the US after Erdogan's famous speech in Davos in January 2009. As Azerbaijan continued its good relations with Israel and resumed those with the US, this factor has been generating additional strains in relations.

Of special interest for the purposes of this chapter are the last two phases. The AKP's unforeseen determination in pushing the gates of the EU cannot be detached from the party's position on the domestic political scene. One of the most definite beneficiaries of the reforms required by the EU was to be the AK Party and the Islamists in general. There are still doubts about their real intention, and the eventual halt in the reform process does not help the optimists much. But at least, to consolidate their legal and political standing, the AKP needed the reforms that happened to be demanded by the EU as well (such as curbing the political power of the military), and they have been successful in that sense. Getting closer to Europeans meant listening to Europeans more and more and, therefore, acting more favourably vis-à-vis Armenia.

The Obama factor needs to be singled out, as it could be considered a trigger for the border blunder. Because of his promise to the Armenian American community to label the 1915 events as genocide before his election in 2008, after the election US president Obama was looking for a more realistic and politically cheaper way of satisfying Armenian demands. Turkish–Armenian rapprochement seemed to be the best option, since the only country that visibly opposed it was small Azerbaijan. But more interesting is the context that made the Obama factor's influence possible. The 'genocide recognition' issue has been creating problems between Turkey and the Western governments for some time, and the border closure was not helping Ankara's hand much. Turkey itself was starting to think that the cost of closing the borders was becoming politically unbearable. The "zero problem" philosophy of Foreign Minister Davutoglu was quite timely in this context, preparing the ideational ground for the bold move by the AKP.

The pressure that the powerful Armenian diaspora could bring to bear on their political leaders in Western countries, the EU's reluctance to accept Turkey and hence willingness to emphasise anything that could serve to delay the process, the implication of Western states in the rebellion of the Ottoman Armenians during the First World War and their eventual deportation and Azerbaijan's relative weakness compared with the politically and discursively powerful Armenian position turned into a great deal of pressure on Turkey. Ankara was expected to better its relations with Armenia without the latter's change of its position on the occupied territories of Azerbaijan.

Turkey's increasingly strategic relations with Russia have served as another, relatively new and potentially unpredictable game-changing factor hurting relations between the two countries (Goksel 2009). Turkey is highly dependent on Russia for its gas and there is an accelerating trend regarding energy deals in general, be it the nuclear power plant in Akkuyu or the musings about the South Stream and Samsun-Ceyhan pipelines. Turkey has gotten much in return economically. Although there is still a big trade imbalance in favour of Russia, Turkish goods are successfully finding their way into the Russian market, Turkish firms are very visible in the construction sector in Russia, and Russia is the source of the second highest number of tourists after Germany.

Another reason for the improved Turkish-Russian relations could stem from the nature of the AKP government, with its independent, the-West-is-not-the-only-place-to-look-at attitude. Turkish willingness to act as a junior partner to Russia may hurt such deals as the Southern Corridor and will create additional problems for Azerbaijan in liberating its territories. One cannot help but recall how the Azerbaijan Democratic Republic was invaded by the XI Red Army, which claimed to use Azerbaijani land to cross over to Turkey to help Ataturk's regime against international imperial aggression. But the Russian–Turkish relationship does not have to hurt Azerbaijan's national interests. A healthy relationship between these two countries could make Russia (which has been afraid of Western incursions through Turkey) more confident and less aggressive in the Caucasus.

Pros and cons of close relations for Turkey and for Azerbaijan

What does Azerbaijan gain from good relations with Turkey and what does it lose? First of all, Azerbaijan has found a powerful diplomatic ally. This diplomatic support has nowhere been more important than in the case of NK, where beyond diplomacy Turkey has kept its borders to Armenia almost closed. By allying itself with Turkey, Azerbaijan finds a relative counterbalance to the Russian and Iranian encroachments. Baku views its neighbours to the north and south with suspicion given their less than fully respectful attitude towards the country's independence.

True, the NK issue has shown the limits of Turkish power vis-à-vis Russia, yet the case with Iran has been slightly different. Turkey resorted to a display of force to send a signal to Tehran when the latter chased away the Baku-authorised

BP vessels exploring Alov prospect in the Azerbaijani sector of the Caspian Sea in 2000: "[T]his was the first – and so far only – time that Ankara stepped in to put action behind its rhetoric of brotherhood and support for Azerbaijan" (Cornell 2011, 374). Yet Azerbaijan never returned to the Alov prospect again. Moreover, counterintuitively, some of the anger Russia and Iran feature for Azerbaijan is due to Azerbaijan's good relations with Turkey and, mainly through Turkey, with the West.

Second, Azerbaijan also gains from a relatively convenient route for the flow of Azerbaijan's oil and gas, which not only uses Turkish territory, but also would have been difficult without Turkish support. Zeyno Baran claims that "without close US-Turkish cooperation, it would not have been possible to pull the multibillion-dollar BTC project together" (Cornell 2011, 116). But this aspect of the relationship, unlike the support on NK, has paid for its own cost. In other words, Turkey gained handsomely as a result of this deal. The same is the case with Turkish investments and trade. Due to language similarities, its economic know-how could be spilling over to Azerbaijan faster than it would have otherwise, although this is hard to measure. But there is hardly any favour in trade relations either, no transfer of sensitive technologies, for instance (News.az 2011). The relationship is no different with any other country Turkey has normal economic relations with.

What about cons? As indicated above, due to the perception of Azerbaijan as a natural and sure ally of Turkey, there is a natural animosity by Russia and Iran. Probably, it is because of this that Russia will not invest effort to resolve the NK problem, since the belief is that a relaxed Azerbaijan will inevitably become an unconstrained ally of Turkey threatening Russia's southern borders in one way or another in the long run. The same applies to Iran. Azerbaijan alone might not be perceived as a threat to the territorial integrity of Iran, but together with Turkish hard and soft power, it could generate enough momentum to at least create trouble in the region.

Elchibey's policies fed such fears on the part of Russia and Iran to the highest extent, but even without that, the situation probably would not have been much different. Despite the fact that Elchibey has been gone for eighteen years now, Russia and Iranian perceptions have hardly changed. This is an indication of how both Russia and Iran look at 'sociology' rather than 'politics,' and 'grassroots' rather than the 'elite' regarding Azerbaijani–Turkish relations. For them, once again, Azerbaijan is a natural and strategic ally of Turkey, and constraining Azerbaijan means constraining Turkish incursion into their immediate neighbourhoods. Armenian perceptions of Azerbaijanis (the former always referring to the latter as Turks) can be understood in the same context (Goksel 2009). This is one of the biggest prices to be paid by Azerbaijan and is almost tragic. For Turkey is never a good enough match for the combined power of Iran and Russia, two dissatisfied members of the international system with enormous regional hard and soft power.

Among Turkey's pros, one could start with the prestige Turkey retains on its eastern borders, where it befriended the largest state in the Caucasus. This sends good signals to everyone somehow associating themselves with Turkey due to history or identity in the Caucasus – Central Asia and wider Eurasia in general. That Azerbaijan is the gateway to the Caucasus and Central Asia for Turkey is not a baseless claim; "the loss of close relations with Azerbaijan" could indeed mean "the loss of access to the Caspian and Central Asia" (Baran 2005, 112). Azerbaijan is the country that provides Turkey with a sense of alternative foreign policy identity when the European option fails or falters, i.e., almost always. Especially for the AKP and many of its supporters, the Caucasus and Central Asia are in third place after the Middle East and Europe, but there is a significant percentage of people in Turkey who would place the Caucasus and Azerbaijan at the top of the list.

Another pro is that Azerbaijan is a relatively big market for Turkish goods. Accounting for 75 percent of the South Caucasus' GDP, Azerbaijan's purchasing power cannot be compared to that of other actual or potential partners in the region. The current trade volume between the countries is around 3 billion USD. Turkey served as the gateway for global corporations entering the Caucasus. As Cornell (2011) puts it, "many large international firms . . . use[d] their Istanbul offices as stepping-stones to the establishment of operations in Azerbaijan, as well as the rest of the Caucasus region" (360). Turkey is the most reliable market in the region, and this makes it a nice destination for the oil money accumulating in Azerbaijan, including both public and private sources. [A]ccording to the Adana Chamber of Commerce, total investment in Ceyhan reached 11 billion USD due to BTC already back in 2007: "Total investment between the two nations has reached 10 billion USD so far and is supposed to increase to 15 billion USD after the SOCAR investment into the Petkim petrochemical complex" (Baguirov 2010).

The Turkish oil company TPAO has 6.75 percent and 9 percent stakes in the Azerbaijani multibillion-dollar ACG oil and Shah Deniz gas projects, respectively. The prevalence of the rule of law and secure property rights are the main reasons for the outflow of investment from Azerbaijan to Turkey. The breakneck pace of investments in Azerbaijan into the infrastructure and construction business has benefited Turkish companies more than those of any other country. While Azerbaijan is currently lacking the capacity to meet its domestic demands, from furniture to lamps, and as there is a need for experienced companies to carry out sophisticated projects, the first country Azerbaijanis turn to is Turkey. Both publicly and privately, the amount would have been less had Turkey not been a special country for Azerbaijan. Case in point: Azerbaijani billionaire Mubariz Mansimov, who resides in Turkey and does not shy away from indicating that all the business in which he is involved in that country is about reciprocating Turkish favour regarding its support on the NK issue.

Azerbaijan has contributed immensely to Turkey's energy security by two huge oil and natural gas pipelines. In the early 1990s, when Turkey was concerned about its global role after the end of the Cold War and the waning of its importance in the eyes of the West, it was counting on its new role as an energy transit country from Eurasia to the West, and Baku's willingness to cooperate was much more than good news. Thus, Azerbaijan meant more than prestige to Turkey during those years. Turkey did have a pipeline from Iraq, but it went out of service after the First Gulf War in 1991. Azerbaijan's entrance onto the scene could not have been timelier. Although it could be claimed that Turkey was the best route anyway, and Azerbaijan was gaining because of this choice too, the eventual selection of Turkey was far from certain at the start.

What does Turkey lose because of very close relations with Azerbaijan?[15] The first and the only thing that comes to mind is bad relations with Armenia. There are two more issues that are behind these bad relations, however. The first is the genocide claim by Armenians (especially those outside Armenia), and the Armenian territorial claims to Turkey (a lesser issue). The second claim has nothing to do with Azerbaijan. But Turkey might have fueled the genocide claim, to an extent, by its bad relations.[16]

Conclusion

In the late 1980s and early 1990s, it was largely the choice of the leadership of Azerbaijan's national liberation movement to look in the direction of Turkey that started it all. The past definitely conditioned this attitude, cultural similarity was significant, but there was nothing predetermined about this choice. Turkey's progressivism and Western orientation were significant factors, yet the degree of reliance on Turkey was a decision made by the Azerbaijani elite. The ultimate goal was Azerbaijan's sovereignty and territorial integrity, where the concrete issue became the Armenian demands on Nagorno-Karabakh.

Ironically, too much reliance on and too much orientation towards Turkey might have been one of the most important reasons for the losses Azerbaijan suffered in Karabakh. An unrestrained alliance between Turkey and Azerbaijan was not acceptable for Russia. Nagorno-Karabakh was a hostage taken to ensure that the feared alliance never got fully realised. Yet Turkey was also the most supportive country vis-à-vis Karabakh and at least by closing its borders to Armenia proved its worth. This, too, was Turkey's choice and the ultimate justification for the affection towards Turkey. Thus followed the biggest energy projects. Therefore, despite the presence of structural reasons, the close relationship is the outcome of choices and depends on tangible acts on both sides. There is nothing that guarantees the continuation of relations at the same level in the future unless proper decisions are made and right actions are taken.

Challenges to the special relationship abound. Turkey will remain a more powerful neighbor with more choices; the asymmetric nature of the relationship will continue to weaken Azerbaijan's hand. There will be bigger factors and actors than Turkey and Azerbaijan pushing the countries in different directions. There are significant cultural (political, social and religious) differences amid the remarkable similarities between the countries. The AKP is different qualitatively and, combined with a changing political mood in Turkey, will modify the character of relations. Time will also play its role in diluting the romantic tone. The only thing Azerbaijan and Turkey can do is to manage these developments carefully and cleverly. There are things that this process of management should take into consideration.

Neither has been a burden for the other. The relationship has been very complex and both nations did big favours for each other. Azerbaijan should be grateful for Turkish diplomatic support and for the border closure. In general, in Azerbaijan, there is a feeling that to the west there is a great country to which they could turn any time they face problems. Turkey does deserve special treatment, within reasonable limits, and at the end of the day, as a sovereign country, it makes its own decisions.

Turkey, in turn, should appreciate the affection it retains in Azerbaijan on a daily basis and at the top of the agenda. At times, Azerbaijanis seem to be "more Turkish" than those in Turkey. Turkey gained from Azerbaijan's energy projects politically and economically more than any other country save Azerbaijan. It needs to be noted that the Armenian problem Azerbaijan has cannot be separated from the history of Turkey itself. The current Republic of Armenia would not have been demographically as strong without the Armenians hailing from Turkey. The current level of hatred towards Azerbaijan would not have been anywhere as high without what happened to Armenians in Turkey. From the Armenian perspective, Azerbaijanis were Turks who deserved punishment for the things that befell them in Anatolia in the early twentieth century.

Azerbaijan should not expect to be treated in a special way and Turkey should not overplay its geopolitical monopoly. Azerbaijan has placed too many eggs into the Turkish basket. Its lifelines, BTC and BTE, pass through Turkey. Vernon, in his famous obsolescing bargaining theory, argues that in such cases, the side that understands that already-made investments are not easily movable starts demanding more from common ventures (Vernon 1971). Turkey seems to be playing similarly. The difficulties in the current gas deals are partly the result of this understanding that Azerbaijan is already overdependent on Turkey and Turkey remains to be the best option for its next pipeline. The fact that Turkey started to talk about opening the borders to Armenia after these projects were completed through Turkey raises eyebrows too. Azerbaijan deserves to be treated better than what OBT suggests. If not, then it should play hardball; Turkey does not hold the key to the gates of Europe – the Black Sea is another one.

One of the problems of Azerbaijani–Turkish relations is that it is difficult to build a healthy relationship with a wounded nation. Azerbaijan is one. And the relationship was forged during the hurting period for Azerbaijan. It is not over yet. This sensitivity needs to be understood well. Otherwise, there is nothing fundamentally contradictory in Turkish and Azerbaijani national interests.

Both sides need to do several things to change the unhealthy situation. What is a favour and what is a mutual interest need to be sorted out. This is a very difficult process, but a candid dialogue should already begin. Sometimes the accusations are the result of ignorance (Goksel 2009), sometimes of a much higher expectation and a sense of entitlement and sometimes of real problems. The boundaries need to be clearly defined, but more is required from Azerbaijan.

The relationship is asymmetric to Azerbaijan's disadvantage. Turkey will not bother to learn Azerbaijan better. It is a larger, more secure state whose main foreign policy direction is not looking eastwards towards Azerbaijan. It is Azerbaijan that should try to change the increasingly dominant, yet misinformed discourse in Turkey, and get real itself.

Romanticism has proven to be a tougher nut than many have thought. It withstood many of the challenges firmly. Cultural affinity intermingled with common aspects of historical experience and blessed with an ideological give-and-take has been the main context where the relationship has been unfolding and will continue to unfold for years to come. There are a lot of voices that want more clarification as to what 'brotherhood' between the countries means, attacking the perception of hallowed romanticism. It is true that 'brotherhood' needs to be supported by clear-cut and formal institutional mechanisms synchronising the policies of the countries where possible and working to minimise damage where necessary. But there is no ground in discounting or criticising the identity affinity and the concomitant affection between the two countries. There is no other country in the world where Turkish soft power reaches the levels it does in Azerbaijan, and there is no other country in the world where Azerbaijani soft power reaches the levels it does in Turkey. This is an invaluable asset in its own right and should be protected and cherished.

The problem is not the affinity and affection, but the gap that could emerge between formal statements and real behind-the-scenes discussions. Popular perceptions and private elite discourse in both countries have started to diverge. Especially in Turkey, among the elite the romance faded rather quickly. The liberal opinion makers and many politicians think of Azerbaijan as a burden, specifically regarding relations with Armenia. But whenever they tried to put their thinking into action, as with Armenian conciliation, it was the perception by the Turkish grassroots of Azerbaijan as part of their 'self' that proved to be the most serious impediment.[17]

A similar situation is present in Azerbaijan. But the ex-communist Azerbaijani elite – with a very different educational background and different values – may not feel much affection for Turks. Here too, the grassroots Azerbaijani population found Turks much closer to their values and more similar to themselves. Given the societal foundations of the 'brotherhood' perception and favourable structural factors tying the countries together, if something goes wrong, the blame will totally and squarely lie with the opinion- and policymakers in Turkey and Azerbaijan.

Notes

1 *Times*, 17 Feb., 1992; *The Daily Telegraph*, 22 Feb., 1993; Baskin Oran in Cornell (2011, 365).
2 From the very beginning, there have been problems between the countries, which are part of any relationship. But the dangerous element with Turkey and Azerbaijan has been the gap between the public narrative of fraternity and the private real

perceptions. As the public discourse was growing increasingly more idealised, in private both sides were complaining about the other more and more loudly. Unable to build mechanisms for an honest dialogue, Turkey and Azerbaijan were heading towards an inescapable crush, which came in 2009 with Armenian–Turkish protocols. Therefore, it is wrong to assume that 2009 was one big misstep by Turkey or, for that matter, Azerbaijan. The problem had been in the making.

3 For example, Azerbaijanis are easily surprised by the degree of religiosity in Turkey, while it is very difficult for a Turk to understand why an Azerbaijani would speak Russian in his/her daily life.
4 For excellent depictions of the identity quest of Azerbaijanis after being torn from Iran by Russian invasion, see Swietochowski (1995) and Altstadt (1992).
5 It is enough to randomly survey Azerbaijani newspapers on 15 September, the anniversary of the liberation of Baku, to see the point.
6 To this day, few in the international community remember that Azerbaijan was the first among the post-Soviet republics to get rid of Russian military bases. As a result, it lost about one sixth of its territory, while one seventh of its population became refugees and internally displaced persons.
7 The other would be the perceived cultural suppression of Azerbaijanis in Iran.
8 The first indication of this was the erection of an impenetrable anti-air-defense system in Karabakh in a matter of two weeks, for which Armenian expertise and technology could not reasonably account. See Waal (2004, 209).
9 The Turkish community of Cyprus would not qualify as a state and, unlike Azerbaijan, was perceived as an extension of Turkey.
10 Turkey was also instrumental in initiating the UN Security Council resolutions that for the first time somehow put a degree of blame on the Armenian side. These resolutions are additional assets in the Azerbaijani arsenal in its conflict with Armenia. However, they did not cost Turkey anything and Turkey was not alone in this move, being supported greatly at least by Pakistan. In terms of their influence, the resolutions are important, but the border closure probably generated more tangible consequences for Armenia and added a sense of legitimacy to the words of the UN documents.
11 Personal discussion in Turkey, Ankara, Mar. 2000.
12 According to Zeyno Baran (2005), even before the AKP, "[t]here were . . . periods of tension, but then-President Suleyman Demirel of Turkey kept bilateral relations on an even keel due to his strong personal relationship with Heydar Aliyev."
13 The notion of 'border closure' needs qualification. Today one can talk of restricted access to Turkey, rather than closed borders. Armenians are coming to and leaving Turkey freely through Georgia and there have been flights between the two countries since 2002.
14 For Turkish politicians, these were "difficult policy choices" given that they were caught between their own isolationist cautiousness and the Western pro-Armenian attitude. See Aydin (2004).
15 The reader probably has already noticed that the question is the pro and cons of the special relations and not relations in general.
16 However, the most tangible expression of bad relations, the border issue, started after the invasion of Kalbajar, an Azerbaijani region sandwiched between NK and the Armenian Republic, which was clearly attacked from the Republic of Armenia and before which the Turkish military observed increased frequency of visits of Russian planes.
17 Thus the greatest institutional support Azerbaijan has in Turkey is Turkish democracy. As long as this country remains democratic, and there is no reason to believe otherwise, as long as the politicians have to rely on public opinion, Azerbaijan will be an expensive sacrifice to make.

References

Altstadt, Audrey. 1992. *The Azerbaijani Turks: Power and Identity under Russian Rule.* Stanford, CA: Hoover Institution Press.

———. 1996. The Azerbaijani Bourgeoisie and the Cultural-Enlightenment Movement in Baku: First Steps toward Nationalism. In: Ronald Grigor Suny, ed. *Transcaucasia, Nationalism, and Social Change: Essays in the History of Armenia, Azerbaijan, and Georgia,* 199–209. Ann Arbor: University of Michigan Press.

Aydin, Mustafa. 2004. *Turkish Foreign Policy: Framework and Analysis.* Ankara: Center for Strategic Research. www.sam.gov.tr/wp-content/uploads/2011/12/mustafaaydin.pdf.

Baguirov, Adil. 2010. Wikileaks Impact on Azeri-Turkish Relations: The Importance of Terminology. *Hurriyet Daily News,* 12 Dec.

Bal, Idris. 2004. *Turkish Foreign Policy in the Post Cold War Era.* Boca Raton, FL: Brown Walker Press.

Balamir-Coskun, Bezen and Birgul Demirtas-Cosgun. 2009. *Neighborhood Challenge: European Union and Its Neighbors.* Boca Raton, FL: Universal Publishers.

Baran, Zeyno. 2005. The Baku-Ceyhan Pipeline: Implications for Turkey. In: S. Frederick Starr and Svante E. Cornell, eds. *The Baku-Tbilisi-Ceyhan Pipeline: Oil Window to the West,* 103–118. Washington, DC & Uppsala, Sweden: Central Asia – Caucasus Institute and Silk Road Studies Program. www.silkroadstudies.org/BTC_6.pdf.

Birand, Mehmet Ali. 2010. Turkiye Cirpiniyor, Azeriler Ise Hic Orali Degiller. (In Turkish.) *Hurriyet,* 15 Apr. http://hurarsiv.hurriyet.com.tr/goster/ShowNew.aspx?id=14423922.

Bolukbasi, Suha. 2011. *Azerbaijan: A Political History.* London: I.B. Tauris.

Bozdaglioglu, Yucel. 2003. *Turkish Foreign Policy and Turkish Identity: A Constructivist Approach.* New York: Routledge.

Cagaptay, Soner. 2009. Assessing Turkish Foreign Policy under AKP. *Jane's Islamic Affairs Analyst,* Nov. http://goo.gl/fISiGP.

Candar, Cengiz. 2009. Tek Millet Iki Devlete Azerbaycan Uyuyor mu? (In Turkish.) *Habernet,* 24 Apr. www.habernet.net/artikel.php?artikel_id=122.

Cornell, Svante. 1998. Turkey and the Conflict in Nagorno-Karabakh: A Delicate Balance. *Middle Eastern Studies* 34:1, Jan., 51–72.

———. 2011. *Azerbaijan since Independence.* New York: M.E. Sharpe.

Goksel, Nigar. 2009. Turkey and Azerbaijan: Passion, Principle or Pragmatism? *On Turkey Series,* 4 Jun. Washington, DC: The German Marshall Fund of the United States.

Hasanli, Jamil. 2011. *Stalin and the Turkish Crisis of the Cold War, 1945–1953.* Lanham, MD: Lexington Books.

Hüzeyinzade, Cingiz. 1998. *Kimsen? Neçisen? Mefkuren Nedir?* (In Azerbaijani.) 21:1.

Inglehart, Ronald F. and Christian Welzel. 2005. *Modernization, Cultural Change and Democracy: The Human Development in Sequence.* New York: Cambridge University Press.

Kanira, Bora. 2009. *Islam Democracy and Dialogue in Turkey: Deliberating in Divided Societies.* Surrey: Ashgate.

Kardas, Saban. 2009. Turkey Prioritizing Its Relations with Azerbaijan. *Eurasia Daily Monitor* 6:87, 6 May.

Larrabee, Stephen F. and Ian O. Lesse. 2003. *Turkish Foreign Policy in an Age of Uncertainty.* London: Rand Corporation.

Mamedov, Eldar. 2011. Turkish-Azerbaijani Relations: Reality Check. *European Dialogue,* 1 Mar.

Milaz. 2011. Ilham Aliyev: Azerbaijan Recognizes PKK as a Terror Organization Officially. *Milaz,* 28 Jul. www.milaz.info/en/news.php?id=6142.

News.az. 2011. Turkey to Sell T-155 Artillery Systems to Azerbaijan. *News.az*, 14 Oct. www.news.az/articles/46717.

Oguz, Cem. 2010. *Türkiye-Azerbaycan İlişkileri ve Ermenistan Faktörü*. (In Turkish.) YT Yayinlari.

Oliker, Olga, Thomas S. Szayna, Scot Pace, and Peter A. Wilson. 2003. *Faultlines of Conflict in Central Asia and the South Caucasus: Implications for the US Army*. Santa Monica, CA: Rand Corporation.

Onis, Ziya. 2006. Globalization and Party Transformation: Turkey's Justice and Development Party in Perspective. In: Peter Burnell, ed. *Globalising Democracy: Party Politics in Emerging Democracies*, 122–140. London & New York: Routledge.

Ortadogu. 2011. AKP KKTC'nin Taninmasini Istemedi. (In Turkish.) 28 Feb.

Radikal. 2009. Azerbaycanin Karsi Atagi: Dogalgaza Zam. (In Turkish.) 18 Oct.

Reynolds, Michael A. 2011. *Shattering Empires: The Clash and Collapse of the Ottoman and Russian Empires 1908–1918*. Cambridge: Cambridge University Press.

Shiriyev, Zaur. 2012. Turkish-Azerbaijani Relations: Beyond Mottos. *Today's Zaman*, 11 Sep.

Suny, Ronald Grigor. 1996. *Armenia, Azerbaijan and Georgia*. Collingdale, PA: DIANE Publishing.

Swietochowski, Tadeusz. 1995. *Russia and Azerbaijan: A Borderland in Transition*. New York: Columbia University Press.

———. 1996. National Consciousness and Political Orientations in Azerbaijan, 1905–1920. In: Ronald Grigor Suny, ed. *Transcaucasia, Nationalism, and Social Change: Essays in the History of Armenia, Azerbaijan, and Georgia*, 211–241. Ann Arbor: University of Michigan Press.

The Economist. 2005. Where Business Meets Geopolitics. 25 May. www.economist.com/node/4008148.

UPI. 2009. Ankara Losing Money on BTC. 28 Dec.

Vernon, Raymond. 1971. *Sovereignty at Bay: The Transnational Spread of U.S. Enterprises*. London: Longman.

Waal, Thomas de. 2004. *Black Garden: Armenia and Azerbaijan through Peace and War*. New York: New York University Press.

———. 2013. *Black Garden: Armenia and Azerbaijan through Peace and War*, 10th anniversary edition, revised and updated. New York: New York University Press.

3 Geopolitics versus ideology
Azerbaijan in Turkish views on Eurasia[1]

Emre Erşen

Introduction

Since the end of the Cold War, politicians and scholars in both Turkey and Azerbaijan have often called attention to close historical and cultural bonds between the two countries. The "one nation, two states" slogan, popularised by the late Azerbaijani president Heydar Aliyev in particular, could be taken as a remarkable indication of cordial relations Turkey and Azerbaijan established in the post–Cold War period. However, political statements and academic studies tend to neglect an important property these two countries share: geographically, both are Eurasian countries with territories lying simultaneously in the continents of Europe and Asia.[2] Today, this distinctive geographical feature compels the leaders of Turkey and Azerbaijan to pursue a multidimensional foreign policy which closely tracks the political and economic trends in Europe, Russia, Central Asia and the Middle East.

This similarity is at the same time a major factor in terms of the positioning of Azerbaijan at the heart of various conceptions in Turkey about the meaning of "Eurasia" (*Avrasya* in Turkish), a concept which has grown vastly popular among the Turkish political, military and intellectual circles to guide their attempts to define new horizons for Turkish foreign policy in the post–Cold War era. Although their ideas about the physical borders of Eurasia as well as the potential roles Turkey might play in this region varied greatly, Azerbaijan received a significant emphasis in all of these intellectual endeavors, which were also heavily influenced by ideological considerations like Turkism, Eurasianism and neo-Ottomanism. In practical foreign policy terms, too, Azerbaijan became a focal point in Ankara's geopolitical outlook towards the former Soviet – especially Turkic – republics. The Caspian's rich oil and natural gas reserves played a particularly important role in this process. Consequently, Turkey–Azerbaijan relations became intrinsically linked to the evolution of the concept of Eurasia in the eyes of Turkish intellectuals and politicians.

This chapter is set to employ a critical geopolitical approach to discuss and analyse Azerbaijan's place in the changing geopolitical conceptions about Eurasia in post–Cold War Turkey. Critical geopolitics and particularly the three types of geopolitical reasoning it offers (i.e. formal, practical and popular geopolitics) have so far failed to generate adequate interest among the academic circles in Turkey. Although there has recently been an increase in the number of studies attempting to analyse geopolitical discourses in Turkey by utilising a critical geopolitical approach, the field is still dominated by traditional notions and understandings, which tend to associate geopolitics with concepts like security, strategy, interest and power.[3]

The prevalence of such a realist approach in geopolitical studies in Turkey is surprising, particularly given that critical theories have now grown nearly as influential as traditional ones in other major fields of the international relations discipline in Turkish academia. In order to initiate a similar trend in the realm of geopolitics, there is a need to deconstruct or at least reinterpret some of the geopolitical themes and concepts that Turkish scholars have frequently invoked. In light of the above, this chapter will elaborate on formal geopolitical representations of the concept of Eurasia in post–Cold War Turkey. Given that the concept of "Turkish Eurasianism" is largely based on the geopolitical narratives developed by Turkish scholars, writers and intellectuals, formal geopolitics appears to be the most elucidatory category of critical geopolitics in terms of shedding light on Azerbaijan's significance in the Turkish views on Eurasia.

Critical geopolitics and Turkish Eurasianism

Although the discipline of geopolitics is mostly associated with authors like Halford J. Mackinder, Alfred T. Mahan, Karl Haushofer and Zbigniew Brzezinski, contemporary geopolitical thinking has moved towards a critical understanding of the relationship between geography and politics in recent years. Also known as "critical geopolitics," this new approach views geography as a construction of the human mind and argues that traditional geopolitical fixations and perceptions of boundaries can change if people alter their current imaginations about geography.[4] It also refuses to view geopolitics exclusively in terms of military power and tries to embrace cultural, economic and social dynamics behind the globalisation of world politics (e.g. Dalby 2008). A major objective of critical geopolitical approaches in this regard is "to examine how it is that international politics are imagined spatially or geographically and in so doing to uncover the politics involved in writing the geography of global space" (Sharp 2003, 333).

Gearóid Ó Tuathail, one of the leading theorists of critical geopolitics, proposes a threefold typology, which he thinks might be useful in problematising the discourses about the geographical features of world politics: formal, practical, and popular geopolitics. Formal geopolitics symbolises the geopolitical reasoning employed by analysts and scholars in academia, strategic institutes and think tanks. Practical geopolitics is to be found in discourses of government representatives and foreign policy bureaucrats. Popular geopolitics, in turn, represents geopolitical narratives reflected in the mass media, cinema, novels and cartoons (Ó Tuathail 1999). Critical geopolitics argues that these three forms of geopolitical reasoning contribute to the "spatialising of boundaries and dangers (the geopolitical map of the world) and the geopolitical representations of self and the other (the geopolitical imagination)" (Mamadouh 1998, 244).

Formal, practical and popular geopolitics are closely linked to each other and it is impossible to draw a clear line between them (e.g. Sidaway 1998). Academics, journalists and intellectuals have regular contacts with each other as well as government officials and other state authorities. These contacts reinforce intensive exchange of ideas on many political and social issues. Geopolitical frameworks shaped in the course of this exchange are processed by the mass media and penetrate into popular culture. Metaphors such as the "iron curtain," "rogue states" and the "axis of evil" aim to simplify international politics for the public and help people make the "us and them" or "friend and enemy" distinctions in a more simplified manner. Politicians also frequently use such abstractions to defend a particular policy. At the same time, these concepts generate popular public debates of a geopolitical nature.

Although there is a growing body of literature on popular geopolitics, most geopolitical reasoning in world politics is believed to take place in the realm of practical geopolitics (Ó Tuathail and Agnew 1998, 81).[5] The latter includes everyday forms of geopolitical reasoning employed by foreign policy decision-makers in defending or explaining their policies to the public. These so-called geopolitical codes are different from the institutional or strategic knowledge produced within the framework of formal geopolitics in that they are based on commonsense geopolitical narratives (Ó Tuathail 1999, 114). There is, however, an extremely close interaction between formal and practical geopolitics, not least because the most important objective underlying the production of theories and strategies in universities and think tanks is to provide guidance to policymakers on one hand and legitimacy to their decisions on the other. In fact, most scholars contributing to the production of formal geopolitical knowledge usually also serve as advisers – or sometimes even ministers – in national governments.[6]

Formal geopolitics is also associated with "geopolitical traditions," which are based on geopolitical narratives developed by intellectuals and scholars in accordance with their state's historical, geographical and cultural features (Ó Tuathail 2003, 89). Since each geopolitical tradition represents a distinct value system, there is normally more than one geopolitical tradition in every country. Graham Smith (1999), for example, analysed three rival geopolitical traditions in Russia: one viewing the country as part of Europe, one believing that it is neither European nor Asian, and one suggesting that it is a bridge between the two continents. A similar study was also conducted by Walter Russell Mead, who identified four distinct US geopolitical traditions – Jeffersonian, Wilsonian, Jacksonian and Hamiltonian (Mead 2002; also Ó Tuathail 2003, 89). Timothy Garton Ash, in turn, classified four geopolitical traditions in the UK as small Britain, cosmopolitan Britain, European Britain and American Britain (cited in Dodds 2007, 47).

Ó Tuathail (2003, 88–90) contends that a geopolitical tradition in a country can only be distinguished from others by revealing its social support base as well as the way it defines national interest and cultural identity. Based on these criteria, one may recognise three major geopolitical traditions attributing a special meaning to this concept in Turkey. Some scholars tend to associate these traditions respectively with three political ideologies: Turkism/nationalism, socialism/Kemalism and conservatism/Islamism (Akgül 2009, 164–165; Eren-Webb 2011, 59; Kılıçbeyli 2003, 326). Others, in turn, call attention to the emergence of a new school of thought called Turkish Eurasianism – a broader concept including various formal geopolitical meanings attributed to the concept of Eurasia in the Turkish context (Aktürk 2004, 207–238; Ismayılov 2011, 275).

Turkish Eurasianism has been subject to heated academic debate due to its vagueness and lack of clear philosophical roots (Aras 2003; Ivanov and Şişin 2002, 80–84; Karasar 2008, 119). This is also because it is usually compared to Russian neo-Eurasianism promoted by nationalist writers like Alexander Dugin in the post–Cold War period as a new national salvation idea for Russia. Although the history of Eurasianist thought in Russia dates back to the 1920s, Dugin's version is unique, as it combines the anti-Western ideas of classical Eurasianist thought with the geographical determinism of traditional Western geopolitical theories and proposes – among other things – the establishment of a continental bloc of Eurasian countries as a geopolitical balance against US domination of world politics (e.g. Dugin 2004).

Although Russian neo-Eurasianism has been met with increasing interest by Turkish political and intellectual circles since the mid-1990s, there is serious confusion about the meaning of Eurasianism in the Turkish context, since it is associated with political ideologies like Kemalism, Turkism and neo-Ottomanism, which are critical not only of each other, but also of the imperialistic designs of Russian neo-Eurasianism. Thus, instead of treating Turkish Eurasianism as a distinct ideology, some scholars believe we can only talk about various "reflections" or "interpretations" of the Eurasia concept in Turkey (Imanov 2008, 293). This approach also seems more suitable for making comprehensive analyses in the light of Ó Tuathail's definition of geopolitical traditions. In this regard, one could identify three geopolitical traditions in Turkey – each attributing a distinct meaning to the concept of Eurasia in the post–Cold War period. Based on their geographical focus rather than ideological roots, one could define these traditions as the Turkic-world-centered geopolitical tradition, the Asia-centered geopolitical tradition, and the Moslem-world-centered geopolitical tradition.[7] Variations among them also provide important clues regarding the geopolitical depiction of Azerbaijan by Turkish intellectuals and policymakers.

Turkic-world-centered geopolitical tradition

The Turkic-world-centered geopolitical tradition identifies Turkey's national interest as integration with the Turkic republics of the former Soviet Union; it enjoys widespread support among groups associated with the MHP and draws upon Turkic ethnic identity in cultural terms.[8] Although this tradition was powerful in the last period of the Ottoman empire, it lost significant influence following the foundation of the Republic of Turkey in 1923 as the leaders of post-Ottoman Turkey chose to distance themselves from political and cultural links with Turkic communities abroad. The collapse of the Soviet Union and the emergence of five independent Turkic states in the Caucasus and Central Asia, however, provided a new boost to this geopolitical tradition, whose supporters have very enthusiastically embraced the Eurasia concept as they attempted to redefine their geopolitical outlook towards this new region.

Especially in the first few years following the collapse of the Soviet Union, practical geopolitical meanings attributed to the concept of Eurasia in Turkey were shaped under the heavy influence of this tradition. For example, the official TV channel founded in 1992 to strengthen relations between Turkey and the Turkic republics was named TRT-Int Avrasya. More significantly, MHP leader Alparslan Türkeş accompanied Prime Minister Süleyman Demirel in the latter's first official visit to the five Turkic republics in April 1992. Demirel also stated frequently that he regarded Turkism as an important element of Turkey's foreign policy towards this region (*BBC Summary of World Broadcasts*, 31 Aug. 1994).

Together with President Turgut Özal, Demirel was at the same time a strong supporter of the idea of a "Turkic world stretching from the Adriatic Sea to the Great Wall of China," which he sometimes alternatively described as "Eurasia" (see his statements in *Cumhuriyet*, 24 Feb. 1992 and *Milliyet*, 1 Nov. 1992). Importantly, such a description associates Eurasia not only with the Turkic republics of Central Asia and the Caucasus, but also with the Turkic minorities living in the Balkans. Noteworthy in this respect are also the activities of the Turkish Agency for Technical and Economic Cooperation (TİKA) founded by the Turkish state in 1992 to provide aid for the economic development of Turkic republics. Not only did TİKA undertake significant projects in Central Asia and the Caucasus, as well as the Balkans, but it also helped popularise the concept of Eurasia in Turkish academic circles by publishing the *Avrasya Dosyası* (Eurasian File) bulletin and *Avrasya Etüdleri* (Eurasian Studies) journal (e.g. Laruelle 2008, 6). The establishment of the Black Sea Economic Cooperation in June 1992 may also be regarded as a sign of Turkish policymakers' desire to view the Balkans within their emerging conceptualisation of Eurasia.[9] However, as the Balkan countries began to develop closer links with the EU, Eurasia became associated in the minds of Turkish intellectuals and policymakers with the Turkic republics of Central Asia and the Caucasus.

The geopolitical tradition centered on the Turkic world and its vision of Eurasia is represented by nationalist journals, including *Türk Yurdu* (Turkish Homeland), *Yeni Avrasya* (New Eurasia), *Ayhaber* and *Asya-Avrupa* (Asia-Europe) (Imanov 2008, 315). The Avrasya Bir Foundation, founded in 1993, may also be taken to represent this tradition, since promoting Turkism around the world and fostering relations between Turkey and the Turkic world were cited among its main goals (Aras 2000, 50).[10] More importantly, the Eurasia Strategic Research Center (ASAM), established in 1999, produced many books not only on Turkic republics, but also on other highly regarded issues of Turkish nationalism, including the Armenian and Kurdish issues. Noteworthy, however, ASAM's quarterly journal (also titled *Avrasya Dosyası*, like the TİKA bulletin), which in time became a leading publication of international affairs in Turkey, was not dominated by a nationalist discourse and, instead, published scholarly articles on political, economic and cultural processes taking place in the former Soviet republics (Aça 2002, 162).[11]

There are two ways in which Eurasia is geographically defined in the Turkic-world-centered geopolitical tradition. The first definition depicts the region quite broadly as a joint Euro-Asian supercontinent or a vast territory located at a meeting point of the two continents of Europe and Asia (Andican 1996, 28; Ilhan 2006, 119). For example, Professor Ümit Özdağ, a longtime leading figure in the Turkish nationalist movement and the ASAM chair between 1999 and 2004, described Eurasia as a region starting from Hungary, covering the entire Balkans, Turkey, the Caucasus, Central Asia, Iran, Russia, Ukraine, Afghanistan, Pakistan and extending into Mongolia (Özdağ 2004, 23).

The second definition treats Eurasia as a region where Turkic/Turkish communities are found in great numbers and, as such, is more ideologically oriented. In fact, Eurasia in this second conceptualisation seems more like a modernised version of the "Turan" – the ancient homeland of Turkic peoples in the steppes of Central Asia – which still enjoys a very important place in Turkish nationalist ideology (Kolobov et al. 2006, 296). Proposals for the establishment of ambitious regional integration schemes such as "Unified Turkestan" or the "Turkestan Confederation" may also be evaluated in the light of this second definition of Eurasia (Andican 1992, 12–18; 1997, 13).

Although some may argue that Eurasia has been favored by some Turkish nationalist figures as a more inclusive concept, open to non-Turkic peoples, "Turkishness" is still at the heart of nearly all variations of this concept in the Turkic-world-centered geopolitical tradition (Imanov 2008, 317; Yeniçeri 2004, 1). The late Muzaffer Özdağ, regarded as a leading activist of Turkish nationalism, for instance, claimed that the Eurasian axis defined as the "heartland" or "geopolitical pivot of history" by writers like Mackinder was at the same time the axis of Turkic history as well as the "living space of the Turkic race" (Özdağ M. 2003, 12). His son Ümit Özdağ similarly asserted that the Turkic peoples were the most important actors in terms of the intellectual, sociological, cultural and economic development of Eurasia (Özdağ Ü. 2003, 14).

Such a heavy emphasis on Turkishness naturally highlights Azerbaijan in this tradition's depiction of Eurasia, since it is geographically and culturally the closest Turkic state to Turkey. Furthermore, a number of Azerbaijani intellectuals, including Hüseyinzade Ali Bey and Ahmet Ağaoğlu, were quite influential in promoting the idea of Turkism in the Ottoman empire. Following the collapse of the Soviet Union, Turkish nationalists showed even greater interest in Azerbaijan given the latter's war with Armenia over Nagorno-Karabakh (e.g. Andican 1996, 29). Eventually, many Turkish nationalist writers began to view Turkish-Azerbaijani relations as a "natural alliance," which should also be regarded as the nucleus of Turkey's geopolitical outlook towards Eurasia. Namık Kemal Zeybek, a leading figure in the Turkish nationalist movement, for example, claimed that Turkey and Azerbaijan should act as a unified state (Zeybek 2006). Ümit Özdağ (2003, 12) also indicated in a similar manner that the seven million Azeri Turks should be regarded as an integral part of Eurasia.

In geopolitical terms, Turkish nationalists define Azerbaijan either as a "bridge" that connects Anatolia with the Turkic world or as a pivotal country in the union of Turkic states to be established under Turkey's leadership. Regarding the first definition, Muzaffer Özdağ called Azerbaijan an "unbreakable hinge" or "sacred bridge" between Turkey and Turkestan, which he believed represented two powerful flanks of the Turkic world (Özdağ M. 2003, 295). Retired general Suat Ilhan, one of the leading geopolitical theorists in Turkey, similarly claims that Azerbaijan is of principal importance to Turkey's Eurasian strategy, as it is both a physical and a cultural link between Turkey and the Turkic world. Representing the second geopolitical definition of Azerbaijan, however, he asserts that this country should be regarded as the focal point of a union of Turkic states (Ilhan 1999, 88; Ilhan 2006, 29). Özcan Yeniçeri, another leading nationalist writer and currently a member of the Turkish parliament under the MHP, too, writes that Azerbaijan has a central position in what he calls the "Western axis" of the Turkic world, which he argues also includes Turkey and the Turkish Republic of Northern Cyprus (Yeniçeri 2006, 33–35).

Yet another nationalist writer, Ali Külebi, contends that the essence of Turkish Eurasianism is the "advancement towards a full integration of Turkey and Azerbaijan," a reality also reflected, Külebi believes, in the "one nation, two states" motto (Külebi 2006). The latter motto also expresses, in the most remarkable way, a geopolitical manifestation of Turkish nationalists' ideas about the special relationship between the two countries. The slogan "brotherly Azerbaijan" is also frequently invoked by nationalist groups in Turkey to emphasise Azerbaijan's special place in Turkey's geopolitical reasoning, including as compared with Eurasia's other former Soviet republics (Işeri and Çelik 2013, 277–278; also see Özdağ Ü. 2003, 293–300).

The above conception of Eurasia, including the notion of Azerbaijan's leading position in the region it embodies, have already had some practical implications on a policy level, including as expressed in the extension by the Turkish government, under the pressure of the MHP, of diplomatic recognition to Azerbaijan almost a month before Turkey recognised the other four Turkic republics (Oran 2001, 377–378) and Turkey's active lobbying for Azerbaijan's inclusion in the Black Sea Economic Cooperation at the time despite the fact that the latter was not a Black Sea littoral state. The importance of Azerbaijan's independence and territorial integrity was also recurrently emphasised during the Turkish Grand National Assembly's sessions that discussed the Eurasian dimension of Turkish foreign policy.[12] In short, under the influence of the Turkic-world-centered geopolitical tradition, Azerbaijan and Eurasia became intertwined in intellectual and political discussions on Turkish foreign policy – particularly in the immediate aftermath of the collapse of the Soviet Union.

Asia-centered geopolitical tradition

Although the Turkic-world-centered geopolitical tradition is also squarely critical of the West and, as such, favors Turkey's distancing – and even turning away – from the US and EU in foreign policy, Eurasianism's anti-Western implications in the Turkish context are rather framed by the Asia-centered geopolitical tradition, which defines Turkey's national interest as its inclusion in an Asian/Eurasian geopolitical bloc against the West and enjoys support from various socialist and neo-nationalist (*ulusalcı*) groups skeptical about Turkey's relations with the US and EU and, as such, promoting in the cultural sphere ideas of anti-imperialism and Kemalism. This tradition especially highlights close relations between the governments of Turkey and the Soviet Union during the period of 1919–1939, calling attention to what it sees as an "anti-imperialist political dialogue" between Atatürk and Lenin.

Although it has been supported by certain opposition groups and parties in Turkey, the influence that the Asia-centered geopolitical tradition enjoyed with Turkish foreign policy makers has been quite limited – especially compared with the Turkic-world-centered geopolitical tradition. One of the rare instances where a top-level figure publicly expressed the views of this tradition was in 2002, when General Tuncer Kılınç, secretary-general of the National Security Council, proposed the formation of a Russian-Turkish-Iranian axis in order to stand against what he called "the EU's unacceptable requests" regarding the Cyprus and Kurdish issues (see *Sabah*, 8 March 2002). Even then, however, both the Turkish government and the general staff immediately rejected General Kılınç's views. Yet, the rapid improvement of Turkish–Russian relations after 2003, coupled with the gradual worsening of Turkey's relations with the US and EU, provided fresh impetus to the Asia-centered geopolitical tradition in debates about the Eurasian dimension of Turkish foreign policy.

The rise of anti-Western sentiment among the Turkish public following the US occupation of Iraq in 2003 and Cyprus' accession to the EU in 2004 brought this tradition closer to the ideas of Russian neo-Eurasianism, which particularly stands out for its anti-Western rhetoric. Indeed, the consensus between Russian neo-Eurasianists and some leftist circles in Turkey began to emerge in the mid-1990s, partly because both groups geopolitically defined Eurasia as the major adversary of the "Atlantic" – a term which denoted the US domination of world politics.

In this regard, one could argue that the view the Asia-centered geopolitical tradition holds of Eurasia actually represents a new conceptualisation of the "third world," in which Eurasia is identified with the oppressed peoples of the post–Cold War world. Hakan Reyhan (1997, 3–4), the founder and editor-in-chief of the journal *Ulusal* (National), for instance, describes Eurasia as "the universal solidarity between the oppressed peoples against neo-imperialism" and claims that even socialist Cuba, in Latin America, could be included in this construct due to its resistance to US imperialism. Such a definition defines the borders of Eurasia in terms of ideology rather than geography.

A similar approach is found in the ideas of Doğu Perinçek, leader of the ultra-leftist Workers' Party, who defines Eurasia as a revolutionary center against US imperialism and Latin America and Africa as its two flanks (1996, 16).[13] Identifying these three continents with the "oppressed world," he believes that Eurasia in particular is the geopolitical adversary of the US, Europe and Japan (Perinçek 1997, 28; 2000, 9). His son Mehmet Perinçek (2006) similarly defines

Eurasia as the enemy of the Atlantic; however, he believes that the latter is represented by the alliance between the US, UK and Israel. In his depiction, Eurasia emerges as an "anti-imperialist geopolitical reservoir" that includes Russia, China, India, Arab countries, Iran and the Turkic world (26).

Another leading figure in this tradition was the late socialist writer and poet Attila Ilhan. Although he described Eurasia as the geographical region including the Central Asian Turkic republics, Iran, Afghanistan, the Commonwealth of Independent States, Turkey, the Caucasus, Syria, Iraq and the Balkans, Ilhan argued that this concept should be understood in the light of the ideas of Bolshevik Tatar politician Mirsaid Sultan Galiev, who advocated the ideology of "national communism" for the Moslem communities of the Soviet Union (Ilhan 1997, 35–36; 2000, 185). His depiction of Eurasia in this regard was squarely similar to Galiev's socialist "Turan Republic" project that aimed to bring all the Moslems of the Caucasus and Central Asia together under one socialist state (Bennigsen and Wimbush 1979, 66–68).

In his thinking of Eurasia, Ilhan – apart from his admiration for Galiev's ideas – was also heavily influenced by Mustafa Kemal Atatürk; a reality reflected in his reference to these two leaders as "heroes of Eurasia" (Ilhan 2000, 185). He also attached great importance to the political dialogue between Atatürk and Lenin during and after the Turkish War of Independence, as he believed this anti-imperialist dialogue formed the core of the Eurasian idea (Ilhan 2004b). A similar emphasis on Atatürk's policies can be found in the works of writer Anıl Çeçen, whose political views fall somewhere between Turkism and neo-nationalism (Çeçen 1999, 335–350). Defining Eurasia as the region formed by Anatolia, the Black Sea basin, Ukraine, Moldova, southern Russia, the Caucasus, Central Asia, the Xinxiang region of China and the Middle East, Çeçen indicates that Atatürk strengthened the Eurasian dimension of Turkish foreign policy through prioritising Turkey's relations with Russia as well as the Middle Eastern and Balkan countries (Çeçen 2006, 390, 406). He also has a more favorable view of Russia's role in Eurasia as he defines Istanbul and Moscow as the two centers of this region (379, 403). Thus, in contrast to anti-Russian ideas of some other writers, Çeçen is closer to the ideological line advocated by Ilhan, a position sometimes also named "Kemalist Eurasianism," which recommends Turkey's inclusion in an alternative model of globalisation together with Eurasian countries like Russia (Perinçek and Akçalı 2009, 565–566).

Çeçen is also among major writers who bring to salience Azerbaijan's importance to Turkey's strategy in Eurasia. However, the emphasis on Azerbaijan within the Asia-centered geopolitical tradition is largely determined in relation to anti-imperialism and Turkish–Russian cooperation, which stands in sharp contrast to the emphasis the Turkic-world-centered geopolitical tradition places on Turkic solidarity and cultural/emotional bonds. The latter tradition is also rather skeptical about Russia's position in Eurasia, including as reflected in MHP leader Devlet Bahçeli's definition of Russian Eurasianism as "EU-Russianism," i.e. a new kind of Russian imperialism (see *Zaman*, 10 Dec. 2004). Writers like Çeçen, in contrast, believe that Turkish and Russian versions of Eurasianism should not counteract each other. In view of this, he suggests that Turkish leaders follow the example of Atatürk's 1937 Saadabad Pact set to engage Eurasia's "southern tier" in a manner less threatening to Russian interests in Central Asia and further proposes the establishment of a "Central States Union," an anti-imperialist bloc including Turkey, Azerbaijan, Iran and Syria (Çeçen 2006, 408–409).

A similar emphasis on anti-imperialism can be found in Doğu Perinçek's "Big Asia Union," which likewise places Azerbaijan in a geopolitical alliance with Turkey, Syria, Iran and Iraq, not least given Perinçek's conviction that "Turks, Kurds, Persians, Arabs, Azeris, Baloch and Turcoman communities are all included in the camp of oppressed nations" and should therefore join their forces against imperialists within a Eurasianist vision (Perinçek 2000, 25). His views are also reflected in the official program of the Workers Party, which similarly proposes the establishment of a "regional alliance" among Turkey, Azerbaijan, Iran, Iraq and the TRNC.[14]

One should particularly mention the TRNC's place in the ideas of Turkish neo-nationalists towards Eurasia. Especially after UN secretary-general Annan announced his plan to facilitate the EU accession of a unified Cyprus, a pragmatic rapprochement took place between Perinçek's Workers Party and Dugin's Eurasian Movement. The latter's support for Turkish neo-nationalists' condemnation of Western policies in Iraq and Cyprus was particularly important in this respect. Consequently, Dugin received numerous invitations to visit Turkey and speak at conferences also attended by high-level Turkish political and military figures. He even paid a visit to Northern Cyprus in late 2004 and held official meetings with the TRNC leaders as if he were an official representative of the Russian state.

A closer look at Eurasianist discourses as presented in Turkey and Russia, however, exposes some very clear differences between the two versions. For example, whereas Dugin continuously advocates a Eurasian empire to be led by Russia, Turkish neo-nationalists formulate their anti-Western ideas around the notion of protection of the Turkish nation-state. More importantly, the initial version of Dugin's neo-Eurasianist project in the 1990s described Turkey as a pro-Atlanticist "scapegoat" to be punished to realise neo-Eurasianist ideals. Dugin also proposed the dismemberment of pro-Turkish Azerbaijan through joint efforts of Iran, Russia and Armenia (Dugin 2003, 78–79). Although he significantly revised his ideas on Turkey and Azerbaijan following his flirtation with Perinçek's Workers Party, such intellectual inconsistencies expose the limits of a possible Turkish–Russian alliance on the basis of neo-Eurasianism.[15]

Furthermore, not everyone in Turkey believes that Asia and Europe should be understood in binary terms as two opposite civilisational alternatives. Especially in the second half of the 1990s, Demirel began to describe Turkey as the West's "gate" opening into Eurasia (*BBC Summary of World Broadcasts*, 20 Oct. 1994). In a similar fashion, the idea of a "Eurasian order" voiced by Ismail Cem, Turkish foreign minister between 1997 and 2002, emphasised Turkey's "two-dimensional identity originating from the privilege of being both Asian and European" (Cem

2009, 105–106). Cem believed that Turkey's membership in the EU and its emergence as the "pivotal, decisive centre" of Eurasia were not "contradictory, but complementary" goals and that Turkey's rise in Asia always resonated in its relations with Europe (Cem 2009, 74; 2001, 60). In this regard, he attributed special importance to the BTC oil pipeline due to its potential to turn the country into a center in the transportation of Central Asian and Caspian energy resources to Europe (Cem 2009, 74). A similar emphasis on Turkey's geo-economic role in Eurasia could be seen in what Demirel called the Eurasian Project, which he described as a bid to link Europe with Asia through various oil and natural gas pipelines to be laid via Turkey (*Cumhuriyet*, 6 Oct. 1999). Since the future of those projects depended primarily on the participation of the Azerbaijani government, Azerbaijan grew to assume a primary position in Ankara's conceptualisation of Eurasia.

Moslem-world-centered geopolitical tradition

The third geopolitical tradition attributing a special meaning to the concept of Eurasia in post–Cold War Turkey is Moslem-world centered. Defining Turkey's national interest in terms of establishing a sphere of influence in the former territories of the Ottoman empire, it enjoys the support of religious and conservative circles close to the ruling AKP and highlights Moslem identity in the cultural sphere. It is particularly associated with the views of Ahmet Davutoğlu, well-known professor of international relations who served first as chief foreign policy adviser with the AKP government and then became Turkey's foreign minister in 2009. As such, Davutoğlu represents and embodies the powerful relationship between formal and practical geopolitics in the Turkish context.

Davutoğlu's seminal book *Strategic Depth* (2001) is regarded as the "bible" of the Moslem-world-centered geopolitical tradition, mainly because it makes a bold call to Turkish policymakers to make peace with the country's Moslem roots and Ottoman past (Davutoğlu 2001, 52–58). Such a strong emphasis on the Ottoman heritage also explains why many scholars, in Turkey and internationally, tend to describe this tradition as "neo-Ottomanism."[16] A similar emphasis prevails in Davutoğlu's conceptualisation of Eurasia as he prefers to use the concept of "Afro-Eurasia," the most important subregions of which he believes were once unified by the Ottoman empire. For Davutoğlu, being heir to such a powerful political and cultural legacy at the heart of the Afro-Eurasian continent gives Turkey a remarkable opportunity to turn itself into a "central country" in world politics (Davutoğlu 2001, 195, 331; also see Davutoğlu 2002).

A similar link between Eurasia and the Ottoman empire was established by the neo-conservative journal *Yarın* (Tomorrow), published between 2002 and 2007. In an interview the journal ran with Attila Ilhan, for instance, Eurasia was defined as the "Ottoman-Russian joint cultural basin" (Ilhan 2004a). Another article in the journal claimed that the Ottoman empire should be revived in order to unify Eurasia, the latter defined as a geographical region upon which a religious/cultural interaction took place between the Turks, Slavs and Arabs (Şamir

2005). Most significantly, the journal's editor, Ahmet Özcan, wrote that Eurasia in the Turkish context should be understood as the farthest borders of the Ottoman empire and that Turkey should follow "an open and consistent policy of Pax Ottomanica" towards these borders (Özcan 2005).

Moslem solidarity and the Ottoman heritage are also highlighted by the activities of *Diyalog Avrasya* (Dialogue Eurasia), a cultural/intellectual platform founded in 1998 by Fethullah Gülen's religious community, which also owns an impressive network of educational institutions in many Turkic republics (Balcı 2003). Although these schools provide high-quality education in line with Western standards and the Gülen community is believed to have a relatively moderate understanding of Islam, the schools sometimes caused uneasiness for the secular-minded ruling elite of the Turkic republics – most notably Uzbekistan (Yanık 2004, 300–301) – but also in some other states where they were recently forced to close, including indeed in Azerbaijan. Still, *Diyalog Avrasya* aims to facilitate intercultural dialogue rather than cooperation in political or religious matters and, as such, brings together intellectuals of diverse political and ideological backgrounds from Turkey, Russia and other former Soviet republics.[17] At the same time, however, its understanding of Eurasia seems to be limited to the Ottoman geographical and conceptual space, as also indicated by some of the articles published in the platform's eponymous journal (Ersanlı and Okman 2000, 29; Karpat 2000, 41).

In many ways, it is the Middle East, rather than the Caucasus or Central Asia, that plays a central role in the view the Moslem-world-centered geopolitical tradition holds of Eurasia. Davutoğlu, for instance, describes the Middle East as the center of the Afro-Eurasian continent (Davutoğlu 2001, 132). Other conservative writers, including Ali Bulaç and Ibrahim Karagül, similarly claim that the Middle East should play the pivotal role in Turkey's policies in Eurasia (Bulaç 2007; Karagül 2010). In practical geopolitical terms, too, one could claim, the focus in Turkey's geopolitical outlook towards Eurasia under the AKP government shifted away from the Turkic republics, and the concept is now viewed in relation to a much larger geography, one including not only Central Asia and the Caucasus, but also the Middle East and even North Africa. Since 2005, for instance, TİKA has been implementing its development aid programs also for the African states. Broadcasts of *TRT Avaz* founded in 2009 to replace the older *TRT Avrasya*, in turn, are available not only in Central Asia and the Caucasus, as was previously the case, but also in the Middle East.

For some Turkish political scientists, the AKP's geopolitical vision represents "civilisational geopolitical thinking" and makes use of the "us versus them" dichotomy by emphasising civilisational differences not only between Turkey and the West, but also between some non-Moslem countries like Israel and Armenia (Bilgin and Bilgiç 2011, 180, 192). Azerbaijan naturally acquires a degree of prominence in such a geocultural approach, as also indicated by some of the articles in *Yarın* and *Diyalog Avrasya* (Mete 2004, 19–20; Uyanık 2007). The latter even has an office in Baku, which coordinates the platform's cultural and social activities throughout Azerbaijan.[18]

At the same time, however, Azerbaijan's principal significance to the AKP government seems to be understood in terms of traditional geopolitical calculations, rather than civilisational affinities. Although the other two geopolitical traditions also draw attention to Azerbaijan's geopolitical importance to the Turkish strategy in Eurasia, their main focus is either on Turkic solidarity or the anti-Western nature of Turkish-Azerbaijani relations. In contrast, Davutoğlu's discourse places a greater emphasis on Azerbaijan's geo-strategic significance to Turkey. For example, defining Azerbaijan as "the most important strategic ally" in the Caucasus, he claims that unless this country acquires a stable and powerful regional position, Turkey will fail to achieve any significant influence in the Caspian basin (Davutoğlu 2001, 127–128). In this regard, he even likens Azerbaijan to the "wing" of Turkey in the Caucasus and Caspian region (*Yeni Akit*, 3 Oct. 2013).

Given the above and not unlike the times of Demirel and Cem, Azerbaijan – given its position at the center of grand transportation projects linking Europe and Asia via Turkish territory, including the BTC oil pipeline, the BTE natural gas pipeline and the BTK railway – still has a strong bearing on the AKP government's geopolitical outlook towards Eurasia. Among the most recent examples is TANAP, set to carry significant amounts of Azerbaijani natural gas through Turkey to Europe, which Davutoğlu hailed as one of the most important projects in the geo-economic map of Eurasia.[19] Erdoğan, too, believed the completion of TANAP would place both Turkey and Azerbaijan in a strategic position with regard to energy supply to Europe, a development he believed was extremely important for the entire Eurasian continent.[20]

Conclusion

Since the collapse of the Soviet Union, Turkey has become home to the rise of various formal and practical geopolitical representations of the Eurasia concept. These can be grouped under three geopolitical traditions, each corresponding to its own temporal boundaries. During the first period, which lasted until around 1995, Eurasia was almost exclusively defined under the influence of the Turkic-world-centered geopolitical tradition and as such was associated with the Turkic republics of the former Soviet Union. The second period, which continued until the early 2000s, was dominated by a pragmatic approach viewing Eurasia in relation to Turkey's geo-economic interests in the Caucasus and Caspian region. It was also during this period, however, that the Asia-centered geopolitical tradition's interpretation of Eurasia as an alternative to or a balance against the West began to attract certain opposition groups, although this view was also challenged by a civilisational approach, which highlighted Turkey's unique geo-cultural identity as a Euro-Asian country. During the third period, which has spanned more than a decade of AKP rule in Turkey, this civilisational approach was merged with the Moslem-world-centered geopolitical tradition, and Eurasia grew to connote a broader region, which included the farthest borders of the Ottoman geo-cultural realm.

Today, each of these three geopolitical traditions, to various extents and in different ways, continues to influence Ankara's understanding of Eurasia. Although the AKP's foreign policy discourse, for example, is largely associated with the Moslem-world-centered geopolitical tradition, its views about Eurasia have not been entirely free from influences of the Turkic-world-centered tradition. In a similar fashion, while the MHP, the third largest party in the Turkish parliament, represents a foreign policy discourse based on Turkic–Moslem solidarity; anti-Westernism features strongly in its discourse on Eurasia as well, and there is also a significant neo-nationalist faction within the main opposition party, Republican People's Party (CHP), which sympathises with the views of the Asia-centered geopolitical tradition.

Similarly, all three Turkish geopolitical traditions emphasise Azerbaijan's prominence in Turkey's strategies in Eurasia, although there are also some important nuances in their understanding of the particular nature of this prominence: close cultural and emotional bonds between the two nations play a critical role in the Turkic-world-centered geopolitical tradition, while the Asia-centered geopolitical tradition attributes additional, anti-imperialist, meaning to Turkey–Azerbaijan cooperation; and the Moslem-world-centered tradition, in turn, interprets Azerbaijan's significance in Eurasia in terms of Moslem solidarity as well as crude geopolitical calculations centered on the Caspian's rich natural resources.

Ultimately, however, and despite their fundamental differences, all three geopolitical traditions invoke the Eurasia concept to highlight the "exceptional geopolitical importance" of Turkey as a country bridging and influencing different regions, continents, religions and civilisations (Yanık 2009, 537). Put differently, whether it connotes the Turkic world, an anti-Western bloc of Asian states or the Moslem/Ottoman geo-cultural realm, Eurasia only acquires geopolitical significance with Turkey imagined as its focus or leader. Such an imagination inevitably attributes to Azerbaijan the role of a supporting actor – rather than a protagonist – in a neo-imperial strategy, which defines Turkey as Eurasia's real center, an outlook introducing a principal tension in Turkey's conceptualisation of Eurasia and its relations with Azerbaijan the latter stands to frame.

Notes

1 This research was supported by Marmara University's Scientific Research Projects Coordination Unit (Project No: SOS-D-080415–0144).
2 The World Factbook of the US Central Intelligence Agency defines Turkey and Azerbaijan as Middle Eastern countries with small territories in Europe. See www.cia.gov/library/publications/the-world-factbook/geos/aj.html#Geo and www.cia.gov/library/publications/the-world-factbook/geos/tu.html. For the UN Statistics Division, however, both are Western Asian countries, which border eastern and southern Europe. http://unstats.un.org/unsd/methods/m49/m49regin.htm.
3 For studies that employ a critical geopolitical approach, see Bilgin (2007), Tank (2006), Yanık (2011, 2009).
4 Among the very first studies based on critical geopolitics was Gearóid Ó Tuathail's doctoral thesis under the supervision of John Agnew at Syracuse University in 1989 (see Mamadouh 1998, 244).

5 For a number of studies employing popular geopolitics, see Dodds (2003), Sharp (1993).
6 Mackinder, for example, was not only an academic, but also a member of the British parliament. Brzezinski and Kissinger, in turn, had direct influence on the formulation and implementation of US foreign policy.
7 The "Europe-centered geopolitical tradition," historically the most powerful geopolitical tradition in Turkey, has not been included in this study. This is because this tradition does not attribute a significant meaning to the Eurasia concept and is largely focused on Turkey's political, economic and cultural integration with the European states. Yet, one should note that a number of scholars sometimes tend to define Eurasianism as the opposite of Europeanism in the Turkish context (e.g. Berkan 2009; Dağı 2002).
8 For Suat Ilhan (2006, 204), the Turkic world consists of Turkey, Azerbaijan, Kazakhstan, Uzbekistan, Kyrgyzstan, Turkmenistan and the Turkish Republic of Northern Cyprus.
9 Foreign Minister Hikmet Çetin, for instance, stated that the Black Sea basin was located at the "heart of Eurasia." See *TBMM Tutanak Dergisi* 11, 204.
10 Also see www.avrasyabir.org.tr/hakkinda.
11 Also see *Avrasya Dosyası (Azerbaycan Özel Sayısı)*.
12 See, for example, Demirel's speech before the Turkish Parliament on 7 May, 1992. *TBMM Tutanak Dergisi* 10, 419–420.
13 He is currently imprisoned due to the criminal case launched against the "Ergenekon" grouping, which was found guilty of organising a coup against the government. The Ergenekon case covers many other neo-nationalist politicians as well as military figures, intellectuals and journalists.
14 See www.ip.org.tr/lib/pages/detay.asp?goster=tbelgeler&belgetur=2.
15 For Dugin's revised ideas on Turkey's position in the Eurasian Bloc, see Dugin (2007, 107–137).
16 For the roots of neo-Ottomanism in Turkish foreign policy, see Yavuz (1998, 19–41).
17 See the platform's official website at www.daplatform.org.
18 See www.diyalogazerbaycan.com.
19 See his remarks at www.mfa.gov.tr/disisleri-bakani-sayin-ahmet-davutoglu_nun-yunanistan-disisleri-bakani-evangelos-venizelos-ile-ortak-basin-toplantisi_-19-temmuz.tr.mfa.
20 See www.caspiantv.net/contentJx.aspx?cID=300.

References

Aça, Mehmet. 2002. Avrasyacı Yaklaşımın Türkiye Çeşitlenmeleri ve Türk Dünyasının Geleceği. In: Emine Gürsoy-Naskali and Erdal Şahin, eds. *Bağımsızlıklarının 10. Yılında Türk Cumhuriyetleri*, 33–62. (In Turkish.) Haarlem: SOTA.
Akgül, Fatih. 2009. *Rusya ve Türkiye'de Avrasyacılık*. (In Turkish.) Istanbul: IQ Kültür Sanat Yayıncılık.
Aktürk, Şener. 2004. Counter Hegemonic Visions and Reconciliation through the Past: The Case of Turkish Eurasianism. *Ab Imperio* 4, 207–238.
Andican, Ahat. 1992. Orta Asya Türk Cumhuriyetlerinden 'Birleşik Türkistan'a: Tarihi Bir Zorunluluğun Sosyopolitik Analizi. (In Turkish.) *Türk Yurdu* 64, 12–18.
———. 1996. Türkiye, Türk Dünyası ve Rusya Üzerine Düşünceler. (In Turkish.) *Ulusal* 1, 25–29.
———. 1997. Avrasya Stratejileri Üzerine (Interview). (In Turkish.) *Ulusal* 4, 13–20.
Aras, Bülent. 2000. Turkey's Policy in the Former Soviet South: Assets and Options. *Turkish Studies* 1:1, 36–58.

———. 2003. Avrasya'yı Yeniden Düşünmek. (In Turkish.) *Zaman*, 4 Jan.
Avrasya *Dosyası (Azerbaycan Özel Sayısı)*. Special issue dedicated to Azerbaijan. Spring 2001. 7:1.
Balcı, Bayram. 2003. Fethullah Gülen's Missionary Schools in Central Asia and their Role in the Spreading of Turkism and Islam. *Religion, State and Society* 31:2, 151–177.
Bennigsen, Alexandre A. and S. Enders Wimbush. 1979. *Muslim National Communism in the Soviet Union*. Chicago: The University of Chicago Press.
Berkan, Ismet. 2009. Avrasyacılık Mümkün mü? (In Turkish.) *Radikal*, 15 Feb.
Bilgin, Pınar. 2007. 'Only Strong States Can Survive in Turkey's Geography': The Uses of 'Geopolitical Truths' in Turkey. *Political Geography* 26:7, 740–756.
Bilgin, Pınar and Ali Bilgiç. 2011. Turkey's 'New' Foreign Policy toward Eurasia. *Eurasian Geography and Economics* 52:2, 173–195.
Bulaç, Ali. 2007. Avrasya'nın Sınırları. (In Turkish.) *Zaman*, 3 Mar.
Çeçen, Anıl. 1999. *Atatürk ve Avrasya*. (In Turkish.) Istanbul: Cumhuriyet Kitapları.
———. 2006. *Türkiye ve Avrasya*. (In Turkish.) Ankara: Fark Yayınları.
Cem, Ismail. 2001. *Turkey in the New Century*. Nicosia & Mersin: Rustem.
———. 2009. *Türkiye, Avrupa, Avrasya: Birinci Cilt*. (In Turkish.) Istanbul: Türkiye İş Bankası Kültür Yayınları.
Dağı, Ihsan. 2002. Competing Strategies for Turkey: Eurasianism or Europeanism? *Central Asia-Caucasus Analyst*, 8 May. www.cacianalyst.org/view_article.php?articleid=1189.
Dalby, Simon. 2008. Imperialism, Domination, Culture: The Continued Relevance of Critical Geopolitics. *Geopolitics* 13:3, 413–436.
Davutoğlu, Ahmet. 2001. *Stratejik Derinlik*. (In Turkish.) Istanbul: Küre Yayınları.
———. 2002. Türkiye Köprü Değil, Merkez Ülkedir (Interview). (In Turkish.) *Yarın* 7, 12–14.
Dodds, Klaus. 2003. Licensed to Stereotype: Popular Geopolitics, James Bond and the Spectre of Balkanism. *Geopolitics* 8:2, 125–156.
———. 2007. *Geopolitics: A Very Short Introduction*. Oxford: Oxford University Press.
Dugin, Aleksandr. 2003. *Rus Jeopolitiği: Avrasyacı Yaklaşım*. (In Turkish.) Istanbul: Küre Yayınları.
———. 2004. The Eurasian Idea. *Eurasia Information Analytical Portal*. http://evrazia.org/modules.php?name=News&file=article&sid=1884.
———. 2007. *Moskova-Ankara Ekseni*. (In Turkish.) Istanbul: Kaynak Yayınları.
Eren-Webb, Ebru. 2011. To Which Eurasia Does Turkey Belong? A Comparative Analysis of Turkish Eurasianist Geopolitical Discourses. *Boğaziçi Journal* 25:2, 59–82.
Ersanlı, Büşra and Cengiz Okman. 2000. Avrasya: Az-i-Ya: Jeopolitikten Diğer Perspektiflere. *Diyalog Avrasya* 1, 28–34.
Ilhan, Attila. 1997. Avrasya Kutbu ve Siyaset Tarihi Üzerine (Interview). (In Turkish.) *Ulusal* 4, 34–38.
———. 2000. *Sultan Galiyef: Avrasya'da Dolaşan Hayalet*. (In Turkish.) Istanbul: Türkiye İş Bankası Kültür Yayınları.
———. 2004a. Maarif, Ekonomi ve Savunma Millileştirilmeli (Interview). (In Turkish.) *Yarın* 3:31. http://goo.gl/sQYfll.
———. 2004b. Ortaklaşa Umut: Avrasya. (In Turkish.) *Cumhuriyet*, 5 Jul.
Ilhan, Suat. 1999. *Türkiye'nin Jeopolitik Konumu ve Türk Dünyası*. (In Turkish.) Ankara: Atatürk Kültür Merkezi.
———. 2006. *Türklerin Jeopolitiği ve Avrasyacılık*. (In Turkish.) Istanbul: Bilgi Yayınevi.
Imanov, Vügar. 2008. *Avrasyacılık: Rusya'nın Kimlik Arayışı*. (In Turkish.) Istanbul: Küre Yayınları.

İşeri, Emre and Nihat Çelik. 2013. Turkish Nation-State Identity and Foreign Policy on Armenia: The Roles of Sèvresphobia and 'Brotherly' Azerbaijan. *Turkish Review* 3:3, 274–281.
Ismayılov, Meşdi. 2011. *Avrasyacılık: Mukayeseli Bir Okuma: Türkiye ve Rusya Örneği.* (In Turkish.) Ankara: Doğu Batı Yayınları.
Ivanov, A. V. and M. Y. Şişin. 2002. Türkiye Avrasyacılığı'nın Tarihi Oluşumu Şüphelidir. (In Turkish.) *Diyalog Avrasya* 6, 80–84.
Karagül, Ibrahim. 2010. Davutoğlu, Avrasya Birliği, 'Kaos Kuşağı'. (In Turkish.) *Yeni Şafak*, 5 Feb.
Karasar, Hasan Ali. 2008. Türk Dış Politikasında Batı'ya Alternatif Arayışları: Avrasyacılık Örneği. (In Turkish.) *Demokrasi Platformu* 4:13, 117–128.
Karpat, Kemal. 2000. Türkiye Açısından Avrasya. (In Turkish.) *Diyalog Avrasya* 1, 38–43.
Kılıçbeyli, Elif Hatun. 2003. 21. Yüzyılda Avrasya ve Avrasyacılık: Rusya, Çin, İran ve Türkiye'nin Jeopolitik Yaklaşımları. (In Turkish.) *Jeopolitik* 2:6, 82–91.
Kolobov, Oleg A., Aleksandr A. Kornilov and Fatih Özbay. 2006. *Çağdaş Türk-Rus İlişkileri: Sorunlar ve İşbirliği Alanları 1992–2005*. (In Turkish.) Istanbul: TASAM.
Külebi, Ali. 2006. The Forgotten Option: Turkish Eurasianism. (In Turkish.) *Turkish Daily News*, 23 Aug.
Laruelle, Marlène. 2008. Russo-Turkish Rapprochement through the Idea of Eurasia: Alexander Dugin's Networks in Turkey. *The Jamestown Foundation Occasional Paper*, Apr. http://goo.gl/xTNnsJ.
Mamadouh, V. D. 1998. Geopolitics in the Nineties: One Flag, Many Meanings. *GeoJournal* 46:4, 237–253.
Mead, Walter R. 2002. *Special Providence: American Foreign Policy and How It Changed the World*. New York: Routledge.
Mete, Ömer Lütfi. 2004. Nevruz Avrasyacılığı. (In Turkish.) *Yarın* 2:25, 19–20.
Ó Tuathail, Gearóid. 1999. Understanding Critical Geopolitics: Geopolitics and Risk Society. *Journal of Strategic Studies* 22:2–3, 107–124.
———. 2003. Towards Conceptual Clarity in the Critical Geopolitical Structures and Geopolitical Cultures: Study of Geopolitics in Geopolitical Perspectives on World Politics. In: Lasha Tchantouridze, ed. *Geopolitics: Global Problems and Regional Concerns*, 75–102. Winnipeg: Centre for Defense and Security Studies.
Ó Tuathail, Gearóid and John Agnew. 1998. Geopolitics and Discourse: Practical Geopolitical Reasoning in American Foreign Policy. In: Gearóid Ó Tuathail, Simon Dalby, and Paul Routledge, eds. *The Geopolitics Reader*, 78–91. London & New York: Routledge.
Oran, Baskın, ed. 2001. *Türk Dış Politikası: Cilt II*. (In Turkish.) Istanbul: İletişim.
Özcan, Ahmet. 2005. Açık Mektup: Üç Tarz-ı Siyaset. (In Turkish.) *Haber 10*, 14 Dec. www.haber10.com/makale/1367/#.UmarHXAtz9M.
Özdağ, Muzaffer. 2003. *Türkiye ve Türk Dünyası Jeopolitiği*. (In Turkish.) Ankara: Avrasya Bir Vakfı.
Özdağ, Ümit. 2003. *Türk Tarihinin ve Geleceğinin Jeopolitik Çerçevesi*. (In Turkish.) Ankara: ASAM.
———. 2004. Türkiye'nin Türk Dünyası Politikasının Teorik Çerçevesi. (In Turkish.) *Asya-Avrupa* 4, 22–30.
Perinçek, Doğu. 1996. Devrimci Atılımın Eşiğinde. (In Turkish.) *Teori* 83, 3–17.
———. 1997. Devrimci Cumhuriyetin Dış Politikası: Avrasya Seçeneği. (In Turkish.) *Ulusal* 1, 26–33.
———. 2000. *Avrasya Seçeneği: Türkiye İçin Bağımsız Dış Politika*. (In Turkish.) Ankara: Kaynak Yayınları.

Perinçek, Mehmet. 2006. *Avrasyacılık: Türkiye'deki Teori ve Pratiği*. (In Turkish.) Ankara: Bilgi Yayınevi.
Perinçek, Mehmet and Emel Akçalı. 2009. Kemalist Eurasianism: An Emerging Geopolitical Discourse in Turkey. *Geopolitics* 14:3, 550–569.
Reyhan, Hakan. 1997. Avrasya Gündemi. (In Turkish.) *Ulusal* 4, 3–5.
Şamir, Israel. 2005. Ey Osmanlı Geri Gel. (In Turkish.) *Yarın* 4:41, 6–8.
Sharp, Joanne. 1993. Publishing American Identity: Popular Geopolitics, Myth and the Reader's Digest. *Political Geography* 12:6, 491–503.
———. 2003. Refiguring Geopolitics: The Reader's Digest and Popular Geographies of Danger at the End of the Cold War. In: Klaus Dodds and David Atkinson, eds. *Geopolitical Traditions: A Century of Geopolitical Thought*, 332–352. London & New York: Routledge.
Sidaway, James D. 1998. What Is in a Gulf?: From the 'Arc of Crisis' to the Gulf War. In: Gearóid Ó Tuathail and Simon Dalby, eds. *Rethinking Geopolitics*, 224–239. London & New York: Routledge.
Smith, Graham. 1999. The Masks of Proteus: Russia, Geopolitical Shift and the New Eurasianism. *Transactions of the Institute of British Geographers* 24:4, 481–500.
Tank, Pınar. 2006. Dressing for the Occasion: Reconstructing Turkey's Identity. *Southeast European and Black Sea Studies* 6:4, 463–478.
TBMM Tutanak Dergisi, Dönem 19, Cilt 10, Birleşim 74, 7 May, 1992.
TBMM Tutanak Dergisi, Dönem 19, Cilt 11, Birleşim 78, 20 May, 1992.
Uyanık, Mevlüt. 2007. Türk(men)lerin Birlik ve Yeniden Diriliş Projesi: İpek Yolu. (In Turkish.) *Yarın* 7:58. http://yarindergisi2007.blogspot.com/2007/05/trkmenlerin-birlik-ve-yeniden-dirili.html.
Yanık, Lerna K. 2004. The Politics of Educational Exchange: Turkish Education in Eurasia. *Europe-Asia Studies* 56:2, 293–307.
———. 2009. The Metamorphosis of Metaphors of Vision: 'Bridging' Turkey's Location, Role and Identity after the End of the Cold War. *Geopolitics* 14:3, 531–549.
———. 2011. Constructing Turkish 'Exceptionalism': Discourses of Liminality and Hybridity in Post–Cold War Turkish Foreign Policy. *Political Geography* 30:2, 80–89.
Yavuz, M. Hakan. 1998. Turkish Identity and Foreign Policy in Flux: The Rise of Neo-Ottomanism. *Critique: Journal for Critical Studies of the Middle East* 7:12, 19–41.
Yeniçeri, Özcan. 2004. Çatışan ve Örtüşen Stratejiler. (In Turkish.) *Asya-Avrupa* 1, 3–21.
———. 2006. Yeni Bir Türk Stratejisi ve Yeni Bir Türk Hamlesi. (In Turkish.) *Asya-Avrupa* 4, 33–35.
Zeybek, Namık K. 2006. Hangi Dış Siyaset? (In Turkish.) *H. O. Tercüman*, 17 Mar.

4 The bilateral origins of South Caucasus trilateralism

Michael H. Cecire

The progressive emergence of trilateral economic and geopolitical coordination among Turkey, Georgia and Azerbaijan ("trilateralism") is a transnational outgrowth of Turkey–Azerbaijan bilateral relations. Turkish foreign policy informed by the "strategic depth" concept and "zero problems" policies towards neighboring regions propelled trilateralism from a series of bilateral ties towards an increasingly coherent grouping. Turkey–Azerbaijan bilateral relations inspired and sustained the emergence of a trilateral grouping that came to include Georgia. However, though bilateralism is the basis of trilateral relations, trilateralism has emerged as an independent geopolitical variable. Rather than an adjunct to Turkish-Azerbaijani relations, trilateralism is itself increasingly reinforcing bilateral ties between the three states rather than the other way around.

In June 2012, Turkey, Georgia and Azerbaijan signed the Trabzon Declaration, which formalised the fast growing economic, social, and diplomatic relations between the three states since the turn of the new century.[1] The declaration served as a statement of shared values as well as for economic, security and diplomatic cooperation, including support for the varying Euro-Atlantic aspirations of the signatories. The Declaration has also been accompanied by a bevy of collaborative projects and initiatives – including the marquee Baku-Tbilisi-Kars railway project, crisscrossing energy conduits and close security cooperation – that offer concrete manifestations of an emerging trilateral entente. In the framework of the Declaration, which established a regular tripartite forum at the foreign minister level, the foreign policies of the three states are being increasingly coordinated and complemented. The first meeting of the "Trabzon 3" took place in March 2013 in Georgia's southwestern port city of Batumi. Multiple successive meetings have taken place since then, gradually encompassing other "power" ministries and government organs – defense, economy and heads of state and government (Cecire 2015b).

The Trabzon Declaration is an exclamation point to the converging interests of Turkey, Georgia and Azerbaijan. The growth and development of this trilateral alignment has its roots in a shared history, which has been of special significance to Turkey in particular. More contemporaneously, the three states also share a number of economic and foreign policy interests that have facilitated an organic and rapid development of interstate relations, including the Caucasus' role as an energy conduit and the role of Euro-Atlantic integration. In this formulation, Turkey–Azerbaijan relations form the core of trilateralism, with Georgia's participation initially derivative of this dynamic. However, trilateralism's development looks to be gradually reinforcing bilateral interstate relations rather than exclusively the converse. Although bilateral national interests gave rise to trilateralism, trilateralism is now a driving force.

However, the three states' expanding ties are not without their obstacles and potential for complications. Despite the upward trajectory of Turkey-Georgia-Azerbaijan trilateralism, Russia's role as the perceived regional hegemon remains an issue of significant consequence. This factors in to the character and ultimate potential of the trilateral alignment. Other possible limits to the nascent grouping include the internal politics of all three countries and the noticeable divide between Moslem Turkic Turkey and Azerbaijan (although predominantly Sunni and Shiite, respectively) and Christian Orthodox Georgia.

From bilateral to trilateral alignment

Ahmet Davutoglu, Turkey's former foreign minister turned prime minister, is widely credited as the architect of Turkish foreign policy under the AKP. In his 2001 book *Stratejik Derinlik Türkiye'nin Uluslararası Konumu* [Strategic Depth: Turkey's International Position], Davutoglu (2001) outlines what would later become the foundational contours of AKP foreign policy. In Strategic Depth, Davutoglu posits that Turkish geography and history (and particularly the role of its Ottoman legacy) grants the country latent reserves of soft power – strategic depth – which can be used as leverage to propel the country forward as a global power in its own right. Critics, both in Turkey and abroad, have noted the similarity of Strategic Depth's geographical pretensions to the old borders of the Ottoman empire, dubbing the doctrine "neo-Ottomanism" – a descriptor Davutoglu, Turkish president Recep Tayyip Erdogan and the AKP vociferously reject (see Davutoglu 2001).

In Davutoglu's formulation, the Middle East, the Balkans, Central Asia and the Caucasus are all part of Turkey's historical neighbourhood and potential spokes in a resurgent Turkish system. In practice, Turkish foreign policy outreach towards these regions – and especially the Middle East – was known internationally as the Zero Problems with Neighbors[2] policy, so called for Ankara's efforts to improve its ties with Strategic Depth states, including normalising relations with erstwhile adversaries such as Syria and Iran. Yet, Turkey's ability to channel its historical legacy into foreign policy successes has been operationally limited, particularly in its approach to the Middle East – the clear primary focus of its strategy. Although Turkey's cultural and soft power assets are unmistakable (Davutoglu 2010), this has not necessarily translated into long-term geopolitical gains. The apparent unraveling of Turkish influence in the Middle East and the escalation of the war in Syria have evoked many an obituary for Zero Problems. The waves of domestic unrest that gripped Turkey in 2013 and 2014 have also been cited as an example of the limits of Turkish foreign policy (Ottens 2013).

Whatever the prognosis of Turkey's Middle Eastern policies, however, Zero Problems has seen relative success elsewhere. More quietly, Turkey's diplomatic charms appear to be having a positive effect in the Balkans, the historical source of much of the former Ottoman empire's bureaucracy, troops and prized Janissary units. Diplomatic relations are strong and rising along with increased trade between Turkey and the Balkan states (Bechev 2012). Some analysts, however, do not see Turkey's increasing Balkans influence as translating into much more than richer trade opportunities at the moment (Rüma 2010).

Even more than the Balkans, the Caucasus benefits from the Turkish Zero Problems policies. Although, like in the Balkans, it has not received nearly the same media coverage or governmental attention from Ankara as the Middle East, it has quietly emerged as something of a success story. If Zero Problems is judged on Turkey's ability to build serviceable or better relationships with its neighbors and increase Turkish geopolitical influence, the Caucasus rates exceedingly well. Compared with the Middle East, where Turkey's foreign policy "successes" in Syria, Iran and Egypt have backfired and its former alliance with Israel has eroded (possibly to the point of no return), the South Caucasus has offered a stabler narrative of upwards-tracking relations. The emergence of trilateralism as a geopolitical grouping, with the three states in an embrace across economic, political and defense sectors, is a manifestation of this trend.

Turkey–Azerbaijan relations

Turkey–Azerbaijan relations are a founding basis for both Zero Problems policies in the South Caucasus and trilateralism. Although aspects of Turkey's practice of Zero Problems led to major disagreements between Ankara and Baku, the endeavor of pursuing Zero Problems in the South Caucasus was ultimately dependent on the bilateral relationship. This may appear counterintuitive on its face, but Turkish strategic confidence to pursue "football diplomacy" with Armenia, in pursuit of groundbreaking bilateral accords, was a risk worth taking only because of the strength of Turkey–Azerbaijan relations. If anything, the strength of bilateral Turkey–Azerbaijan relations that preceded Zero Problems exemplified the promise of Strategic Depth before the term was even coined. Secondarily, Turkey's subsequent abandonment of its normalisation initiative with Armenia, following Azerbaijani pushback, is yet a further expression of the strength of those ties. Overall, Turkey's interests in the South Caucasus region are, at least from a superficial reading, reducible to its long-standing partnership with Azerbaijan. Interests derived from the bilateral alliance – economic, geopolitical and security considerations – directly incentivise and sustain trilateralism.

Turkey's relationship with Azerbaijan rests on pillars of state secularism, a common Turkic identity and geopolitical alignment. Turkey was the first state to recognise the Republic of Azerbaijan's independence in 1991 and supported it, if somewhat tacitly, in its war with Armenia over the separatist territory of Nagorno-Karabakh. The common mantra for the bilateral partnership has been "one nation, two states," underlining their common Turkic cultural heritage. Since independence, bilateral relations have steadily increased, with trade volume having expanded by 2012 to US$4.2 billion³ and culminating in the 2010 strategic partnership that includes, among other things, a mutual defense clause. However, even this somewhat understates the prominence that Azerbaijan enjoys within Turkish foreign policy making. Although Ankara has traditionally prioritised the Middle East and the Mediterranean in the conduct of its foreign policy, Baku retains a significant level of pull relative to its modest size and location apart from these more "traditional" regions. One reason is, again, the sense of fraternity between the two states.

The other reason for Azerbaijan's outsized position in the Turkish foreign policy firmament is the centrality of Azerbaijani hydrocarbons in Turkish geopolitical aspirations to regional power. Although Turkey's energy relations with Azerbaijan have fluctuated since the latter's independence, it has recently come to rely on the stable flow of Azerbaijan-sourced energy (Yılmaz and Kılavuz 2012). With the construction of the BTC oil pipeline, the South Caucasus gas pipeline, the planned expansion of the latter to accommodate TANAP, and the Trans-Adriatic interconnecting pipeline (TAP) – which will ferry energy to southern European markets – bilateral energy relations have grown from minimal to robust in the span of little more than a decade.⁴

While energy relations have catapulted Azerbaijan from poor cousin to crucial ally, the socio-cultural links that bind "fraternal" relations deepen the relationship beyond the high-level interconnections necessitated by national interests and geopolitics. While it is no coincidence that a mutual defense agreement was not inked until 2010 – by which point Azerbaijan's utility as energy supplier had become fully realised – there is no question that socio-cultural ties made the strategic partnership possible. Turkey maintains no comparable level of ties with any of its other trade partners or energy suppliers outside of its alliance obligations to NATO, which largely preceded Ankara's now expansive economic relations with the Euro-Atlantic space. Conversely, with the possible exception of North Cyprus (though a special case in many respects), Turkey maintains no comparable level of sponsorship towards any other Turkic community. Exceptionally, Azerbaijan's Turkic identity and abundant energy reserves serve as mutually force-multiplying factors that elevate Baku well beyond the role of a "conventional" junior partner or client.⁵

Azerbaijan's relatively outsized position vis-à-vis Turkey is well illustrated in the 2008–09 crisis in bilateral relations between Ankara and Baku. Turkey, seeking to more proactively insert itself as a player in South Caucasus politics, pursued a policy of outreach and normalisation with Armenia, with which it has no diplomatic relations. Ultimately, however, the initiative collapsed under its own weight. Azerbaijan, which strongly and publicly opposed the measure, given Armenia's occupation of its territories, was able to play a major role in the formation of public opinion and the eventual scuttling of the initiative (Chatham House 2012). However, Azerbaijan's opposition was not to Zero Problems as a concept – Baku has embraced other expressions of it in the Caucasus – but rather the tactical effort to normalise Turkey–Armenia relations without preconditions.

Economic growth, which relies on the stability and growth of cheap energy, is the single most important means to Turkey's great-power aspirations. A 2011 announcement by Prime Minister Erdogan outlined a list of goals for 2023, the centennial of the republic's founding, which was dominated by economic targets. This included the much-quoted mission to make Turkey a top-ten global economy by that point. The Turkish economy's reliance on energy supplies to fuel its economic growth makes Azerbaijan, and the South Caucasus overall, an essential means to that goal. This, perhaps, is Strategic Depth ideally illustrated: the residues of a bygone Pax Turkana form the foundations for a modern strategic partnership with Azerbaijan that confers Ankara access to badly needed strategic resources.

In this sense, the bilateral Turkey–Azerbaijan partnership is the kernel of the Turkish strategy in the South Caucasus and allows its other partnership with Georgia to be possible. By extension, ties between Turkey and Azerbaijan are the heart of Turkey-Georgia-Azerbaijan trilateralism; the latter will likely rise or fall based on the stability and development of the former. Were bilateral relations to hit rocky shoals, Georgia's position within the trilateral grouping would also be concomitantly impacted. Turkey's need for hydrocarbons, and the means to extract and transit them, makes Turkey–Azerbaijani relations the strategic driver of trilateralism. Azerbaijan's perceived role as both an energy supplier and a potential transit state for energy flows from elsewhere, like Central Asia and Iran, augments a relationship of shared values with strategic importance. The 2008–09 experience also demonstrates the limits and the strengths of Strategic Depth in the Caucasus: its close tethering to Turkish-Azerbaijani relations.

Georgia: strategic corollary to partner

Current Turkey–Georgia ties, in turn, are mostly an outgrowth of Turkish relations with Azerbaijan. While Ankara and Tbilisi would likely have cultivated neighborly relations, and even some measure of interdependency, without Azerbaijan, Georgia's elevated role as Turkish strategic partner and trilateral participant is arguably a function of geographical happenstance, linking Turkey to Azerbaijan. Over time, however, Tbilisi has well leveraged its position of strategic corollary into that of a genuine partner.

Unlike Azerbaijan, which can point to a common, if distinctive, socio-cultural identity with Turkey, the conventional Georgian narrative of historical relations with Turkey is largely adversarial. Given this history, prevailing cultural predispositions in Georgia, even today, are primarily negative towards Turkey as well as Azerbaijan. Polling conducted by the Tbilisi-based branch of the Caucasus Research Resource Centers illustrate this predilection through the regular Caucasus Barometer surveys, which, among other things, gauge Georgians' attitudes towards foreigners through proxy indicators, such as the percentage that approve of doing business with various foreign nationalities or approve of Georgian women marrying various foreign nationalities. However, the most recent Caucasus Barometer, released in 2013, shows that while Georgians may be predisposed to skepticism towards their Turkic neighbors, they are also able to differentiate between geopolitical interests and their opinions of neighbors.[6] This would seem to suggest that Georgians make a powerful distinction between their perceptions of people and those of their governments.

It is this distinction, possibly rooted in a historical need to adapt to rapidly changing political conditions, which allows Georgians to accept a strong degree of strategic realism in their foreign policy. Whatever the Georgian people's ideals about interactions with Turks and Azerbaijanis, they have countenanced successive governments that have presided over dramatic expansions of ties with both states. Although Georgian democracy is still in its infancy, state policy has had a way of regressing to popular opinion, whether through revolutions, upheaval, or democratically conducted elections (Cecire 2013a). Even despite public anti-Turkish sentiment voiced within its diverse ranks, Georgia's ruling Georgian Dream coalition has maintained a strong policy that favors continued and expanded economic and geopolitical cooperation with Ankara and Baku (Cecire 2012).

Turkey–Georgia relations, as noted, might be described as mostly an outgrowth of Turkish interests in Azerbaijan and the Caspian. Being the most logical conduit between Turkey and Azerbaijan, and ideal as a transit route for goods and energy, Georgia has been instrumental in the construction of the BTC pipeline, the South Caucasus pipeline, and the planned development of TANAP. Bilateral relations have expanded particularly rapidly since the AKP's election in 2002 and Georgia's 2003 Rose Revolution, which saw a pro-West government come to power. While AKP-ruled Turkey has embraced Georgia as fertile territory for Strategic Depth,[7] Georgia has looked to Turkey as a means to economic development and a window to the Euro-Atlantic.

Today, Turkey–Georgia relations not only boast a bevy of joint infrastructure projects, but have also made Turkey a leading source of foreign direct investment and overseen the establishment of a free trade area in 2007 and passport-free borders. In many ways, at least in terms of bilateral economic initiatives, Turkey–Georgia relations might be considered more progressive than Turkey's economic relations with Azerbaijan (Cecire 2013b). Unlike Azerbaijan, Georgia's troubled relationship with Russia and its pro-West political consensus allow Tbilisi more flexibility to integrate with Turkey. Though Georgia and Azerbaijan are connected to Turkey through different means and motivations, the end result has been warm relations that have gradually parlayed into increasingly robust trilateral engagement.

Self-sustaining trilateralism

While the June 2012 Trabzon Declaration might be noted as the formal unveiling of Turkish-Georgian-Azerbaijani trilateralism, it only made official what had, by that point, already become an increasing reality. Yet while trilateralism was driven by key interests and was founded on the basis of Turkey–Azerbaijan relations, it has begun to achieve a critical mass by which it now represents an organic aspect of the three states' national interests rather than merely an expression of them. Converging economic and geopolitical interests incentivised trilateralism, which now reinforces and conditions each individual state's interests.

Economic factors

Trilateral economic integration, a product of energy integration largely (but not exclusively) through pipelines, exemplifies the amplification of Turkey–Azerbaijan relations. Simply, Azerbaijan is the energy producer and Turkey is the downstream consumer and distributor. Georgia, at least initially, was little more than the convenient (if enthusiastic) transit state.

However, the pipelines not only tethered the three states to a common energy source, but represented the beginnings of a kind of economic integration through mutual dependence. For Turkey and Georgia, the pipelines carried much-needed energy. For Azerbaijan, the pipelines not only ferried its hydrocarbons to market, but enhanced the geopolitical stature of the South Caucasus by connecting Caspian energy to European markets. Indeed, there is convincing evidence to suggest that the BTC pipeline was primarily a project of geopolitical importance rather than economic (Cecire 2015b). While Turkey's economy has required cheap energy to be sustained and grow, the greater problem was more related to its crushing dependence on imports from the likes of Russia and Iran than the availability of supplies (Baran 2005). BTC offered an opportunity to ease that dependence through some measure of alternative supply while also elevating Ceyhan's potential as a world-class oil terminal and meeting Turkey's economic aims to fashion itself as a regional energy hub. By the time the BTC pipeline began operations, Azerbaijan, and to a lesser extent Georgia, saw new strength in its geopolitical profile. Azerbaijan, for its part, was no longer bound to Russian-backed pipelines – and the below-market rates that often accompanied them – to bring its energy products to market. This trend has only accelerated as other pipelines have been developed in the region.

A more recent example of trilateral economic cooperation is the BTK railway, also known as the Kars-Akhalkalaki-Tbilisi-Baku railway. BTK builds on the foundation laid by BTC and other Caucasus-transiting pipelines and takes the concept a step further. BTK, set to begin operations in late 2016, is envisaged to carry energy supplies as well as trade goods from the Caspian region and Central Asia to European markets via the Caucasus and Turkey. Though it cannot match pipelines for volume, the BTK would provide Azerbaijan with an added flexibility in transporting oil and natural gas westward. Conceivably, the railway could also transport smaller quantities from fresh sources in the Caspian or even Central Asia (Khankishiyeva 2012).

Crucially, BTK is being cast as a means to economically integrate not only Turkey, Georgia, and Azerbaijan, but also the Eurasian landmass. With an initial operating capacity for 1 million passengers a year annually, 6.5 million tons of freight (30 million at full capacity), and enabling the shortest distance between markets in Asia and Europe, the connector would serve as an alternative rail link between Europe and the far east (Ismayilov 2007) – essentially a competitor

Table 4.1 Georgian foreign trade, 2014 (USD)

	Imports	Exports	Total
Turkey	1.7 billion	239 million	1.97 billion
Azerbaijan	638 million	545 million	1.18 billion
Russia	575 million	275 billion	850 million
China	733 million	90 million	823 million
Ukraine	546 million	140 million	686 million

Source: Geostat.Ge

to Russia's Trans-Siberian railway. The circulation of goods and people offers the three states the potential for added depth to their economic and social integration (Lussac 2008). If the development of BTC and other pipelines was the first phase of fortifying the South Caucasus' geopolitical case, BTK represents a subsequent level of this concept.

There are also less formal developments in the economic relations of the three states. Though pipelines and the BTK dominate high-level discourse, informal business relationships and tourism are bringing the three states together. Today, for example, Turkey and Azerbaijan are Georgia's top two trade partners, accounting for approximately US$2 billion and US$1.2 billion, respectively, in 2014 trade volume.[8]

Although Georgia does not feature as centrally in the trade balances of either Turkey or Azerbaijan, both of which have significantly larger economies with a more sophisticated exports base, it is considered by both states to be a key emerging market. This is evidenced by Turkey and Azerbaijan's status as two of the largest and most consistent sources of foreign direct investment in Georgia. According to the Georgian statistics office, in 2014, Turkey and Azerbaijan invested some US$67 million and US$300 million, respectively, in Georgia, and the five-year FDI average between 2009 and 2014 is US$83 million and US$117 million, respectively – the third and second highest averages. No less importantly, Turkish citizens and Azerbaijanis are emerging as the top visitors to Georgia, topping the lists in 2011 and 2012.[9] Perhaps equally interesting is that Georgians accounted for the fifth largest group of foreign visitors to Turkey between 2010 and 2012. Azerbaijan, by contrast, which has not signed a comparable open border protocol with Turkey, was thirteenth.[10] These figures are expected to rise with the opening of the BTK in late 2014. Former Turkish president Abdullah Gul, an enthusiastic supporter of the project, has called for establishing a joint economic zone among Turkey, Georgia and Azerbaijan to take advantage of the BTK's anticipated economic potential (Ibrahimov 2007).

Geopolitical factors

The trilateral trend is not just limited to economic integration. Although many of the joint projects among Turkey, Georgia and Azerbaijan have a geopolitical character, they are not necessarily in themselves geopolitical developments. Yet, concrete forms of geopolitical cooperation abound among the three states. And trilateralism itself, although perhaps facilitated by economic interests, is a consequence of geopolitical aims. Ad hoc collaboration should be sufficient to meet all three countries' economic objectives, and yet they have opted to push forward with integration beyond economic necessity. In effect, trilateralism is an increasing reality because it is a means of satisfying each country's national interests.

Turkish involvement has served as the major catalyst. Prior to 2008, Turkish focus on the region assumed an overwhelmingly commercial character. Although aware of the geopolitical undertones of its projects, Turkey's inherent economic utility did not signal explicit geopolitical designs on the Caucasus.

This shifted following the 2008 war between Russia and Georgia. Ankara, alarmed by Russia's incursion and understandably frustrated by its limited ability to influence the situation, despite the obvious geographical proximity (Torbakov 2008), sought to remedy its relative separation from the region. Turkey's proposal, the Caucasus Stability and Cooperation Platform (Şen 2008), was meant to insert Turkey into a regional brokering role. Although Russia responded positively, the CSCP never took root, as Russia saw little incentive to permit Turkey's political involvement in the region. And Georgia, though aware of Turkey's economic dependence on Russia, was nevertheless unhappy with Ankara's muted public reaction to the invasion and the equivocating language that accompanied the CSCP's unveiling (in Moscow, of all places).

Although the CSCP concept was quietly abandoned, the experience was nonetheless instructive for Turkey, which recognised that Russia, in spite of its decline since the Soviet era, remained the dominant power in the Caucasus. And conversely, Turkey, for all of its purported rise, was ill-equipped to take a leading role in its own backyard, upon which it had invested its hopes as a long-term energy and transit corridor (Aydin 2010). This proved to offer Turkey a newfound impetus for engagement. In the period following the August 2008 war, Turkey took a stronger approach in deepening its bilateral relationships in the region – including the ill-fated rapprochement with Armenia as well as the emerging trilateral grouping of Turkey, Georgia and Azerbaijan manifested in the Trabzon Declaration. Turkey opened a new consulate in Batumi, visa and then passport requirements with Georgia were lifted and bilateral trade grew dramatically. Turkey has yet to sign a visa-free[11] or free trade agreement with Azerbaijan, but recent talks suggest that both could be on the horizon (Akhundov 2013; Anatolia News Agency 2012). And Georgia, at least until the change of power in October 2012, repeatedly raised an offer of confederating ties with Azerbaijan and even Turkey (Civil Georgia 2010).

Defense and security cooperation is another major aspect of geopolitical trilateralism. Many developments in this sphere have also grown exponentially since 2008 due to a confluence of factors. Prior to 2008, one major obstacle to closer defense cooperation between Georgia and Azerbaijan was reportedly over Armenia's use of a Russian munitions factory in Georgia to service its armored vehicles. However, the 2008 war rendered this dispute moot, and defense relations subsequently grew rapidly (Kucera 2013). In addition, the 2008 war underscored the vulnerability of the South Caucasus transit corridor absent Turkish engagement. Since that point, Ankara has been a diligent supporter of trilateral defense cooperation.

One aspect of that cooperation is military interoperability. For the first time, in September 2012, Turkey, Georgia and Azerbaijan participated in joint, trilateral military exercises aimed at protecting pipeline infrastructure (RFE/RL 2012). Though the objective was innocuous enough, the subtext of the three states cooperating to protect a geopolitically force-multiplying infrastructure is potentially significant. The three states did not have to wait long for the joint Caucasus Eagle 2012 exercises held in Turkey that November (TRT.Net.Tr 2013). In addition, underscoring all parties' enthusiasm for trilateral security cooperation, joint trilateral military exercises have become routine affairs, as have regular meetings among the three states at the defense ministerial level (Cecire 2015a).

Georgian officials across the domestic political spectrum have expressed support for strong relations with Turkey and Azerbaijan (though with allowances for friendly ties with neighbouring Armenia). This has extended beyond joint military exercises. In particular, trilateral coordination has reportedly expanded into Georgia's indigenous defense industry through cooperative ventures with Azerbaijan and Turkey. Reportedly, a joint defense industry working group was established with Azerbaijan, and the two states are collaborating closely in developing their domestic defense industries with significant assistance from Turkey (Shiriyev 2013). Already, plans have reportedly been discussed for the Georgian–Azerbaijani production of armored vehicles and warplanes with technical input from Turkey.

Euro-Atlantic integration and trilateralism

Although trilateralism includes a number of tactical developments in the economic and defense spheres, the question of Euro-Atlantic integration was once a decisive strategic factor within the initiative. Euro-Atlanticism added a powerful impetus to the raison d'être for trilateralism, as it previously factored strongly into each of the three states' strategic aims. However, as the three states have extended their interdependence, Euro-Atlantic integration has become an increasingly less important realm of mutual interest. This, however, does not mean that Euro-Atlantic integration is not important for any of the individual states. AKP Turkey has sometimes challenged its Euro-Atlantic moorings, but Middle Eastern contingencies have reemphasised the role that NATO continues to play in Turkish strategic interests. Meanwhile, despite growing domestic uncertainty, Georgia has maintained a deep and surprisingly resilient political consensus in favor of Euro-Atlanticism.

Euro-Atlantic integration may have been a driver for trilateralism at its outset, but trilateralism has sufficiently developed independently of each government's Western integration aspirations. Turkey has sought to orient itself as an independent pole of power, though the events of the Arab Spring seem to have helped Ankara reconcile its long-term strategic aims within the framework of NATO, which it has called upon to help guard against possible Syrian missile threats (Reuters 2013). For its part, Georgia has been an enthusiastic aspirant to Euro-Atlantic structures, including NATO and the EU. Azerbaijan, by comparison, has been decidedly cooler to the idea of joining within Euro-Atlantic structures and is increasingly at odds with its erstwhile Western partners.

For Turkey, which officially continues to seek European Union membership, solidifying the South Caucasus corridor as a stable and indispensable energy supply route – and Turkey as the hub state facilitating the flow of energy – would elevate its position regionally and within Euro-Atlantic structures. It might also potentially mitigate opposition within the EU to Turkish membership in the medium term. Turkish strategic goals depend on the ability to facilitate steady trade flows for hydrocarbons and the two-way movement of goods through its growing pipeline and transit infrastructure, including the BTK railway when it is completed in late 2016.

Extending the frontiers of Euro-Atlantic interests eastward is in Ankara's interest, as it shifts Turkey from the Euro-Atlantic periphery closer to the geographic center. Given its position of proximity to the South Caucasus and the Caspian, an expanded Euro-Atlantic space furthers Turkey's aims to serve as a "hub" state as envisaged by the Strategic Depth concept. This helps explain Turkey's support for Georgian NATO membership and the Eastern Partnership initiative in the South Caucasus.

For Georgia, still smarting from its 2008 war with Russia, trilateralism is also tightly bound with its Euro-Atlantic aspirations for two primary reasons. First, Georgia regards a close grouping with Turkey and Azerbaijan as being geopolitically advantageous in its hopes to join with Western structures. Turkey, a longtime NATO member and participant in the EU customs union, is a logical advocate for Georgia's process of integration (Mutlu 2011). And recognising Azerbaijan's cognate post-Soviet experience and its perceived strategic importance to the West, Tbilisi also sees Azerbaijan as a means to elevate its own geopolitical value in Western capitals. Taken together, Turkey and Azerbaijan are two elements of a single goal to cultivate Georgia's value proposition to the West.

In addition, Georgia looks to Turkey and Azerbaijan as local sources of geopolitical patronage. Turkey's emergence as a regional power in its own right incentivises Georgia to cultivate interdependencies with Ankara in an effort to hedge against Russian primacy in the Black Sea region. By serving as a critical interconnector to vital resources in Azerbaijan and the Caspian, Georgia has at least partially succeeded in maximising its regional role. To many Georgian policymakers, supporting Turkey's rise would extend rules-based norms to the Caucasus while mitigating any Russian threat – both of which contribute to its chances of Euro-Atlantic accession in the medium to long term.

Azerbaijan's case differs in that it does not appear to be ready to commit to joining Euro-Atlantic structures and prioritises relations with great powers over that of institutions (Strakes 2013). This is partially a consequence of its multi-vector foreign policy, which prioritises balance and is sensitive to Russia's residual power in the region. However, Azerbaijan does embrace its role as a supplier and transit route for goods and natural resources to the West.

At the same time, Azerbaijan fastidiously maintains close relations with Russia, although there is a subtext of mistrust given the latter's patronage of Armenia and Moscow's custom of retaining a constellation of leverage points throughout the region – such as Abkhazia and South Ossetia in Georgia, Transdniestria in Moldova, eastern Ukraine, and more indirectly in Azerbaijan's Nagorno-Karabakh – to maximise its own regional influence (Valiyev 2011). Baku accepts the reality of Russia's regional influence, but it actively supports a multi-polar regional order as an alternative.

Euro-Atlanticism is not the basis for trilateralism, but it was once a powerful driver within each state. The three states each see trilateralism as a means to achieve their national interests, which are all closely intertwined with Euro-Atlantic integration in some form or another – even Azerbaijan. However, trilateralism is not beholden to Euro-Atlanticism and would not be displaced if the three states' Euro-Atlantic agendas were realised or spoiled; trilateralism has achieved sufficient strength to be sustained under its own power.

Challenges to trilateralism

Trilateralism, though demonstrably in the ascendant, is not without its obstacles and potential pitfalls. Given that it relies on the convergence of three sovereign states' national interests, the initiative could falter should conditions change in any one of the three states. Overall, challenges to trilateralism can be categorised in terms of internal/domestic factors and external factors.

Internally, each of the three countries possesses domestic variables that could derail trilateralism. In Turkey, although the public opinion of Turks is generally positively disposed to their Azerbaijani cousins (Hurriyet Daily News 2011), there is no comparable history of popular affection for Georgians. With millions of Georgians visiting Turkey annually, and a significant number staying illegally, there is potential for public backlash. A highly publicised Istanbul murder perpetrated by two Georgians in 2011, for example, caused significant outcry in Turkey against unchecked Georgian immigration (Kirtskhalia 2011).

However, the situation in Georgia is potentially more severe. While Turkish citizens have brought significant investment and tourism to Georgia's cities – and particularly its historically Sunni Moslem region of Adjara – the influx of visitors has reportedly stoked some resentment among Georgian residents (Imedaishvili and Bigg 2012). Of greater concern, however, has been anecdotal evidence of growing tensions between Georgians, predominantly devout Orthodox Christians, and Georgia's not inconsiderable Georgian Moslem community. Prior to the 2012 parliamentary elections, certain figures from the challenging Georgian Dream coalition voiced anti-Turkish statements as part of their campaigns (e.g. Georgia Online 2012). More recently, Georgian Moslem villagers were harassed by Orthodox neighbours over their use of a house as a gathering place for prayer

(Democracy and Freedom Watch 2013). And in early September 2013, Georgian authorities forcibly removed a minaret from a mosque in the Samtskhe-Javakheti region, provoking protests from the Georgian Moslem community, which makes up at least 10 percent of the population (Blua 2013). While tensions do not seem to have reached a point where they are damaging relations with Azerbaijan and Turkey, such an eventuality is entirely conceivable without stronger action from Tbilisi.

Externally, the most potent obstacle to trilateralism is likely to be Moscow's opposition to a regional grouping – formal or informal – from which it is excluded and which promotes a strategic alternative to its domination. Russia, the presumed regional hegemon, is inherently opposed to every major pillar of the trilateral project: first, it opposes regional multipolarity, given its presumption to a special status throughout its "near-abroad"; second, it opposes the expansion of the Euro-Atlantic space into and throughout the Caucasus; and third, Moscow has no wish to see a bloc formed among Turkey, the only nearby state with the capacity to challenge its position, Georgia, its perennial adversary, and Azerbaijan, which it increasingly sees as a friendly state, if not future ally. Perhaps tellingly, Russia began massive war games to coincide with the first meeting of the Trabzon 3 in March 2013 (Agence France-Presse 2013).

Russia, being a major trading partner with Azerbaijan and a key energy supplier to Turkey – to say nothing of its strategic leverage in Karabakh, the eastern Mediterranean (as evidenced by its role vis-à-vis the question of Western intervention in Syria), and Georgia's separatist regions – has the ability to play spoiler. However, the trilateral partnership has been careful to avoid outright competition for this very reason. Instead, it is likely that the trilateral grouping will lack certain coherence, while Ankara, Tbilisi and Baku learn to work together and are able to assess Russia's likely role. Meanwhile, the shifting regional energy landscape, which places a higher priority on unconventional energy plays versus the conventional pipeline paradigm, is helping to mitigate Russia's ability to wield its energy production as a geopolitical spanner (Cecire 2013c).

Conclusion

Trilateralism is already reconfiguring interdependencies in the South Caucasus by empowering Turkey's development as a regional power and, in some respects, even serving as an eastward carrier of Euro-Atlanticism. Built on the foundations of Turkey's Strategic Depth concept and the ongoing strength of Turkish-Azerbaijani relations, the grouping is an outgrowth of the converging national interests of all three powers. While it is only quasi-formal at this point through the Trabzon 3, the trilateral relationship is an increasingly important variable in the economic, security and political spheres of all three states.

Understanding the motivating variables and drivers of South Caucasus trilateralism can help the West to serve as a positive force in the grouping's development. Trilateralism should not be confused with a Caucasus-oriented version of Turkish reimperialisation or "neo-Ottomanism," given that it is largely animated by the three states' converging national interests. Trilateralism remains almost entirely interests based and, beyond bilateral ties between Azerbaijan and Turkey, is not burdened with any overwhelming sense of sentiment. This, on one hand, speaks to the gravity – and durability – of the national interests at stake. At the same time, however, the project suffers from a lack of depth beyond the governmental and economic realms. This will likely be mitigated with time, as people-to-people contacts among the three states increase. But lingering societal prejudices, such as in Georgia, could undermine or even derail the project if left unabated. Whether through the Trabzon 3 format or other existing channels, these societal factors should be addressed if trilateralism is to develop into a long-term arrangement.

Russia's residual presence in the region is also a potential obstacle, given Moscow's potential suspicions of regional balancing. While trilateralism is certainly a means to mitigate the adverse effects of Russian influence, it should not be seen as an anti-Russia bloc. Accordingly, the West should not seek to label it or treat it as such, and local actors should continue their growth in a way that does not evoke a strong reaction from the north.

Notes

1 Republic of Turkey Ministry of Foreign Affairs. Trabzon Declaration of the Ministers of Foreign Affairs of the Republic of Azerbaijan, Georgia and the Republic of Turkey, 8 June 2012. http://goo.gl/VCXmFZ. Accessed 14 Aug. 2013.
2 Republic of Turkey Ministry of Foreign Affairs. Policy of Zero Problems with Our Neighbors. http://goo.gl/jQ0cS0. Accessed 16 Aug. 2013.
3 Azerbaijan. *Republic of Turkey Ministry of Economy*. http://goo.gl/lrZ8y2. Accessed 13 Aug. 2013.
4 *Azerbaijan*. US Energy Information Administration. http://goo.gl/CIENUW. Accessed 19 Aug. 2013.
5 For example, the eventual scuttling of Turkey's diplomatic overtures to Armenia in 2009 might be attributed, at least in some large part, to protests by Azerbaijani authorities against the measures due to Armenia's continued occupation of Nagorno-Karabakh and a surrounding "buffer zone" of undisputed Azerbaijani territory. This illustrated Azerbaijan's ability to leverage its strategic assets as well as tap into pro-Turkic sentiment within Turkey.
6 CRRC Georgia. Online Data Analysis. http://crrc.ge/oda/. Accessed 21 July 2015.
7 Despite initial enthusiasm after the fall of the Soviet Union, Turkey–Georgia relations were in a period of semi-dormancy during most of the 1990s as Georgia was embroiled in successive civil wars and Turkish attention in the Caucasus was focused on Azerbaijan. It was not until Georgia achieved some measure of stability in the late 1990s (and became a realistic option as a transit state) that Turkey–Georgia ties saw a noticeable boost. This was especially true following the AKP's rise to power in 2002 and following Georgia's 2003 Rose Revolution.
8 GeoStat.Ge. საგარეო ვაჭრობა [sagareo vachroba] [External Trade]. http://geostat.ge/?action=page&p_id=136&lang=geo. Accessed 21 July 2015.
9 Georgian National Tourism Administration. Statistics. http://gnta.ge/stats/portal/. Accessed 17 Aug. 2013.
10 T.C. Kültür ve Turizm Bakanlığı. Number of Arriving-Departing Visitors, Foreigners and Citizens. http://goo.gl/bLJmN5. Accessed 27 Sep. 2013.

11 Turkey attempted to broker a visa-free regime with Azerbaijan, but the deal was reportedly scuttled by Iran, which threatened to block the link between Azerbaijan and its Nakhchivan enclave (Bozkurt 2011).

References

Agence France-Presse. 2013. Putin Orders Surprise Black Sea Military Exercises Amid Georgia Meet. *Hurriyet Daily News*, 28 Mar. http://goo.gl/hC45eC.

Akhundov, A. 2013. Minister: Turkey, Azerbaijan to Sign Free Trade Agreement. *Trend*, 25 May. http://goo.gl/66tj3Y.

Anatolia News Agency. 2012. Minister Wants Free Trade with Georgia, Azerbaijan. *Hurriyet Daily News*, 17 Feb. http://goo.gl/HXwpYI.

Aydin, Mustafa. 2010. Turkey's Caucasus Policies. *UNISCI Discussion Papers* 23, 177–192. http://goo.gl/mm4EPG.

Baran, Zeyno. 2005. The Baku-Tbilisi-Ceyhan Pipeline: Implications for Turkey. In: S. Frederick Starr and Svante E. Cornell, eds. *The Baku-Tbilisi-Ceyhan Pipeline: Oil Window to the West*, 103–118. Washington, DC: Central Asia-Caucasus Institute & Silk Road Studies Program.

Bechev, Dimitar. 2012. Turkey's "Zero-Problem" Foreign Policy Is Working. *European Council on Foreign Relations*, 21 Mar. http://goo.gl/2GXfz0.

Blua, Antoine. 2013. Coming or Going, Georgian Minaret Draws Ire. *Radio Free Europe/ Radio Liberty*, 2 Sep. http://goo.gl/LPkgcK.

Bozkurt, Abdullah. 2011. Azerbaijan Says Visa-Free Regime with Turkey Fell Victim to Iranian Pressure. *Today's Zaman*, 19 Jul. http://goo.gl/ZJpJxv.

Cecire, Michael. 2012. Turkish-Georgian Ties after Elections. *Hurriyet Daily News*, 22 Oct. http://goo.gl/ATOKTS.

———. 2013a. Georgia's 2012 Elections and Lessons for Democracy Promotion. *Orbis* 57:2, 232–250.

———. 2013b. Georgia–Turkey Relations in a Georgian Dream Era. *Caucasus Analytical Digest* 48, 3 Mar. http://goo.gl/p4r7JT.

———. 2013c. The Black Sea: Energy Security Fault Line? *Natural Gas Europe*, 26 Feb. http://goo.gl/DnkxwU.

———. 2015a. A New Partnership for Co-Operation in the Black Sea. *Open Democracy*, 18 May. https://goo.gl/ymAAxM.

———. 2015b. A Trilateral Moment. *Business New Europe*, 27 Aug. http://goo.gl/LLeJX9.

Chatham House. 2012. Ways Forward for the Turkey-Armenia Rapprochement. Meeting Summary, 1 May. http://goo.gl/ufgMQ0.

Civil Georgia. 2010. Azerbaijani, Georgian Leaders Meet in Batumi. 18 Jul. http://civil.ge/eng/article.php?id=22524.

Davutoglu, Ahmet. 2001. *Stratejik Derinlik Türkiye'nin Uluslararası Konumu*. (In Turkish.) Istanbul: Küre Yayinlari.

———. 2010. Turkey's Zero-Problems Foreign Policy. *Foreign Policy*. 20 May. http://goo.gl/6CIK6z.

Democracy and Freedom Watch. 2013. Muslims Afraid to Attend Friday Prayer in Kakheti Village. (In Tbilisi.) 6 Jul. http://goo.gl/lw9GuF.

Georgia Online. 2012. Georgian Dream Apologizes for Earlier Xenophobic Statements. 18 Sep. http://goo.gl/vc0NMS.

Hurriyet Daily News. 2011. Turkish Citizens Mistrust Foreigners, Opinion Poll Says. 2 May. http://goo.gl/V9gIdH.

Ibrahimov, Rovshan. 2007. Baku-Tbilisi-Kars: Geopolitical Effect on the South Caucasian Region. *Turkish Weekly*, 25 Nov. http://goo.gl/rA8QV4.
Imedaishvili, Nata and Claire Bigg. 2012. Locals Helpless as Sex Tourism Hits Georgian Black Sea Village. *Radio Free Europe/Radio Liberty*, 8 Jul. http://goo.gl/9fWz1P.
Ismayilov, Rovshan. 2007. Azerbaijan, Georgia and Turkey: Building a Transportation Triumvirate? *Eurasianet*, 6 Feb. http://goo.gl/sZ9vTd.
Khankishiyeva, Ellada. 2012. Central Asia's Market to Open with Baku-Tbilisi-Kars Railway. *Trend*, 22 Oct. http://goo.gl/oVSoOG.
Kirtskhalia, N. 2011. Georgian Speaker Expresses Condolences with Murder Committed in Istanbul. *Trend*, 1 Apr. http://goo.gl/QitrJR.
Kucera, Joshua. 2013. Georgia and Azerbaijan Strengthening Military Ties? *Eurasianet*, 5 Jun. www.eurasianet.org/node/67076.
Lussac, Samuel. 2008. The Baku-Tbilisi-Kars Railroad and Its Geopolitical Implications for the South Caucasus. *Caucasus Review of International Affairs* 2:4. http://goo.gl/IpYosI.
Mutlu, Can E. 2011. A De Facto Cooperation? The Increasing Role of the European Union in Improved Relations Between Georgia and Turkey. *Comparative European Politics* 9:4–5, 543–561.
Ottens, Nick. 2013. Zero Problems Abroad Made Many Problems at Home. *The National Interest*, 12 Aug. http://goo.gl/laikMu.
Reuters. 2013. Patriots in Turkey Send Clear Warning to Syria: Germany. 23 Feb. http://goo.gl/2uePf6.
RFE/RL. 2012. Azerbaijan, Georgia, Turkey Hold Pipeline-Security Exercises. *Radio Free Europe/Radio Liberty*, 24 Sep. http://goo.gl/TvOzLa.
Rüma, İnan. 2010. Turkish Foreign Policy Towards the Balkans: New Activism, Neo-Ottomanism or/so What? *Turkish Policy Quarterly* 9:4, 133–140.
Şen, Erdal. 2008. Turkey Steps into Georgia Conflict. *Today's Zaman*, 14 Aug. http://goo.gl/9wvsgf.
Shiriyev, Zaur. 2013. Azerbaijan-Georgia Military Cooperation and Turkey's Influence (2). *Today's Zaman*, 30 May. http://goo.gl/HC4F7C.
Strakes, Jason E. 2013. Situating the 'Balanced Foreign Policy': The Role of System Structure in Azerbaijan's Multi-Vector Diplomacy. *Journal of Balkan and Near Eastern Studies* 15:1, 37–67.
Torbakov, Igor. 2008. *The Georgia Crisis and Russia-Turkey Relations*. Washington, DC: Jamestown Foundation.
TRT.Net.Tr. 2013. Turkey, Azerbaijan and Georgia to Hold Joint Military Exercises. 7 Feb.
Valiyev, Anar. 2011. Neither Friend Nor Foe: Azerbaijanis' Perceptions of Russia. *PONARS Eurasia Policy Memos* 147, May. http://goo.gl/2ouypc.
Yılmaz, Şuhnaz and Tahir Kılavuz. 2012. Restoring Brotherly Bonds: Turkish-Azerbaijani Energy Relations. *PONARS Eurasia Policy Memos* 240, Sep. http://goo.gl/Uao5um.

5 Azerbaijan–Turkey relations through the prism of economic transactions
A view from Azerbaijan

Elkin Nurmammadov

Introduction

Is there a gap between the actual and potential levels of bilateral economic relations between Azerbaijan and Turkey, two countries characterised by a strong degree of cultural affinity, strong political ties and geographic proximity? Are these favorable characteristics of a bilateral relationship *not* translated into strong economic ties, contrary to what academic literature predicts? High-ranking officials from both countries, while appreciating the current level of economic relations between the countries, claim that such a gap exists. For example, Turkey's trade minister Zafer Caglayan, in his speech at the Azerbaijani–Turkish business forum held in Ankara in 2011, noted that the Azerbaijani–Turkish trade volume could potentially reach US$10 billion as opposed to US$2.5 billion in 2010. At the same forum, Shahin Mustafayev, Azerbaijani minister of economic development, stressed that there is huge unexploited potential of cooperation, especially in such spheres of the non-oil sector as food processing, information technologies and tourism. Notwithstanding the importance of ministerial remarks, they hardly qualify as an academic answer to the question above. Nor is there any academic study on this particular topic. This chapter aims to fill this void.

Does such a gap indeed exist? If so, what factors can explain it? What can be done to bridge it? This chapter seeks to address these questions by examining the nature and dynamics of Azerbaijani–Turkish economic relations. It follows three steps in answering the questions. First, the chapter examines whether there is a gap between the actual and potential levels of the bilateral economic relations. Second, it explores potential explanations of the alleged gap. Finally, drawing on the preceding analysis, the chapter concludes with recommendations as to how to bridge the gap.

It is worthwhile to explicitly define at the outset what the paper means by "economic relations." The study focuses on two dimensions of international economic relations that matter the most for economic growth: cross-border trade in goods and services and foreign direct investment. Both trade and FDI are generally led by the private sector and market-oriented initiatives that promote economic efficiency. Although there are other important aspects of international economic relations, such as labor migration, flow of remittances and knowledge sharing, lack of systematic data only allows for marginal coverage of these aspects.

The study relies on three major sources in analysing bilateral economic relations between Turkey and Azerbaijan. First are interviews I conducted with various experts to collect anecdotal evidence and learn their views on the actual and potential levels of bilateral economic relations. These experts represent the government of Azerbaijan, the Turkish business community and the Turkish diplomatic circle in Azerbaijan. Second, I draw on secondary literature to identify theoretical and empirical studies on what level of economic relations a pair of countries with ethnic and cultural affinity can have, despite disparities in the levels of economic development and institutional quality. Third, I analyse actual data on bilateral economic relations between Turkey and Azerbaijan from a comparative perspective, by looking at the performance of similar pairs of countries.

It turns out that not only do the ministers recognise the gap in bilateral economic relations, the overwhelming majority of experts interviewed as part of this study think along similar lines, even though their explanations of the gap vary. Also, comparison of Azerbaijani–Turkish bilateral economic relations with those of similar pairs of countries lends another piece of support for the existence of the gap.

I suggest several hypotheses to explain the gap. These hypotheses can be classified in two categories. Whereas one set of hypotheses, the *subjective* hypotheses, stem from the factors specific to Azerbaijani–Turkish bilateral relations, the other group, the *objective* hypotheses, stem from factors that can be equally applied to all trade partners of Azerbaijan. The latter set of hypotheses prevail, indicating that a true solution to the existing gap in Azerbaijani–Turkish economic relations lies mainly in addressing structural impediments to the competitiveness of the Azerbaijani economy in general. Put differently, there is no general trend distinguishing Azerbaijani–Turkish bilateral economic relations from Azerbaijan's bilateral economic relations with other countries. Once the structural impediments to the Azerbaijani economy's competitiveness are overcome, Azerbaijani–Turkish bilateral economic relations will prosper as well, perhaps at a magnified rate, taking into account favorable initial conditions. Nevertheless there is still a certain set of measures that can be taken within the specific domain of Azerbaijani–Turkish relations.

I must also note the limitations of this study at the outset. I investigate bilateral economic relations between the two countries while being physically in Azerbaijan. Hence, policy recommendations arising from the analysis in this chapter to a large extent concern policymakers in Azerbaijan. To be sure, this does not mean that the chapter provides only an Azerbaijani perspective: as noted above, the interviewees also include representatives of the Turkish business and diplomatic community in Azerbaijan. Nonetheless, to get a more comprehensive picture of bilateral economic relations, this study needs to be complemented with one based in Turkey.

Potential state

To understand whether there is a gap between the actual and potential levels of economic relations, the "potential level" and its determinants must be defined. By potential level, I mean the one expected to exist given the common cultural, ethnic and linguistic heritage, the track record of strong political relations and the geographic proximity of Turkey and Azerbaijan. Academic literature shows that bilateral relations characterised by even one of these favorable characteristics are in general associated with stronger trade and investment relations

How to quantify the potential level of potential economic relations between a pair of countries? One way would be to use sophisticated statistical techniques to estimate it. Yet the problems with data in our case make outcomes of such an exercise somewhat less reliable. The second-best solution is to rely on expert opinion. Hence, I have conducted a number of interviews with government officials, academics and representatives of the Turkish business and diplomatic community in Azerbaijan. There is a general consensus that bilateral economic relations between the two countries are below their potential. Another way would be to look at this relationship in a comparative perspective.

To that end, I compare Azerbaijan's economic relations with Turkey with those with Russia and Turkey's economic relations with Azerbaijan with those with Georgia and Kazakhstan. A simple exercise, using absolute and relative-to-GDP figures for bilateral trade volumes, allows a comparison of bilateral relations while controlling for size and cultural affinity effects. Russia, like Turkey, can be considered a relatively large trading partner of Azerbaijan; Georgia, like Azerbaijan, can be considered a relatively small trading partner of Turkey; and Kazakhstan, like Azerbaijan, can be considered to have a common ethno-cultural heritage with Turkey.

According to the Turkish Statistical Institute, in 2010 the bilateral trade volume between Azerbaijan and Turkey was more than twice that of Georgia and Turkey, as shown in Table 5.1. However, drawing conclusions based on these numbers may be misleading, as they do not take into account the difference in economic

Table 5.1 Comparison of Turkey's trade with Azerbaijan and Georgia

Year	Partner	Trade Volume	GDP	Volume/ GDP	Factor
2005	Azerbaijan	800.33	13.25	60.43	
2005	Georgia	574.73	6.41	89.65	1.48
2006	Azerbaijan	1035.77	21.03	49.26	
2006	Georgia	752.78	7.77	96.91	1.97
2007	Azerbaijan	1377.32	33.09	41.62	
2007	Georgia	935.65	10.22	91.52	2.20
2008	Azerbaijan	2595.78	46.38	55.97	
2008	Georgia	1521.76	12.87	118.24	2.11
2009	Azerbaijan	2151.31	43.08	49.94	
2009	Georgia	1031.42	10.77	95.79	1.92
2010	Azerbaijan	2416.34	54.37	44.44	
2010	Georgia	1060.17	11.67	90.88	2.04

Source: UN Comtrade

sizes of the individual countries. To correct for this bias, I normalise the numbers by GDP. In this case, the Azerbaijani–Turkish trade volume in 2010 becomes almost half rather than two times larger than the Georgian–Turkish trade volume. Looking at the dynamics of these numbers in the years 2005–2010, one can see that the Georgian–Turkish bilateral trade volume has exceeded that of Azerbaijan and Turkey roughly by a factor of 2 throughout the period, when measured as a share of GDP.

This indicates that despite the lack of common cultural and ethnic heritage in Turkish–Georgian relations, bilateral economic relations between these countries are stronger than those between Turkey and Azerbaijan. Although one could attribute this finding to the shorter trade route between Turkey and Georgia compared with that of Turkey and Azerbaijan, distance alone can hardly explain such a consistent variation.

Next, I compare the Azerbaijani–Turkish trade volume to the Azerbaijani–Russian trade volume, both in absolute numbers and relative to GDP. According to the State Statistics Committee of Azerbaijan, bilateral trade volume between Azerbaijan and Turkey totaled US$942 million in 2010, whereas that of Azerbaijan and Russia totaled US$1.9 billion. Thus, Azerbaijan traded at least twice as much with Russia. However, if we express these numbers as a share of GDP, they become almost equal, as shown in Table 5.2. This is an interesting case, as Azerbaijan also has a lot in common with Russia, mainly the Soviet heritage acquired over seventy-one years during which Azerbaijan was part of the Soviet Union. One is tempted to conclude that these trade volumes become equal after controlling for economic size, because the effects of the cultural affinity of Turkey and Azerbaijan and that of Russia and Azerbaijan simply offset each other. However, this conclusion neglects the positive effect on bilateral trade coming from institutional homogeneity and being members of the same

Table 5.2 Comparison of Azerbaijan's trade with Turkey and Russia

Year	Partner	Trade Volume	GDP	Volume/ GDP	Factor
2005	Turkey	588.96	482.69	1.22	
2005	Russia	1002.63	763.70	1.31	1.08
2006	Turkey	773.18	529.19	1.46	
2006	Russia	1525.84	989.93	1.54	1.05
2007	Turkey	1681.01	649.13	2.59	
2007	Russia	1531.01	1299.70	1.18	0.45
2008	Turkey	1433.50	730.32	1.96	
2008	Russia	1932.62	1660.85	1.16	0.59
2009	Turkey	1013.66	614.42	1.65	
2009	Russia	1815.90	1221.99	1.49	0.90
2010	Turkey	942.34	735.49	1.28	
2010	Russia	1918.56	1479.83	1.30	1.01

Source: UN Comtrade

Table 5.3 Comparison of Turkey's trade with Azerbaijan and Kazakhstan

Year	Partner	Trade Volume	GDP	Volume/ GDP	Factor
2005	Azerbaijan	800.33	13.25	60.43	
2005	Kazakhstan	1018.85	57.12	17.84	0.30
2006	Azerbaijan	1035.77	21.03	49.26	
2006	Kazakhstan	1690.55	81.00	20.87	0.42
2007	Azerbaijan	1377.32	33.09	41.62	
2007	Kazakhstan	2363.94	103.14	22.92	0.55
2008	Azerbaijan	2595.78	46.38	55.97	
2008	Kazakhstan	3222.59	135.23	23.83	0.43
2009	Azerbaijan	2151.31	43.08	49.94	
2009	Kazakhstan	1710.58	115.31	14.83	0.30
2010	Azerbaijan	2416.34	54.37	44.44	
2010	Kazakhstan	3290.86	148.05	22.23	0.50

Source: UN Comtrade

trade bloc, characteristics of the Russia–Azerbaijan trade relationship, but not of Turkey–Azerbaijan. Thus, the fact that these figures are equal indicates that, if anything, Turkey and Azerbaijan are not utilising the potential of economic cooperation to the fullest

I also examine how Turkey's bilateral economic relations with Azerbaijan compare with those with Kazakhstan. Relations between Azerbaijan and Turkey and Turkey and Kazakhstan have similarities and differences. As for the former, from the Turkish perspective, both Kazakhstan and Azerbaijan are considered Turkic nations. They have a common Soviet history and are energy-rich countries of the Caspian region. The difference lies in the fact that Kazakhstan is bigger and richer than Azerbaijan and naturally are expected to trade more with Turkey. However, since I normalise by GDP, this effect must go away. Also, Azerbaijan is probably a more 'Turkic' nation than Kazakhstan, where the majority of the population speaks Russian. This means that the cultural affinity factor should play a much bigger role in Azerbaijani–Turkish economic relations. Looking at Table 5.3, we find support for this conclusion: when controlling for economic size as measured by GDP, the Azerbaijani–Turkish bilateral trade volume is consistently larger than that of Kazakhstan and Turkey, albeit the latter is consistently lower in absolute terms.

Trade flows

This section examines actual trade flows between Azerbaijan and Turkey after considering briefly what academic literature would predict these flows to be. Trade literature mainly uses the gravity equation to empirically understand what drives bilateral trade flows. Introduced by Jan Tinbergen (1962), the gravity equation draws an analogy from Newtonian physics, stating that the force of gravity between any two objects is proportional to the product of their masses and is inversely proportional to the distance between them. When applied to international trade, the basic gravity equation implies that the bilateral trade volume between a pair of countries is proportional to the product of their economic sizes (as measured by GDP) and is inversely proportional to the distance between them. That is, the closer any two countries are, the more they tend to trade with each other, because transport costs are lower. Moreover, the larger they are, the more they tend to trade with each other, because large countries both have more to offer as exports and, being richer, have the means to import more. Modifications of the gravity equation identify additional determinants of bilateral trade flows, such as religion, language, common history, trade policy, common colonial past, membership in international organisations, trade blocs and others. More recent studies emphasise the importance of cultural and institutional differences between countries. Based on the above, Turkey and Azerbaijan may trade more, because they are neighbors and have strong cultural and ethnic ties, yet trade less than they could because there are significant differences in their economic sizes and their levels of economic and institutional development. I address these predictions as separate hypotheses later in the chapter.

Let us first have a detailed look at the nature and dynamic of bilateral trade flows. In 2010, the Azerbaijani–Turkish bilateral trade volume amounted to US$942 million and US$2.4 billion, respectively,[1] according to Azerbaijani and Turkish sources. When decomposed into components, these numbers exhibit differential trends for exports and imports. While Turkey has secured its ranking among Azerbaijan's top import sources, it does not rank even as one of the top ten export destinations of Azerbaijan. Moreover, Azerbaijan's exports to Turkey have been declining over time (Table 5.4).

The non-oil export numbers in Table 5.5 show a more realistic picture of Azerbaijan's relations with its trading partners, given that the share of oil exports in Azerbaijan's total exports has been above 90 percent in recent years. Europe is the main market of destination for Azerbaijani oil, while

Table 5.4 Turkey's share in Azerbaijan's trade

Year	Exports, %	Imports, %	Trade Volume, %
2005	6.3	7.4	6.9
2006	6.1	7.3	6.6
2007	17.4	10.9	14.3
2008	1.3	11.3	2.6
2009	0.7	14.8	4.9
2010	0.8	11.69	3.37

Source: State Committee on Statistics of Azerbaijan

Russia and Turkey are the two most important export destinations for non-oil products. Non-oil exports, despite their small share in total exports, have increased in absolute terms: their value more than tripled between 2003 and 2010. Since 2010, non-oil export growth has surpassed oil export growth, albeit starting from a low base. It is also noteworthy that even though Azerbaijan's non-oil exports to Turkey have been rising in absolute terms, they have actually been falling as a share of GDP. By contrast, non-oil exports to Russia have been rising both in absolute terms and as a share of GDP, as shown in Table 5.5.

Turkey is Azerbaijan's second largest import partner after Russia, as shown in Table 5.6. The dynamics and composition of Azerbaijan's import numbers in fact mirror the country's development. Over time, Azerbaijan has reduced the

Table 5.5 Non-oil exports of Azerbaijan, 2003–2010 (in US$millions)

Year	Russia	Turkey	Total Non-Oil	Russia's Share, %	Turkey's Share, %
2003	125.5	52.2	362.6	34.6	14.4
2004	185.7	57.2	642.9	28.9	8.9
2005	275.5	73.1	1010.1	27.3	7.2
2006	334.4	86.8	981.9	34.1	8.8
2007	517.7	84.1	1126.9	45.9	7.5
2008	569.2	121.9	1393.2	40.9	8.7
2009	578.3	41.7	1049.2	55.1	4.0
2010	556.9	63	1168	47.7	5.4

Source: UN Comtrade

Table 5.6 Imports of Azerbaijan, 2003–2010 (in US$millions)

Year	Russia	Turkey	Russia*	Turkey*	Total*	Russia's Share, %	Turkey's Share, %
2000	134.9	229.7	249.3	128.5	1172	21.3	11.0
2001	130.9	225.2	153	148.2	1430.8	10.7	10.4
2002	273	226.9	280.9	156.2	1665.6	16.9	9.4
2003	407.8	315.5	383.9	195.1	2626.4	14.6	7.4
2004	606	404	569.4	225	3515.9	16.2	6.4
2005	835.4	528.1	717.2	313	4211.2	17.0	7.4
2006	1035.6	695.3	1181.6	385	5266.7	22.4	7.3
2007	1371.2	1047.7	1003.9	624.7	5712.2	17.6	10.9
2008	1930.4	1667.3	1349.7	807.3	7161.9	18.8	11.3
2009	1468	1398.4	1066	906	6114.2	17.4	14.8
2010	1476.9	1551.2	1145	771.4	6596.8	17.4	11.7

* Reported by State Committee on Statistics of Azerbaijan; otherwise, UN Comtrade

share of its low-value-added imports from the former Soviet Union countries in favor of a higher share of high-value-added imports from the EU and Turkey. Yet, Turkey's share in Azerbaijan's imports in turn has relatively declined in the face of increasing imports from EU countries.

Azerbaijani–Turkish trade is dominated by inter-industry trade, where exported and imported goods are different, as opposed to intra-industry trade, where exported and imported goods are of the same kind. Azerbaijan imports mainly manufactured goods from Turkey while exporting commodities, as shown in Tables 5.7 and 5.8. This trade pattern is an outcome of Azerbaijan's trouble with diversifying the economy – the country simply lacks competitive items to export outside the energy sector. Moreover, Turkey's dependence on energy exports is high and continues increasing. The Ministry of Energy of Turkey estimates the country's energy import dependence to rise from the current 72 percent to 80 percent by 2020 (Yilmaz and Izmen 2009, *passim*). As the Azerbaijani non-oil economy develops, the composition of its export and import baskets changes accordingly, though at a slow pace. For instance, Azerbaijan now exports some of the goods it used to import from Turkey (World Bank 2009, *passim*).

Table 5.7 Composition of Azerbaijani exports to Turkey (in US$millions, unless otherwise noted)

Commodity	2008	2009	2010	Average, 2008–10	Share in Total, %
Food and live animals	1.51	2.12	2.21	1.95	0.65
Beverages and tobacco	0.00	0.00	0.01	0.00	0
Crude materials, inedible, except fuels	3.62	15.72	8.26	9.20	3.05
Mineral fuels, lubricants and related materials	504.31	65.93	107.86	226.03	74.96
Chemicals and related products	46.12	9.80	32.51	29.47	9.77
Manufactured goods	68.02	13.29	17.88	33.06	10.96
Machinery and transport equipment	2.41	0.66	2.00	1.69	0.56
Miscellaneous manufactured articles	0.17	0.07	0.17	0.14	0.05
Total	626.16	107.59	170.89	301.55	100

Source: UN Comtrade, Standard International Trade Classification

Table 5.8 Composition of Turkish exports to Azerbaijan (in US$millions, unless otherwise noted)

Commodity	2008	2009	2010	Average, 2008–10	Share in Total, %
Food and live animals	109.52	101.92	119.99	110.48	8.54
Beverages and tobacco	5.74	6.35	9.11	7.07	0.55
Crude materials, inedible, except fuels	15.57	23.51	18.93	19.34	1.49
Mineral fuels, lubricants and related materials	15.09	16.40	21.29	17.59	1.36
Chemicals and related products	2.66	1.06	3.55	2.43	0.19
Manufactured goods	224.45	229.89	263.90	239.41	18.5
Machinery and transport equipment	565.78	448.48	490.30	501.52	38.75
Miscellaneous manufactured articles	497.66	324.16	367.40	396.41	30.63
Total	1436.48	1151.77	1294.48	1294.24	100

Source: UN Comtrade, Standard International Trade Classification

FDI flows

This section examines FDI flows between Azerbaijan and Turkey. FDI is a measure of the foreign ownership of a country's productive assets, such as factories, mines and land. Higher FDI stock is associated with faster economic growth through both direct and indirect effects on the host economy.[2] Along with adding to the capital stock and providing financing to private business, FDI may boost productivity of the host economy through new know-how, such as new products, production methods and marketing techniques, better inventory management and quality control. Another important direct effect of FDI comes through higher employment and skills development opportunities for the local labor force. In addition to direct effects, FDI flows may contribute to the host country's growth and development through positive productivity spillovers to domestic companies and may lead to lower prices and higher-quality goods and services for consumers through increased competition.

Most importantly, as FDI includes direct ownership control, it assumes a long-term commitment to operating in the host country and therefore it is much less volatile and less responsive to shocks compared with other investment flows, such as portfolio investment, bank investment and financial derivatives investment.

For the reasons above, developing and emerging countries are keen on attracting FDI. Yet not every country has succeeded in this effort. The literature lists three major economic motives for a country's attractiveness as an FDI destination: resource seeking, market seeking and efficiency seeking. The resource-seeking motive refers to FDI that flows to resource-abundant countries, serving to extract and export that resource. A huge FDI boom in Azerbaijan aimed at exploitation of the Azeri-Chirag-Guneshli oil field in the second half of the 1990s is a case in point. Market-seeking FDI usually flows to countries with an already existing, or rapidly rising, middle-income population to exploit an expanding consumer market or to countries that are located next to large markets. US investment in the Irish economy is a good example here. Finally, efficiency-seeking FDI aims at exploiting a country's lower factor costs or opportunities for economies of scale to produce and export goods and services. EU investments in eastern Europe illustrate this case.

Although economic motives play a primary role in attracting FDI, in case they are equal between a pair of countries, other factors may tip the balance. *Institutional motives* refer to economic, social and political stability; a favorable tax regime and policy; FDI-friendly labor and product market regulations; a strong overall business climate and competition policy. *FDI-specific motives* include the general investment climate, financial sector development, marketing of the country as an FDI location, investment incentives such as import duty exemptions, income tax holidays and low income and corporate taxes.

It is important to bear in mind that institutional and FDI-specific motives matter only if economic motives are held constant. Hence, without favorable economic and institutional conditions, no FDI will flow into a country even if there is a perfect investment climate. FDI may be influenced by other factors as well. For example, ethnicity and social connection have played important roles in Singapore's FDI in China and Malaysia.

In the context of this study, it would be useful to evaluate the motives for the existing stock of Turkish FDI in Azerbaijan and to compare it with other countries' FDI in Azerbaijan. Of equal importance is how Azerbaijani companies have been investing in Turkey, especially given the recent surge in outward FDI activity by SOCAR.

For most of the period since Azerbaijan became independent in 1991, Turkey has been the largest source of FDI in the non-oil sector of Azerbaijan. In 2010, Turkey ranked as the second largest FDI source for Azerbaijan after the Netherlands, accounting for 22.4 percent of total non-oil FDI flows, as shown in Table 5.9. Over 1,000 Turkish companies operate in Azerbaijan, with a total employment of 60,000. According to the Undersecretariat of the Treasury of Turkey, Turkish FDI stock in Azerbaijan totals US$3.8 billion, and it is the second largest destination for Turkish FDI after the Netherlands.[3] Turkish companies have been in the Azerbaijani market since the collapse of the Soviet Union in 1991. The Turkish Business Association in Azerbaijan, established in 1994, was in fact the first non-governmental organisation established in Azerbaijan since the country became independent in 1991.

Attracting FDI is one of the key steps in diversifying the Azerbaijani economy. Although Azerbaijan has been increasingly using its oil revenues to meet domestic investment needs, especially in building much-needed physical infrastructure and investing in health and education, FDI is important, because it brings new

Table 5.9 Turkey's non-oil FDI in Azerbaijan

Year	Amount, US$ million USD)	Share in Total, %	Rank
2002	17.2	37.6	1
2003	17.1	37.6	1
2004	80.1	76.9	1
2005	96.2	41.7	1
2006	136.6	37.0	1
2007	109.2	24.8	1
2008	60.8	12.3	3
2009	76.8	12.3	3
2010	147.5	22.4	2

Source: Ministry of Economic Development of Azerbaijan

technology, managerial skills and facilitates integration into the global economy along the way. Azerbaijan has succeeded in attracting FDI in the oil sector, including that from Turkey. Existence of substantial natural resources and the absence of considerable political instability is sufficient to make FDI to the oil sector a self-running process. This type of FDI is classified as resource seeking. The real question, however, is how to stimulate investment in the non-oil sector. A recent report argues that even though there is a considerable potential for market-seeking FDI in Azerbaijan, as the country gradually moves towards a lower poverty rate and higher average salaries, attracting efficiency-seeking FDI does not seem possible in the near future (Günther and Björn 2009, *passim*).

Without doubt, Turkey's FDI in Azerbaijan has been strong. There are reasons to believe that Turkish non-oil FDI is especially important for Azerbaijan compared with FDI flows from other countries, because it is generally less capital intensive and more suitable to local conditions. Yet many Turkish interviewees believe that the current numbers are below the potential and with certain structural reforms in place they could substantially rise. The absence of a free trade agreement between the countries, tight migration regulation, lack of skilled labor, problems with customs and lack of strong physical infrastructure are major obstacles to further strengthening Turkish FDI in Azerbaijan. It is worth noting that Turkey is not only capable of being a source of FDI in Azerbaijan, but also can serve as a bridge for European, and especially Middle Eastern, investors (particularly from Gulf Cooperation Council countries) who seek to expand to Azerbaijani and Central Asian markets.

In recent years, Azerbaijan has increased its outward FDI activity, carried out mainly by SOCAR. After investing in certain projects in Georgia, close political and cultural ties paved the way for Azerbaijan's FDI in Turkey as well. According to the Undersecretariat of the Treasury of Turkey, Azerbaijan ranks as the sixth major foreign investor in Turkey, behind only such advanced and/or large economies as the US, UK, Germany, the Netherlands and Iran. As noted above, a lion's share of Azerbaijan's FDI in Turkey is due to SOCAR, which has invested approximately US$5 billion in Turkey. Yet there are other, smaller companies that have invested around US$1.5 billion in Turkey. In April 2011, these companies established the Azerbaijani Business Association in Turkey, which aims to coordinate and facilitate business operations of some 850 Azerbaijani companies in Turkey.

Azerbaijan's FDI in Turkey can be mostly classified as market seeking. STEAS, a joint venture by SOCAR and Turcas Petrol, its strategic partner in Turkey, in 2008 bought a 51 percent share in Petkim, Turkey's major petrochemical company, which controls 25 percent of the Turkish market.[4] SOCAR's Petkim investment is a first step in the company's ambitious plan to become a major player in the energy market in the Black Sea region (Lussac 2011, *passim*). As part of this plan, a new oil refinery for Petkim in Izmir is due to begin construction by 2014.

As for problems voiced by the Azerbaijani side, SOCAR officials were unhappy with the monopolistic environment of Turkey's internal energy market, which jeopardised the financial viability of SOCAR's investment in Petkim. Despite these problems, there are two concrete signs that political ties between the countries eventually paved the way for stronger cooperation in energy policy. First, despite the fact that SOCAR's initial bid for Petkim fell short of that made by a Russian-led consortium, the Turkish Investment Authority subsequently reversed the decision in favor of SOCAR. Second, the problems above were resolved in June 2010, as the Turkish Energy Market Regulatory Authority granted a thirty-year gas-marketing license to STEAS, a "rare privilege for a foreign company" (Lussac 2011).

Reasons behind the gap

In this section, I propose and discuss several hypotheses aimed at explaining the alleged gap in Azerbaijani–Turkish bilateral economic relations.

Hypothesis 1: "crowding out" by energy projects

One possible reason that bilateral economic relations between the two countries are below their potential level is that the energy trade and FDI may "crowd out" the non-energy trade and FDI. Put differently, this is a manifestation of the institutional Dutch disease hypothesis in international trade and FDI.

The argument is as follows: the presence of large rents attracts foreign investors, hence energy trade and investment continue even under unfavorable conditions – oil extraction in war-torn African countries being a case in point. Traditional Dutch disease literature argues that in a country with abundant natural resources, the non-oil tradable sector shrinks as financial and labor resources are diverted toward the oil and non-tradable sectors. More recent studies emphasise that not only are financial and labor resources leaving the non-oil tradable sector, but so is the appetite for policy and institutional reforms which are essential pre-conditions for stronger non-oil trade and FDI. Natural-resource-rich countries tend to be complacent in establishing such an environment.

In the same vein, Azerbaijan and Turkey's joint involvement in such large energy projects as the construction of the BTC oil pipeline and the BTE natural gas pipeline, prospective cooperation in the construction and operation of other gas pipelines, such as Interconnection Turkey-Greece-Italy, the Nabucco project, the Trans-Adriatic Pipeline and TANAP, as well as Azerbaijan's huge investment in Turkey's energy sector, may have acted as a deterrent to a potentially more fruitful cooperation in non-oil trade and investment spheres. Put differently, in the absence of energy cooperation on such a massive scale, political and social capital in bilateral relations could have been directed at developing trade and investment relations in the non-energy sector.

Turkey and Azerbaijan indeed depend on each other when it comes to energy policy. While Azerbaijan's motives for energy cooperation are rather straightforward given the country's high dependence on energy exports and given Turkey's strategic location as a bridge for Azerbaijani gas and oil to reach European markets, Turkey also has strong reasons for energy cooperation with Azerbaijan. Turkey has an energy-intensive economy and given the fact that the country is not rich in natural resources, it is highly dependent on oil and gas imports. As noted above, the Ministry of Energy of Turkey estimates the ratio of energy import dependence to reach 80 percent by 2020. Turkey also wants to capitalise on its favorable geography and historical role as the bridge between West and East and Europe and Asia and become an energy hub in its own right. Last but not least, Turkey wants to reduce its dependence on Russia, which is currently the main supplier of natural gas to Turkey.

The experts I interviewed do not think that the energy cooperation between Azerbaijan and Turkey has diverted political and social resources away from developing cooperation in non-oil spheres. If anything, energy policy has had a positive impact: it seems that SOCAR's problems with the uncompetitive nature of the Turkish internal petrochemical market were resolved as part of broader negotiations over energy issues. Also, as noted above, there are over 1,000 Turkish firms operating in Azerbaijan and there have been few to no cases where Turkish companies have suffered from unfair treatment by Azerbaijani authorities.

Hypothesis 2: dominance of political issues

Energy policy nowadays cannot be completely understood without taking into consideration the influence of politics. Hence my next hypothesis: perhaps there are a number of outstanding political issues in bilateral relations that overwhelm the prospects and opportunities for economic cooperation.

So, did political relations hamper economic relations between Azerbaijan and Turkey? Let us first refer to the literature to understand the link between politics and economics. The literature does not provide a clear-cut answer: causality may run in both directions. There is both empirical and anecdotal evidence that problems in political relations can increase uncertainty and lower economic exchange between a pair of countries. On the other hand, as trade volumes and investment flows increase among countries, payoffs to maintaining and deepening ties rise correspondingly. Trade and FDI are usually forerunners of deeper and broader socio-cultural and political international relations.

The effect of a political relationship on an economic relationship is not homogeneous across different types of economic relations: trade appears to be less sensitive to increases in political uncertainty than is investment. Evidence shows that, on average, political distance does not matter for an exporter: more policy and political control is likely to be exercised over import activities. On the other hand, investment and in particular FDI flows are affected by the political relationship between a pair of countries. This is because FDI requires more time and commitments in a domestic political setting of the destination country and because FDI flows, unlike trade flows, are not secured against discriminatory behavior, due to the absence of a WTO-type rule-based multilateral organisation.

In practice, there are well-known examples of political relations hampering economic relations, such as US–Iran, Iran–Israel, US–Cuba and Azerbaijan–Armenia. Despite these notable exceptions, there is evidence that, in general, economic interests seem to overcome political tensions. A good case of how economic relations dominate political tensions is the Chinese–Japanese relationship. Ever since normalisation of relations in 1978, this relationship has experienced a steady positive trend despite minor political tensions. Chinese–Japanese bilateral trade volume ranks third in the world after the US–Canada and US–China relationships. Another example could be the German–Russian relationship, where economics drives politics once again.

This hypothesis may come as a surprise, because one would expect such ostensibly strong political allies as Azerbaijan and Turkey to enjoy stronger economic relations as well. During the interviews, I specifically asked whether political relations have had a negative impact on economic relations. The answer was unanimously negative for Turkish and Azerbaijani interviewees: if anything, political closeness has paved the way for stronger economic ties. However, there is one notable exception to this general trend – the energy policy. In negotiations over gas import prices and transit terms, as one Azerbaijani official noted, Turkish authorities seemed to treat Azerbaijan as a "junior brother" that has to succumb to whatever the "senior brother" tells him. This was not in line with Azerbaijan's willingness to negotiate as an equal partner. Thus, despite the strong ethnic, cultural, historical and political ties, the two countries experienced serious disagreement over the gas import and transit prices. Meanwhile, political tensions arose as Turkey started normalisation of bilateral relations with Armenia, further exacerbating the negotiations.

The fact that the Turkish–Armenian normalisation process started amid Azerbaijani–Turkish negotiations on the revision of gas import and transit prices induced some analysts to argue that this particular political event caused subsequent economic tensions. They have argued that Azerbaijan was using the energy card to pressure Turkey out of rapprochement with Armenia. However, there are strong reasons to believe that this is not the case: economic problems between the two countries have their own dynamics and the Turkish–Armenian rapprochement does not appear to be the root cause.

Saban Kardas (2011) argues that the energy dispute between Turkey and Azerbaijan was caused by incompatibility, and the increasing divergence, between energy policies of the two countries, rather than by political developments in bilateral relations. Turkey wants to expand its role as simply a transit country to become a hub country. A hub country essentially capitalises on its favorable geographic position by buying a commodity from the producer and reselling it to consumers on its own terms. This practice is different from that of a transit country, which simply receives transit fees for transportation of the commodity over its territory, without reaping extra benefits. Such a setup contradicts Azerbaijan's plans to become a direct supplier of gas to Europe.

Moreover, the gas price dispute actually predated the Turkish-Armenian rapprochement. Rapprochement efforts might have exacerbated already heated tensions over gas prices and, ultimately, might have created a momentum in bilateral relations that pushed the two countries, especially the Turkish side, to reconsider its overall strategy toward Azerbaijan and energy cooperation in particular. However, even without the rapprochement, the gas import price dispute would be there, awaiting resolution. Nevertheless, in the long term the Turkish attitude toward normalisation of relations with Armenia might have challenged its right to commercial exclusivity in the eyes of the Azerbaijani government.

Despite the fact that in the particular case above, politics has not dominated economics, on the whole the Nagorno-Karabakh conflict has had a negative impact on the economic performance and economic relations of regional countries. Evgeny Polyakov (2001) applies the gravity model to the regional trade in the South Caucasus and finds that regional conflicts adversely affect trade there. In regard to the Azerbaijani–Turkish trade in particular, he argues that a shorter transport route via Armenia would substantially bring trade costs down. Right now trade between Azerbaijan and Turkey must traverse either Iran or Georgia.

On a positive note, the fact that Turkey is doing so well on investment in Azerbaijan is actually a sign of political closeness between the two countries. There is evidence that important effects of political relations on economic relations are realised more through FDI than through trade in goods and services. Therefore, if anything, there is a positive link between politics and economics in bilateral relations. Moreover, the way the Turcas-SOCAR bid for Petkim was handled in Turkey may be a good indicator of how political relations between the countries in fact improved economic cooperation.

Hypothesis 3: lack of bilateral agreements that facilitate trade and FDI

Another hypothesis is that the two countries may lack the necessary bilateral legislative base that would reduce transaction costs for trade and FDI. The Turkish side especially mentions shortcomings in three areas: migration code, visa regime arrangements and free trade agreements, the latter being cited as the most important.

Turkish experts argue that without such a free trade agreement Turkish exports to Azerbaijan lose in competitiveness in comparison with exports from Russia and other former Soviet Union countries that benefit from having FTAs with Azerbaijan. Signing an FTA, according to the Turkish side, will boost trade volume between the two countries and attract Turkish FDI in the non-oil sector alike. Minister Zafer Caglayan, in particular, remarked that the trade volume could more than double from the current US$2.4 billion to US$5 billion if an FTA is signed. Moreover, such a trade agreement would benefit Azerbaijani exports to Turkey, which are currently at a disadvantage, other things equal, vis-à-vis EU exports to Turkey. Similarly, this trade agreement would benefit Turkish exports to Azerbaijan, which are currently at a disadvantage, other things equal, vis-à-vis Russian or Ukrainian exports to Azerbaijan.

Turkish companies believe they are hurt by recently updated migration legislation in Azerbaijan that makes it harder and more expensive for foreign citizens to work in the country. Because the local, Azerbaijani labor force mostly lacks the managerial and vocational skills necessary for business operations, Turkish companies have long relied on bringing in Turkish workers. With new migration legislation in place, it is now burdensome and more costly to bring in these workers. Azerbaijani officials argue that the current migration policy aims at developing local human capital which otherwise would be crowded out by foreigners.

Hypothesis 4: disparity in the levels of economic and institutional development

Another hypothesis is that Azerbaijan and Turkey may lag behind the potential level of economic relations simply because they are at different levels of economic and institutional development. This disparity more than offsets the positive initial effect of cultural affinity and geographic proximity between the countries, and as a result, these factors could lead to a volume of bilateral trade and investment levels lower than their potentials. Let us compare the economies of Turkey and Azerbaijan according to these different aspects of development.

Economic development

According to the World Bank country classification, both Azerbaijan and Turkey fall under the "upper middle income country" category. Yet it would not be accurate to treat these countries as equal in terms of economic development. Looking at Table 5.10, Turkey is way ahead by many indicators: its GDP per capita in 2010 was almost twice that of Azerbaijan. Its total trade volume with the world is ten times as large as Azerbaijan's. It is already a member of OECD and the G20 club of rich countries and is likely to become one of the top ten economies in the world by 2023. Azerbaijan, despite its spectacular growth in the first decade of the twenty-first century, has yet to diversify away from being an oil-dependent country towards a productive-sector-led, non-oil export-based modern economy.

Table 5.10 Selected macroeconomic indicators, 2010

Statistic	Turkey	Azerbaijan
Nominal GDP (US$billions)	735.49	54.37
GDP per capita (US$)	10,309	6008
Total export (US$billions)	113.97	21.28
Total import (US$billions) USD)	185.54	6.59

Source: International Monetary Fund, World Economic Outlook Database

The Turkish economy is much more diversified, its export basket much more sophisticated than Azerbaijan's, as is the range and economic development of its export destination markets. As discussed above, the gravity model suggests that richer countries tend to trade more with each other, thus given disparities in economic sizes and the levels of development of Azerbaijan and Turkey, their potential level of economic cooperation may not be that high at this stage of Azerbaijan's development. Does this mean there is actually no gap between the actual and potential levels of bilateral economic relations between the two countries? This would contradict the unanimous opinion of the experts coming from different backgrounds, who think that such a gap exists, although for different reasons. Moreover, in the comparative analysis in the beginning of the chapter, even after controlling for economic sizes the Georgian–Turkish trade volume was almost twice as large as the Azerbaijani–Turkish trade volume. Perhaps having a look at the role of institutions in the bilateral economic relations will shed more light on the existence of the gap.

Institutions and business climate

Azerbaijan and Turkey may be behind their potential level of bilateral economic relations because of different levels of institutional development. Recent economic literature emphasises the role of institutions in promoting economic growth and development in addition to traditional drivers such as investment in physical and human capital, as well as technological innovation. Without strong institutions in place, it is very difficult to achieve sustained growth in standards of living. Poor institutions negatively affect private transactions, leading to higher transaction costs with negative effects on growth and development. This argument can also be extended to international trade and investment. Factors such as quality of governance, institutional homogeneity, and institutional quality are among those that may affect bilateral trade flows.

The role of institutions in bilateral trade flows is twofold. First, institutional *quality* matters. Empirical studies find that the institutional quality of exporters and importers has a positive effect on the amount of trade between them. A stronger institutional framework reduces uncertainty about contract enforcement and general economic governance. Security of private property is essential for international trade. The degree of mutual trust may be important in an environment where contracts are poorly enforced (Guiso et al. 2007). Lack of trust will prevent otherwise profitable trade and investment opportunities. Some of the determinants of trust are history of war, commonality of religion and genetic distance.

Second, institutional *homogeneity* matters. Countries with similar levels of institutional quality incur low transaction costs in economic exchange. Similar norms of behavior and institutional environment lead to similar levels of trust, thereby reducing transaction costs. On the other hand, countries with substantially different levels of institutional quality tend to trade less with each other. It is mostly countries with poor institutions that suffer: they cannot benefit from knowledge spillovers, large sales markets and other advantages of trading with more economically advanced countries.

Turkey's institutional quality is higher despite notable developments in Azerbaijan in recent years. Turkey has a relatively long history of a market economy, while Azerbaijan has yet to complete its transition from a centrally planned economy to a market economy with an adequate number and quality of institutions. Azerbaijan continues to suffer from corruption, bureaucracy and poor enforcement of the rule of law.

Poor institutional quality in Azerbaijan is a serious impediment to realising its trade potential and becoming an attractive FDI destination. Azerbaijan's trade and custom facilitation processes are way below competitive levels. Azerbaijan is one of the 10 hardest countries in trading across borders: the country ranks 177th out of 183 in the World Bank's *Doing Business 2011* report (see Table 5.11).

Table 5.11 Doing Business rankings for Azerbaijan, Turkey and Georgia, 2010–11

Topic	Azerbaijan		Turkey		Georgia	
	2011	2010	2011	2010	2011	2010
Starting a business	15	17	63	56	8	6
Dealing with construction permits	160	157	137	133	7	7
Registering property	10	8	38	35	2	2
Getting credit	46	44	72	69	15	30
Protecting investors	20	20	59	57	20	41
Paying taxes	103	107	75	73	61	61
Trading across borders	177	178	76	72	35	31
Enforcing contracts	27	27	26	25	41	41
Closing a business	88	85	115	119	105	96
Overall rank	54	55	65	60	12	13

Source: www.doingbusiness.org

106 *Elkin Nurmammadov*

Doing Business provides further data on the ease of trading across borders. According to the 2011 report, compared with a firm in Turkey, an Azerbaijani firm must spend 29 and 31 additional days to complete an export and an import transaction, respectively (see Table 5.12).

Azerbaijan's trade logistics infrastructure is weak, leading to high transactions costs both for exporters and importers. The value of Azerbaijan's Logistics Performance Index (LPI) – a trade logistics "friendliness" index computed by the World Bank based on a worldwide survey of global freight forwarders and express carriers – is low even in comparison with other post-Soviet countries. Turkey and Azerbaijan score 3.22 and 2.64, respectively, while the regional average for Europe and Central Asia is 2.74, as shown in Table 5.13.

One can also claim that Turkey and Azerbaijan are far from being institutionally homogeneous by observing that while the former is both a member of the WTO and a customs union with the EU, the latter is a member of neither.

Azerbaijan is one of a few countries in the world that is not a WTO member: the accession process has been going on for over fourteen years. Turkey, on the other hand, has been a WTO member since 1995. This hampers the competitiveness of Azerbaijani exports to WTO member countries because these exports are not protected by multilateral rules, leaving the governments of importing

Table 5.12 Trading across border rankings, 2011

Indicator	Azerbaijan	Turkey	Eastern Europe and Central Asia	OECD
Documents to export (number)	9	7	6.4	4.4
Time to export (days)	43	14	26.7	10.9
Documents to import (number)	14	8	7.6	4.9
Time to import (days)	46	15	28.1	11.4

Source: www.doingbusiness.org

Table 5.13 Logistics Performance Index (LPI) for selected countries

Country	LPI	Customs	Infra-structure	Int'l shipments	Logistics competence	Tracking	Timeliness
Turkey	3.22	2.82	3.08	3.15	3.23	3.09	3.94
Azerbaijan	2.64	2.14	2.23	3.05	2.48	2.65	3.15
Georgia	2.61	2.37	2.17	2.73	2.57	2.67	3.08
Russia	2.61	2.15	2.38	2.72	2.51	2.6	3.23
EECA*	2.74	2.35	2.41	2.92	2.6	2.75	3.33

*Eastern Europe and Central Asia region average

Source: World Bank

countries unconstrained to impose protectionist measures. Without WTO membership, Azerbaijan also loses in investment in the export sector, because potential investors face uncertainty regarding current tariffs and other trade- and investment-related regulations. Thus, Azerbaijan's joining WTO would, at least to some extent, "level the playing field" in bilateral trade between the two countries. A case in point is brought out in my interviews in the Nakhchivan Autonomous Republic, the only part of Azerbaijan that has direct borders with Turkey. Keen on developing its export potential, this region of Azerbaijan wants to target the eastern provinces of Turkey. However, officials were unhappy about non-tariff barriers erected by Turkey in regard to Nakhchivani exports. Were Azerbaijan a member of the WTO, these barriers could probably be easily lifted.

Turkey joined a customs union with the EU in 1996. In the run-up to 1996 and especially since 2002, Turkey's export industries have gained experience producing and exporting goods and services and meeting the standards and norms of advanced countries. The customs union assumes the adoption of a common customs policy and thus common tariffs against third countries. EU regulations, such as a common external tariff, wide use of quotas, special restrictions on agricultural products and very high quality standards, appear to be too big a hurdle to Azerbaijani exporters.

Azerbaijani exporters in Nakhchivan mention the difficulties of getting into the Turkish market due to non-tariff barriers. Also, as noted earlier, SOCAR officials voiced their complaints about inadequate regulations in Turkey's energy sector.

EU membership negotiations with Turkey triggered a host of bold structural reforms in the country. Turkey's competition policy legislation was harmon- ised with that of the EU. EU standards regarding industrial products and consumer rights were adopted as well. This also increased Turkey's attrac- tiveness as an FDI destination. By contrast, Azerbaijan's business environment has yet to improve to attract new domestic and foreign players. Joining the WTO could be an important step in this direction, as it would entail passage of important anti-monopoly and investment protection legislation in the parliament.

Hypothesis 5: inadequate infrastructure and human capital in Azerbaijan

The inadequate level of human capital and poor physical infrastructure are among the major obstacles to efficiency-seeking FDI. Despite Azerbaijan's growing market as well as its proximity to other former Soviet Union countries, the non-oil sector has not been successful in attracting efficiency-seeking FDI. Experts from the Turkish side have cited these factors in explaining why big Turkish companies are virtually nonexistent in Azerbaijan. As noted above, there are two motives for non-oil FDI: market seeking and efficiency seeking. Although there is a growing potential for market-seeking FDI as per capita income in Azerbaijan

Table 5.14 World Economic Forum Competitiveness Report 2011: rankings for selected items for Azerbaijan and Turkey

Item	Azerbaijan	Turkey
Infrastructure	76	56
Health and primary education	83	72
Higher education and training	77	71

steadily increases, there are yet no signs for substantial improvement in the efficiency-seeking area. Table 5.14 compares Turkey and Azerbaijan in terms of the level of infrastructure and human capital, the latter consisting of the measures of education, training and health. Rankings are based on the annual report by the World Economic Forum, prepared for 139 countries. Azerbaijan seems to lag behind Turkey on both infrastructure and human capital.

Good physical infrastructure is essential for spurring private activity. Turkey has a highly developed infrastructure, a rail link to central and eastern Europe and a relatively low cost sea transport infrastructure. Azerbaijan still needs to improve its physical infrastructure, particularly roads and railways, despite considerable steps taken in this direction. Completion of the BTK railroad project is expected to significantly contribute to bridging the gap between the actual and potential levels of bilateral economic relations between Azerbaijan and Turkey. The unresolved Nagorno-Karabakh conflict significantly increases the trade costs between Azerbaijan and Turkey, as exports and imports must transcend Georgia to reach the country of destination. There is a huge trade diversion to the conflict. Although one could argue that even if this constraint were lifted, Azerbaijani goods are not competitive enough to enter the Turkish market – this does not mean that this situation cannot change in the future. Also, the amount of Turkish imports and FDI in Azerbaijan would definitely increase as a result of reduced transportation costs.

Research shows that FDI contributes to economic growth in a country mainly when there is an adequate level of human capital (Borenzstein et al. 1998). In Turkey, there are approximately 24.7 million young, well-educated professionals and around 450,000 graduates from some 150 universities. There are a considerable number of internationally recognised, world-class universities in Turkey. The country has been sending its students for education abroad from the beginning of the twentieth century, whereas a similar state program in Azerbaijan was launched only in 2007. Half of Turkey's population is under 28.3 years old; the country is rapidly transforming into a middle-class consumer economy.

Although Azerbaijan also benefits from having a large share of a young population, the latter often lack the knowledge and skills required to support a diversified market economy. A recent comprehensive study of the Azerbaijani economy by the World Bank (2009) emphasised the problems with human capital in the country. There is a serious mismatch between what is taught at the universities and what the economy demands in terms of knowledge and skills. For example, there is an excess supply of graduates in education, health and manufacturing, while the majority of the labor force is employed in agricultural and service sectors of the economy. Even those who graduate with degrees in disciplines demanded by the market rarely meet the requirements of the workplace, indicating a problem in the quality of their education. Diplomas granted by Azerbaijani universities have been losing their value in the eyes of employers. The private sector faces a severe shortage of highly skilled labor. Interviews have shown that the business sector is strongly in need of people with competitive managerial skills. Business owners in general have complained that most of the job seekers lack even basic soft skills. There is also an important dearth of technical labor, as vocational education has virtually disappeared in Azerbaijan since the demise of the Soviet Union.

Bridging the gap

Azerbaijani–Turkish bilateral relations from time to time have not been as smooth as the "one nation, two states" formula commonly used to characterise these relations would imply. Is this also the case in economic relations? Is there a serious gap between the potential and actual levels of bilateral economic relations? This chapter has explored whether such a gap exists and, if so, what the underlying reasons are.

My conclusion, supported by interviews with Azerbaijani government officials and the Turkish business and diplomatic community in Baku, as well as the analysis of the data and literature, is that such a gap exists. I have proposed and discussed several hypotheses attempting to explain the gap.

While some hypotheses point at the existence of issues specific to Azerbaijani–Turkish relations, the most likely explanation turns out to be that problems hindering Azerbaijan's trade and FDI potential in general, with respect to *all* trade partners, seem to exert a major negative effect on Azerbaijani–Turkish bilateral economic relations as well. Even though there are certain short-term steps that can boost bilateral trade and FDI between Azerbaijan and Turkey, I stress that the main reason for the weak export performance of Azerbaijan vis-à-vis Turkey comes down to the lack of internationally competitive goods in the country. Azerbaijan needs to undergo serious structural reforms to boost competitiveness, and if properly done, that will boost bilateral economic relations with all trading partners, including Turkey. I would even argue that once these structural impediments are addressed, the pace of improvement in Azerbaijani-Turkish economic relations will exceed those in Azerbaijan's other bilateral relations, as this particular relationship has huge potential given such favorable characteristics as cultural affinity, strong political ties and geographic proximity.

I proceed with policy recommendations for Azerbaijani policymakers based on the hypotheses developed above. Most of these recommendations replicate those listed in the reports prepared by major international organisations and aim at improving the overall competitiveness of the country's exports. However, as noted above, there are also recommendations aimed at specifically improving bilateral economic relations with Turkey.

Recommendation 1

Azerbaijan should join the WTO as soon as possible. Although the country may have some rationale for delaying the accession, mainly protecting the non-oil sector, according to many analysts the costs of the delay outweigh the benefits. As a WTO member, Azerbaijan could create positive momentum for economic development by implementing and, more importantly, locking in trade-facilitating reforms. Along with gains from increased transparency, this would also send positive signals to foreign investors. On top of facilitating trade and investment, WTO accession would bring such indirect benefits as increased domestic competition, knowledge spillovers to local firms and thus stronger competitiveness of surviving firms in the non-oil tradable sector. In regard to Azerbaijani–Turkish relations, WTO membership by Azerbaijan will remove disadvantages faced by Azerbaijani and Turkish exporters alike, as discussed above. This is likely to bring investments in the non-oil sector by big Turkish business, resulting in much-needed technology transfer and better prices for customers. Moreover, Nakhchivani exporters will be able to target a bigger market in the East Anatolian provinces of Turkey.

Recommendation 2

With or without joining the WTO, Azerbaijan is in great need of reforming customs. To some extent, problems in customs can be attributed to the general poor institutional infrastructure in the country, as well as the lack of skilled labor: there is a shortage of trained customs brokers and customs experts, creating further bottlenecks in the customs clearance process. Nevertheless, as noted earlier when discussing divergence between Azerbaijani and Turkish statistics, there is a significant undervaluation and most probably differential treatment of imports, indicating the major cause of inefficiency in customs procedures: the strong influence of major monopolists in the country at the expense of consumers and other firms that actually comply with foreign trade regulations.

Recommendation 3

Both sides need to invest more resources in infrastructural development. Completion of the BTK railroad project as soon as possible will have a major impact on the bilateral trade volume between Turkey and Azerbaijan, especially to realise the growing non-oil export potential of Nakhchivan targeting eastern provinces of Turkey.

Recommendation 4

Azerbaijan needs to speed up human capital development in the country, placing more emphasis on vocational training. Besides obvious gains to the Azerbaijani economy from a larger stock of human capital, this will have a positive effect on foreign trade and FDI in Azerbaijan, including that from Turkey. Interviews show that small and medium-sized Turkish companies operating in Azerbaijan have to import skilled labor from Turkey, which increases their costs of production given tighter migration regulation in Azerbaijan. Moreover, this will create more incentives for large Turkish companies to work in Azerbaijan. Azerbaijan should not delay investment in vocational education in the meantime.

Recommendation 5

The two countries should negotiate the terms of and sign a free trade agreement, unless Azerbaijan becomes a WTO member in the near future. This agreement should also have sections on facilitation and protection of investment to further aid Azerbaijani and Turkish investors. This will have an immediate positive impact on Turkey's exports to Azerbaijan but will also facilitate Azerbaijani exports to Turkey once Azerbaijani exporters are able to produce internationally competitive goods.

Recommendation 6

The two states could consider setting up joint ventures to invest in third countries. Azerbaijan could tap into Turkey's strong trade and FDI links with neighbouring countries, especially those in the Middle East and EU, as Azerbaijan improves the composition and diversity of its export basket.

Appendix

Aside on statistics

It is important to have reliable statistical data to guide analysis and policy recommendations. Numbers on bilateral trade volume reported by Azerbaijani and Turkish official sources differ somewhat oddly, complicating the analysis of bilateral economic relations. For example, while the State Committee on Statistics of Azerbaijan reports the bilateral trade volume of US$942 million in 2010, the same statistic reaches approximately US$2.4 billion according to the Turkish Statistical Institute.

It seems like the main problem is with Azerbaijani statistics. A recent World Bank report points to so-called positive mirror trade gap in Azerbaijan, the case that the total value of all exports to Azerbaijan from the rest of the world, as reported by trading partners, is much larger than the total imports of Azerbaijan, as reported by the State Committee on Statistics.

One can notice a huge positive mirror gap in Azerbaijan's trade with Russia and Turkey by looking at Table 5.3, which shows imports of Azerbaijan as reported by Turkish, Russian and Azerbaijani statistics agencies. For the period 2003–9, the value of official imports from Russia amounted to US$6.3 billion, as reported by Azerbaijan, whereas the value of official exports to Azerbaijan, as reported by Russia, amounted to US$7.6 billion, leading to a positive mirror gap of US$1.3 billion. The same applies to the case of Turkey: the difference between the value of official imports to Azerbaijan and the official exports to Azerbaijan over the same period is equal to approximately US$2.5 billion. In fact, the mirror trade gap must be *negative*, as imports include the cost of insurance and freight and exports are free on board. One other observation is that the positive mirror gap appears to emerge with respect to trade with Russia from 2005 onwards, whereas it exists with respect to trade with Turkey for the whole period of 2000–9. Going beyond purely statistical problems, the positive mirror gap actually hints at the existence of a large amount of unreported imports to Azerbaijan, or the fact that there is a differential treatment of imports at the border. This is also an implicit sign of distorted competition and higher prices for consumers in the market.

Notes

1 I discuss why such a divergence between official numbers exists in the Appendix.
2 See Borenzstein et al. (1998, *passim*), among many others on this topic.
3 According to the Ministry of Economic Development of Azerbaijan, this number is about US$2 billion over the years 2002–2010.
4 SOCAR plans to raise Petkim's share in Turkey's petrochemical market to 40 percent, according to the company representative who spoke at an Azerbaijani–Turkish business forum held in Baku in November 2011. http://contact.az/docs/2011/Economics&Finance/112912197ru.htm.

References

Borenzstein, Eduardo, José de Gregorio, and Jong-Wha Lee. 1998. How Does Foreign Investment Affect Economic Growth? *Journal of International Economics* 45, 115–135.
Guiso, Luigi, Paolo Sapienza, and Luigi Zingales. 2007. *Cultural Biases in Economic Exchange*. Mimeograph, University of Chicago.
Günther, Jutta and Björn Jindra. 2009. *Investment (FDI) Policy for Azerbaijan*. Halle Institute for Economic Research Report.
Kardas, Saban. 2011. Turkish-Azerbaijani Energy Cooperation and Nabucco: Testing the Limits of the New Turkish Foreign Policy Rhetoric. *Turkish Studies* 12:1, 55–77.
Lussac, Samuel. 2011. Azerbaijan, Turkey, and Energy Markets: The Evolution of a Complex Relationship. *Azerbaijan in the World* 4:10, 6–10.
Polyakov, Evgeny. 2001. *Changing Trade Patterns after Conflict Resolution in South Caucasus*. Washington, DC: The World Bank.
Tinbergen, Jan. 1962. *Shaping the World Economy: Suggestions for an International Economic Policy*. New York: 20th Century Fund.
World Bank. 2009. A New Silk Road: Export-Led Diversification. *Azerbaijan Country Economic Memorandum, Report 44365-AZ*. Washington, DC: The World Bank.
Yilmaz, Kamil and Umit Izmen. 2009. Turkey's Recent Trade and Foreign Direct Investment Performance. *Economic Research Forum Working Paper 0902*. Istanbul: TUSIAD – Koc University.

6 State–business relations in Azerbaijan through the eyes of Turkish businesspeople

Pınar Bedirhanoğlu

Introduction

Turkish entrepreneurs were among the first foreign investors to display an interest in doing business in Azerbaijan in the early 1990s despite the political and economic turmoil prevailing in the country in the aftermath of independence. The entrepreneurial rationale of these early-comers is questionable, for their political motivations to help liberate their Azerbaijani brethren from communist rule possibly exceeded their concerns for profit-making at that time due to their self-proclaimed "passionate love for these lands." Once conditions for relative stability in the country started to set in later, language and cultural affinity as well as geographical proximity between the two countries encouraged more Turkish people and companies to search for new beginnings in Azerbaijan. As of this writing, in early 2013, there are 1,266 Turkish companies paying taxes to Azerbaijani authorities, according to information collected by the Turkish Trade Consulate in Baku.[1]

This chapter aims to identify and problematise the historically specific characteristics of state–business relations in Azerbaijan through the lens of Turkish businesspeople, with a particular emphasis on the question of corruption. This will be done on the basis of a critical analysis of twelve in-depth interviews conducted in Baku in August 2011, ten of which were with either the representatives or the owners of some selected Turkish companies. The remaining two interviews were with the representatives of two influential business associations, namely the International Association of Azerbaijani and Turkish Industrialists and Businessmen (TUSIAB)[2] and the Azerbaijan–Turkey Business Association (ATIB).[3] The main consideration underlying the selection of interviewees was to reach relatively long-standing and/or institutionalised Turkish companies operating in Azerbaijan. To this end, ATIB's and TUSIAB's initial directives, as well as recommendations made by some of the interviewees themselves, were utilised. The full list of these interviews is provided in the appendix, and references to these interviews throughout the paper will be made by mentioning their sequence number. It is important to recognise that out of these ten businesspeople interviewed, eight came to Baku in the 1990s, with four having come in the first half of that decade. Hence, the selected interviewees are quite experienced, as they have proved to be successful in earning profits in Azerbaijan, in addition to having an opportunity to observe, and live through, the transformations taking place in politics and the business environment in the country.

The focus on corruption was not intended at the beginning of the research. Indeed, corruption was only one among several topics interviews sought to cover. There was also a concern that the interviewees would not be very willing to discuss this issue. Contrary to this assumption, however, the Turkish interviewees – when asked – did not seem to be very disturbed by the topic and, indeed, provided quite detailed comments on it. Their tendency to view the so-called corruption problem in Azerbaijan as a political system, rather than an issue reduced to bribery, inevitably informed their overall assessment of the Azerbaijani state. The latter position ultimately served to set corruption as the central discussion of the research.[4]

Problematising the question of corruption in Azerbaijan through the eyes of businesspeople has both advantages and disadvantages. On one hand, as they have faced the impact of corruption directly, they might provide us with a rather detailed picture of the issue in question. Indeed, the interviews were very informative in this regard. On the other hand, given the fact that the businesspeople interviewed were those who themselves had been doing business in Azerbaijan, and indeed corruption is a "tango by two,"[5] some were likely to be among those actively involved in such practices, with implications for their own perceptions of corruption. Indeed, this becomes ever more probable given the fact that since 2001, Azerbaijan has not reached beyond the level of 3 on a scale of 1 to 10 in Transparency International's annual corruption perception indexes.[6] Moreover, it is possible that the interviewees were afraid of making negative remarks lest they disturb their established links within the Azerbaijani state. All these mean that the arguments made by the Turkish businesspeople, however informative they are, have to be considered in the light of these reservations. Thus, their evaluations should rather be viewed as contributing to our understanding of how practices perceived as corrupt are also legitimised as normal and acceptable on the basis of various political and economic arguments.

This cautious stand towards the views the Turkish businesspeople provided on corruption in Azerbaijan should also be preserved when considering the anti-corruption agenda pursued by the so-called international community,[7] for it is possible to identify various limitations, inconsistencies, biases and contradictions in this endeavour that stem from the underlying theoretical assumptions, problematic historical conclusions and specific political concerns of the neoliberal perspective informing it. Put briefly, what might be termed "the neoliberal discourse on corruption," which has been produced and reproduced by various international actors since the mid-1990s, is ahistorical, as it fails to differentiate between modern and pre-modern forms of corruption. It is biased, as it associates corruption with historical and cultural specificities of less developed and post-Soviet states only. Finally, it is politicised, as it has redefined and expanded the scope of "corruption" as "rent-seeking," turning the anti-corruption agenda into a comprehensive yet rather ambiguous political reform process aiming ultimately at the wholesale restructuring of some targeted state structures.[8] All of these problematic characteristics underlying this discourse have been reproduced within the context of Azerbaijan, although some historically specific features of the Azerbaijani case seem to drive the international community into a sort of manic-depressive mood. Azerbaijan was identified as the "world's top regulatory reformer" in the *Doing Business 2009* report by the World Bank and International Finance Corporation (TI 2012), while another World Bank report – published just the following year – displayed a far more pessimistic attitude, emphasising the seriousness of the problem of corruption (The World Bank 2010, 8). Such volatilities in the anti-corruption agenda highlight its political character and, consequently, invite one to reject it as a legitimate referent to be approved without questioning. Hence, while trying to make sense of the so-called corruption issue in Azerbaijan, this paper aims to follow an alternative, critical stand by recognising the interest-driven character of different perspectives on it, voiced not only within Azerbaijan, but also at the international level.

The chapter is organised in two main parts. The first part will try to picture changing conditions of doing business in Azerbaijan on the basis of the experiences of the Turkish businesspeople since 1991. An attempt will also be made to problematise their background and the specific advantages they have enjoyed while doing business, as well as the prevailing business practices in Azerbaijan in general. The second part of the chapter will focus on state–business relations in the country to understand how the so-called corruption in Azerbaijan is experienced and perceived by the Turkish businesspeople. Besides the comments made by the interviewees, both parts of the paper will also offer some discussion of the international and domestic determinants that shape and influence transformations in the business environment and corruption in Azerbaijan, in efforts to provide the reader with some basic information on the social, economic and political context in which these comments were made. The final part aims to rethink the political implications of the neoliberal discourse on corruption in Azerbaijan within the context of the broader process of the establishment of the rule of law in the country.

Turkish businesspeople and changing conditions for doing business in Azerbaijan

The period from independence to Heydar Aliyev's consolidation of power in the mid-1990s was certainly not favourable for a business startup in Azerbaijan.[9] The Ebulfez Elchibey–led Popular Front which came to power in June 1992, following the incapable rule of independent Azerbaijan's first president, Mutallibov, failed to ensure internal political stability in the country. During his short-lived presidency, until Aliyev's advent to power in 1993, Elchibey proved incapable of preventing the expanding Armenian invasions in Karabakh or the state's rapid loss of monopoly over coercion at the expense of various ethnic or Russian-supported armed groups ultimately challenging his own rule (Cornell 2011, 72–77). It is interesting to note that two of the interviewees

(2, 10) came to Azerbaijan during these uncertain years to support Elchibey's pan-Turkist rule, and their adventurous but ultimately successful business engagements thereafter have enabled them to stay in the country despite the fall of the Popular Front. One of them (2) said this openly and obviously took pride in it, while the other (10) was more cautious and preferred to associate his interest in Azerbaijan with his concern to initiate conditions of a free market economy in this beloved country. Still, the latter's argument that the early romanticism was over in Azerbaijan and that, consequently, everything has now come to be determined by the market sheds more light on the initial considerations that underlay his decision to come to Azerbaijan. These must have been among the Turkish people who, as mentioned by the TUSIAB representative (12), had come to the country with feelings of fraternity after independence, but then quickly moved to adapt themselves to business conditions in Azerbaijan. Hence, they have arguably grown into "those romantic, dedicated members of the Azerbaijani business community who put Azerbaijani interests even before the Turkish ones" (11).

Besides this latter group, the Turkish business community in Azerbaijan today also comprises those who had come to study at Azerbaijani universities (5, 8), those who worked initially in big construction companies as architects or engineers (1) and those who wanted to try their fortune in Azerbaijan after being hit by economic crises in Turkey like the one in 1994 (3) or came to make a living from Turkey's Black Sea, eastern and southeastern regions in the 1990s (12).

Until the end of the 1990s, the Turkish businesspeople had no rivals in the chaotic, but unexploited Azerbaijani market (11). Svante Cornell (2011, 360) mentions their earlier experience in the market economy and their ability to do business in corrupt environments as specific assets in these early years. However, the majority of them were either individual entrepreneurs or small companies with limited experience; as such, they ended up abusing their unrivaled position by pumping low-quality products into the Azerbaijani market and, consequently, losing prestige towards the end of the decade. Some interviewees suggested that the image of Turkish businesspeople was only able to recover following the boom in the construction sector after the mid-2000s, when more experienced and qualified companies established their business in Azerbaijan (11).

One of the important functions that the Turkish companies fulfilled in Azerbaijan in the early 1990s was to work as intermediaries between the Azerbaijani and Western companies, which lacked common standards and rules to direct their relations. While the Azerbaijani companies would prefer to work with Turkish companies to overcome their international accreditation problems (12), many large Western firms operating in Turkey launched their first businesses in Azerbaijan through their settlements and Turkish staffs in their Istanbul offices (Cornell 2011, 360). The reliance of Western firms in Azerbaijan on well-equipped Turkish companies and engineers still holds, particularly in the construction sector, which, in addition to oil-related works, builds high-tech residences for the wealthy of Azerbaijan. Furthermore, interviewees also mentioned that many European companies hire Turkish managers to expedite their business contacts in Azerbaijan, as they seem to be better at managing unusual state–business practices in the country (11).

In general, Turkish businesspeople are said to bring more knowledge and experience than capital to Azerbaijan through two channels. First, the expertise and professional style of the Turkish managers enjoy such a high level of trust that most of the big Azerbaijani companies have preferred to employ Turkish CEOs or experts to run their businesses (5, 6). This trust is attributed to the high-quality management and organization skills that the Turkish businesspeople allegedly possess (11). Second, it is stated that the lack of qualified labour was among the major problems in Azerbaijan in the 1990s, and the Turkish businesspeople have helped overcome this problem by either bringing over a labour force from Turkey or enhancing their local labourers' expertise through effective training. As the Azerbaijanis have become qualified enough to meet the expectations of the Turkish and other foreign companies, they have begun to replace foreign workers of not only Turkish but also Indian, Pakistani and even Moroccan origin (7). Besides the Turkish businesspeoples' training merits, this change is attributed to the alleged capacity of Azerbaijanis to learn quickly (1). Consequently, as one interviewee mentioned, by the early 2010s, the majority of the labour force employed in Turkish factories in Azerbaijan was composed of locals (11).

Indeed, this latter tendency has been strengthened by state policies as well, given the limited capacity that Azerbaijan's oil-rich economy has displayed for job creation. The oil sector, while producing one third of the national GDP, creates only 1 percent of the jobs in Azerbaijan (Cornell 2011, 240). Hence, besides encouraging the development of non-oil sectors such as agriculture, tourism and services (information technologies and transportation in particular), the Azerbaijani state has been pressuring companies to use as much Azerbaijani labour as possible, rather than hiring people from other nationalities. This pressure has been primarily applied by introducing stricter migration regulations, which now require a minimum of 1,000 AZN per head for the extension of work visas; given that smaller companies can hardly afford this amount, they are prompted to search for local labourers to continue business in Azerbaijan (9). These measures seem to be successful in that the unemployment rate has been in steady decline in Azerbaijan, having dropped from 11 percent in 2001 to 5.3 percent in 2012, according to official statistics (World Bank 2012, 4).

Besides labourers from Turkey, small-scale Turkish companies, as well as Turkish artisans and craftsmen working in the Azerbaijani service sector have also been negatively affected by this tendency, such that interviewees with such affiliations draw a relatively pessimistic picture of their future in Azerbaijan. As they put it, it is impossible to employ a person for more than five years in the service sector, for, once they learn the job, they leave to establish their own businesses (2, 3). This group of Turkish businessmen are planning to move their wealth and investments to Turkey as soon as they manage to resolve various problems related to their property in Azerbaijan, including the acquisition of secure ownership of their shops to enable them to formally sell or transfer them at a later stage (2).

In contrast to this group, the owners or representatives of relatively big and well-established Turkish companies, operating mostly in the construction sector, tend to define the Azerbaijani market as rapidly developing, with more projects expected in future. According to them, Azerbaijan promises high profits, secure payment and the capability to move across the region due to the country's free trade agreements with Russia, Ukraine, Georgia, Moldova and Kazakhstan (6, 7, 9). High profit rates in Azerbaijan have possibly been among the most important motivations that have attracted many Turkish companies to the country since the 1990s. Profits are said to have been at their peak between 2005 and 2007, given high oil prices in the world and resultant huge revenues for the Azerbaijani state. Even though profit rates have declined since then, they are still considered to be very high compared with many other countries in the region (4, 7, 8). In an attempt to continue attracting experienced and institutionalised foreign companies to the country, the Azerbaijani state has been trying to ensure a market-friendly environment by simplifying business and investment regulations since 2008.[10] To appreciate the sheer scale of progress achieved to this effect, suffice it to mention that the process of establishing a company took at least six months ten years ago, while now the entire process is completed online within only three days (11).

Despite such formal improvements, however, there are still risks that big and institutionalised Turkish companies do not want to take in Azerbaijan. According to one interviewee, it was this latter group of risks that had caused Koç Holding to sell its big supermarket chain, Ramstore, to Azersun and consequently leave the Azerbaijani market. Similar considerations also allegedly prompted Sabancı Holding to refrain from realising its investment plans in the country. The discouraging stories of two Turkish companies – Barmek, an electric company whose owner was sentenced to five years in jail following its controversial financial engagement with the Azerbaijani authorities in 2007 (Radikal 2007), and DHT Metal, whose brand-new iron and steel factory was appropriated by the state immediately following its opening by the Turkish president Abdullah Gül during his official visit to Azerbaijan in August 2010 (Sabah 2010) – are cited as examples attesting to the validity of such negative perceptions of the investment climate in the country (1, 2).

It is this duality in the business climate – formal improvements in regulations on one hand and discretionary interventions therein by informal power structures on the other – that Turkish businesspeople, just like their foreign counterparts, have to come to terms with in Azerbaijan if they are to continue doing business there. Their persistent desire to stay in this market despite all the problems they face might be related to various economic as well as personal reasons, which this paper will not problematise. Instead, the next section will attempt to make sense of the experiences the Turkish businesspeople have had with what is commonly referred to as corruption in Azerbaijan and will critically engage with the question so as to identify some of the historically specific reasons that have led to the emergence of such practices in the country.

Understanding state–business relations in Azerbaijan through *hörmet*

> Rule of law is possible but not probable in Azerbaijan, for it does not ensure order and rule here.
>
> (9)

> Here your word is valuable like 'namus.'[11] If you keep your promises, you don't face much problem. Indeed, you solve your problems much easier than you would through law.
>
> (4)

These two quotations from the interviews imply that what is discussed as corruption in Azerbaijan by various international actors is far more complex a phenomenon than its conventional definition – the "use of public office for private gain" (Huther and Shah 2000, 1; Jain 2001, 73) – would have us believe. It can be argued that the emphasis put on "word" rather than "contract" in the second quotation above implies the regulatory importance of personal relations in contemporary Azerbaijan, also explaining why the "rule of law," a modern regulatory principle implying the existence of a public domain, does not ensure order and rule there. Indeed, the Azerbaijani expression of *hörmet* wrongly translated as "bribe" in English, has similar connotations. In its classical meaning, *hörmet* refers to a hierarchical power relation between master and subject, in which, by giving presents in different forms such as money or goods, the subject is meant to recognise the respectful authority of the master, and the master in return takes care of the subject's well-being. Consequently, rather than referring to a non-hierarchical monetary exchange for personal gain, as the conceptualisation of a bribe would imply, *hörmet* is a reflection of underlying power relations of a pre-modern kind. This is certainly not meant to suggest that the institution of *hörmet* in contemporary Azerbaijan is reproduced exactly in its pre-modern content. Rather, it is to suggest that we need to be careful in taking for granted the modern definition of corruption while trying to make sense of a society wherein the boundaries between the public and the private have not been drawn in a way that they have been in the idealised, if historically specific, Western model.[12]

This argument might help one understand why the majority of the Turkish businesspeople interviewed prefer to define what has been conventionally called corruption in Azerbaijan as a system of rule to which one should adjust rather than a problem one should tackle, and they attribute it to the specific way power is practiced in the country to ensure order and rule. For them, this is evident due to their observations that all the *hörmet* collected in Azerbaijan is well documented and controlled within the established political hierarchy and works as a system of collecting and pooling money for the reproduction of the "informal state" (5, 7). Its order-ensuring function is also reflected in the notion that "[i]f you accept it, you don't face much problem" (3).

Turkish businesspeople explain the logic behind the *hörmet* practice in Azerbaijan with reference to either monopolisation from an economic point of view or a family-dominated state structure in political terms, although the latter two phenomena are closely interrelated. They argue that all the major contracts are acquired by four or five families in Azerbaijan, which then distribute the tasks comprised by the contracts to various subcontractors. Consequently, it is impossible to talk about competition in Azerbaijan, for if you do not enjoy some high-level contacts, you can neither have peace in business nor win the tenders (1, 4). One of the interviewees noted that he had had to spend three years jumping from one sector to the other until he was finally employed by a big Azerbaijani company. His fate substantially changed thenceforth, for the new employment has provided him with some powerful high-level contacts (3). The monopolisation argument, in turn, points to the particular limits of "independent" profit-making in Azerbaijan. Some interviewees suggested, for example, that when one's business in one sector begins to make a profit, that sector's monopoly power comes and expropriates it. Thus, one needs to move to another sector if one is to continue business in Azerbaijan (3, 6). The latter means that businessmen in Azerbaijan can make only short-term plans and must always be prepared to leave when the time comes (5). The entire system is viewed by some as an attempt to keep economic and political power in specific hands in crude terms (2), or by others as a specific development model in which big business groups identified by specific families monopolise different sectors in a more sophisticated language (6).

An interesting aspect of the views of the Turkish businesspeople on the *hörmet* practice in Azerbaijan was their legitimisation of it from a clearly statist perspective – a stand which would be accepted as rather strange from a liberal point of view, given that for liberals state and market exist in an antagonistic relation to each other, and hence, businesspeople are assumed to be inherently anti-statist unless they have clear benefits to gain otherwise. To this end, they propose two different explanations. First, *hörmet* arguably helps the Azerbaijani state prevent companies from evading tax payment. It is argued that legally 22 percent of company *profits* have to be paid as income tax to the state, whereas informally 6 percent of the *revenue* is appropriated in cash, though this is said to be ultimately equal to the 22 percent of profits anyway (7). The advantage of this mechanism for the state is that companies do not enjoy the chance of reducing their profits on paper through various accounting tricks, for there is no bargaining in the informal *hörmet* system. This is also viewed as evidence that the Azerbaijani authorities are well aware of profit rates in different sectors and are capable of carefully monitoring the business activities of different companies. Given the high rates of profits available in the Azerbaijani market, it is a given that "if you earn, then you will pay" (5). And second, the *hörmet* system arguably works as a mechanism that wards off the intervention of international financial institutions and their control over the state budget. Hence, a big portion of the collected *hörmets* goes to such informal pools as the Heydar Aliyev Fund, which are out of reach of formal inspection and can use these funds towards the construction and funding of public infrastructure such as hospitals, schools, universities and parks as well as restoration works (1, 2, 10).

These apparently paradoxical statist legitimations proposed by the Turkish businesspeople in relation to the *hörmet* practice can be attributed to their internal and established relationship with the Azerbaijani state on one hand and their Turkic-nationalist stance against such "outsiders" as the IMF and the World Bank on the other, if not to the practical advantages they receive. Indeed, the interviews help also identify some concrete benefits that particularly small and medium-scale Turkish enterprises enjoy due to the *hörmet* practice in Azerbaijan. It is argued that formalisation means an increase in the number of documents to be collected and more complicated processes to be completed. Hence, increased bureaucratisation creates more difficulties for them, in contrast to the proven advantages of having face-to-face relations (4, 8). One interviewee complained sarcastically that in state institutions that are attempting to meet international standards at the expense of *hörmet* practices, everything becomes messy (9). Moreover, it is underlined that the availability of a cheap and informal labour force would disappear if the Western good governance requirements were fully met in Azerbaijan, in that these would lead to a significant loss of profit by eliminating the use of an unregistered labour force and hence increasing the relevant labour costs for the businesses (1, 4).

The preference of some of the Turkish businesspeople for face-to-face *hörmet* relations rather than professionalised ones based on the rule of law could be a function of their desire to keep on enjoying the advantages they have had as first-comers, closely linked to the commonality of cultural characteristics between Azerbaijan and Turkey. They clearly see that professionalisation would bring new and powerful competitors to the market that would ultimately leave no room for small companies, which still manage to survive today, if only by residual income, thus escaping the attention of Azerbaijani monopolists (8).

When looked at from the converse perspective, the international anti-corruption agenda linked to governance could be understood as an endeavour to turn all the world into a "home" for transnational corporations by eliminating transaction costs and problems emanating from societal and cultural differences by moulding common standards, rules and procedures abstracted from a combination of Western best practices, of which they have better knowledge than the locals. This is certainly not to suggest that transnational and institutionalised companies never engage in *hörmet* practices, for it is possible to assume that the oil sector in Azerbaijan, in which powerful Western oil multinationals have been enjoying high profits since signing the "Contract of the Century" in 1994 (Ergun 2003, 649), enjoys the largest capacity for *hörmet* creation. Although this latter question is beyond the scope of this study, interviews conducted with the representatives of well-established and relatively bigger Turkish companies suggest that *hörmet* collection might take different forms in bigger projects, like those in the construction or oil sector. In the latter sectors, the formal price offers are kept artificially high in tenders, so that the relevant Azerbaijani monopoly at the top acquires a particular flexibility to directly arrange the informal wealth redistribution activity without an overt *hörmet* exchange practice with the contractor (1, 7).[13] Hence, one could argue that the question of either eliminating or keeping *hörmet* relations in Azerbaijan is also a matter of broader competition among capitalist interests on different levels and with different capabilities, besides being a question of rule limited to the state only.

By way of conclusion: prospects for rule of law in Azerbaijan

Azerbaijan has been passing through a radical capitalist transformation since independence, with significant restructuring taking place in the political and economic spheres. As discussed in this chapter, Turkish businesspeople have been both close observers and directly affected subjects of this process, given their presence in the Azerbaijani market from the early 1990s onwards. This chapter has attempted to problematise changing state–business relations in Azerbaijan through the lens of business experiences, with a particular focus on the *hörmet* practice and with a view to drawing attention to some of the explanatory and ideological limitations of the anti-corruption discourse reproduced by international actors to make sense of such practices in the country. Indeed, similar critical investigations of post-Soviet transformation could be conducted by focusing on experiences acquired from various other subjective positions. The arguments of the Turkish businesspeople as to the experiences of the transformation of Azerbaijani labourers into qualified workers during the country's post-Soviet transition could well serve as yet another angle from which to study these processes. It is possible to identify the reproduction of a similar "technicised" language in the relevant studies in economics, which persistently emphasise "the task of increasing labour productivity" in Azerbaijan and in other post-Soviet countries (Aliyev 2009, 131). Given the fact that Azerbaijani society in Soviet times comprised a well-educated population, the notion of increasing the qualifications or productivity of labour possibly refers in this context to a substantial social restructuring within the Azerbaijani labour force, whereby – given the changes in technology, standards and work practices following the collapse of the Soviet system – some well-educated representatives of labour grew redundant, while the young generation have to be trained anew in line with the specific requirements of the emergent capitalist market.

The capitalist transformation in Azerbaijan, as well as in other post-Soviet states, has been taking place in the name of "transition towards the market economy" and "democratisation," targets which have become general mottos domestically and internationally, although the question of where this whole process really leads is controversial. This is a process with many of its contingencies – those emanating from its political and class-driven character – continuously subjected to manipulation from different power positions, and what is presently reproduced as the mainstream governance and transparency discourse is nothing but a reflection of one such position. The Council of Europe, in which Azerbaijan acquired membership in 2001,[14] the European Union through its partnership and neighbourhood policies since 2004, the OECD through its Anti-Corruption Network for Transition Economies (OECD 2005, 3) and NATO through its Partnership for Peace[15] emerge as important multilateral institutions that have been creating different forms of joint action programs, financial and technical incentives, directives and limitations, to ensure Azerbaijan's practical and ideological commitment to the principles of governance and transparency. The issue of corruption in Azerbaijan, which assumes a core position in the discourse advanced by the Turkish businesspeople interviewed as part of this study, also forms the cornerstone of the multilateral initiatives these international institutions launched in the name of governance and transparency, where anti-corruption has ultimately been associated with a wholesale transformation of the Azerbaijani state structure.[16] This is indeed a confirmation of the soundness of the views of the Turkish businesspeople arguing that *hörmet* in Azerbaijan denotes a political system rather than a simple corrupt exchange exercised for personal gain only.

If what is defined as corruption in Azerbaijan is indeed a socio-political system that ensures the loyalty of the people from the lower strata of society to the top through a feudal-like chain, then what are the prospects for the establishment of order in Azerbaijan through transparency and the rule of law? Addressing this question is certainly beyond the scope and limits of this conclusion, although the discussion above can be revised in relation to it.[17] Thus, on one hand, one could argue that legitimating discourses developed on issues like corruption will have a decisive impact on the multi-scale political struggles through which the conditions of rule of law are likely to be ultimately determined in Azerbaijan. On the other hand, given the fact that competing conceptions of corruption and hence anti-corruption have been produced mainly by powerful capitalist and statist interests on different levels and in various forms, the prospects for the "ruling" law to appeal to the labour classes in Azerbaijan are rather low, for when elephants fight, it is ultimately the grass that suffers.

Appendix

Interview details

1. Owner of a construction company, 2 August 2011
2. Owner of a company in the service sector, 3 August 2011
3. Owner of a marketing company, 10 August 2011
4. Owner of a textile company, 11 August 2011
5. Owner of an advertising agency, 13 August 2011
6. Representative of a bank, 15 August 2011
7. Representative of an electrical engineering company, 15 August 2011
8. Owner of a tourism company, 16 August 2011
9. Representative of a construction company, 17 August 2011
10. Owner of a construction company, 23 August 2011
11. ATIB representative, 4 August 2011
12. TUSIAB representative, 11 August 2011

Notes

1 Interview with the representative of the Turkish Trade Consulate in Baku on 6 March 2013. It was stated that not all of these companies are thought to be active. Actively operating companies are assumed to be around 700.
2 TUSIAB, established in 1994, sees its mission as facilitating cooperation among Turkish businessmen in Azerbaijan and providing them with information and legal assistance to strengthen their businesses. It is defined as independent from all political and ideological interests (12), though an overview of the TUSIAB publication *Diyalog* shows that the organisation promotes an Islamic-Turkic identity as an important defining feature of Turkish businessmen.
3 ATIB, established in 2004, has a defined mission to improve Azerbaijan's economic, social and cultural relations with other countries, although the priority is given to Azerbaijan–Turkey relations. In comparison with TUSIAB, ATIB aims to engage in high-level diplomatic contacts and projects to promote some key issues dominating the foreign policy agendas of the two states, among which the Armenian question seems to come first (11). That is, unlike TUSIAB, with its Islamic bent, ATIB seems to exhibit a rather nationalist stand, even though its members – likely driven by a desire to distance themselves from the pan-Turkists who had supported Rovshan Javadov's failed coup against Heydar Aliyev in October 1994 (Cornell 2011, 85) – prefer to define the organisation's identity as "Ataturkist and statist," rather than nationalist.
4 This echoes the results of Sian Lazar's anthropological study on Bolivia, based on which Cris Shore and Dieter Haller (2005, 6) noted that "people [in Bolivia] just talked about corruption non-stop: corruption was how they made sense of politics and state" everywhere, including parts of Europe.
5 Prominent Turkish economist Korkut Boratav defined corruption as such in his keynote speech to the conference "'Acts of Resistance' against Globalisation from the South," organised by the Turkish Social Sciences Association, 5–7 September 2005, in Ankara, Turkey.
6 A score of 10 indicates the best country performance in terms of transparency. See www.transparency.org.
7 The term "international community" has specific ideological connotations, as it presumes the existence of a common culture shared by various international, national, local and transnational actors, the main tenets of which are the free market economy and liberal democracy.
8 See Bedirhanoglu (2007) for a comprehensive discussion.
9 For a detailed analysis of how Heydar Aliyev succeeded in ensuring political stability in Azerbaijan, see Altstadt (2003).
10 See www.doingbusiness.org/reforms/overview/topic/starting-a-business.
11 *Namus* in Turkish can best be explained as honour with a patriarchal content.
12 Derluguian (2003, 1001–1002) explains how this pre-modern institution was reproduced during Soviet times within the local administrative structure in Azerbaijan. It would be interesting to extend this research by questioning how the *hörmet* institution has been reproduced since independence throughout the capitalist transformation process in Azerbaijan.
13 For a more positive role attributed to the BP oil company in enhancing transparency in Azerbaijan, see Gulbrandsen and Moe (2007).
14 See the Council of Europe's (2012) recent overview of political developments in Azerbaijan. The report identifies the current conditions of human rights as alarming in relation to basic freedoms of speech, expression and the press, as well as of the judiciary.
15 Cornell (2011, 423) underlines that even though generally underestimated, NATO fulfills a crucial role in pursuing the governance agenda in Azerbaijan through its Individual Partnership Action Plans tailored specifically for each partner country.

16 A quick look at the reports published under the title of governance and anti-corruption in Azerbaijan would easily display the wide scope of political reforms promoted. Transparency International (2011) and Martini (2012), for instance, provide good overviews for one to see how the European Neighbourhood Policy links the issue of corruption to state restructuring in Azerbaijan and promotes specific programs to this end.
17 Apart from research conducted by relevant international institutions, there are some independent academic studies that attempt to address this question from a critical point of view. See Ergun (2003) and Rasizade (2004), for two examples.

References

Aliyev, Shafa. 2009. The Issues of Employment and Importance of the Effective Use of the Manpower in Azerbaijan in Conditions of the World Financial Crisis. *International Journal of Academic Research* 1:1, 129–135.

Altstadt, Audrey L. 2003. Azerbaijan and Aliyev: A Long History and an Uncertain Future. *Problems of Post-Communism* 50:5, 3–13.

Bedirhanoğlu, Pınar. 2007. The Neoliberal Discourse on Corruption as a Means of Consent-Building: Reflections from Post-Crisis Turkey. *Third World Quarterly* 28:7, Oct., 1239–1254.

Cornell, Svante E. 2011. *Azerbaijan since Independence*. Armonk, NY: M.E. Sharpe.

Council of Europe. 2012. *The Honouring of Obligations and Commitments by Azerbaijan*. Doc. No. 13084, prepared by the Parliamentary Assembly, 20 Dec.

Derluguian, Georgi. 2003. How Soviet Bureaucracy Produced Nationalism, and What Came of It in Azerbaijan. In: Leo Panitch and Colin Leys, eds. *Socialist Register 2003: Fighting Identities*, 93–113. Winnipeg: Fernwood Publishing.

Ergun, Ayça. 2003. International Challenges and Domestic Preferences in the Post-Soviet Political Transition of Azerbaijan. *Perspectives on Global Development and Technology* 2:3–4, 635–657.

Gulbrandsen, Lars H. and Arild Moe. 2007. BP in Azerbaijan: A Test Case of the Potential and Limits of the CSR Agenda? *Third World Quarterly* 28:4, 813–830.

Huther, Jeff and Anwar Shah. 2000. *Anti-corruption Policies and Programs: A Framework for Evaluation*. http://econ.worldbank.org/files/1311_wps2501.pdf.

Jain, Arvind K. 2001. Corruption: A Review. *Journal of Economic Surveys* 15:1, 102–103.

Martini, Maira. 2012. *European Union Strategies to Support Anti-Corruption Measures in Neighbouring Countries*. U4 Anti-Corruption Resource Centre, Transparency International. www.transparency.org/files/content/corruptionqas/345_EU_strategies_to_support_AC_measures_in_neighbouring_countries.pdf.

OECD. 2005. *Azerbaijan, Fighting Corruption in Transition Economies*. Paris: OECD Publishing.

Radikal. 2007. Azerbaycandan Barmekin Patronuna Beş Yıl Hapis. (In Turkish.) 25 Sep.

Rasizade, Alec. 2004. Azerbaijan Descending into the Third World after a Decade of Independence. *Journal of Third World Studies* XXI:1, 191–219.

Sabah. 2010. Cumhurbaşkanı Gül, Azerbaycanda. (In Turkish.) 17 Aug.

Shore, Cris and Dieter Haller. 2005. Introduction – Sharp Practice: Anthropology and the Study of Corruption. In: Dieter Haller and Cris Shore, eds. *Corruption: Anthropological Perspectives*, 1–26. London: Pluto Press.

Transparency International. 2011. *European Neighbourhood Policy: Monitoring Azerbaijan's Anti-Corruption Commitments in 2010*. Baku. http:www.transparency.org/files/content/pressrelease/20110504_enp_azerbaijan.pdf.

———. 2012. *Azerbaijan: Out of Tune?* www.transparency.org/news/feature/azerbaijan_out_of_tune.

The World Bank. 2010. *Country Partnership Strategy for Azerbaijan for the Period FY 11–14*. International Bank for Reconstruction and Development, International Development Association and International Finance Corporation, Report No. 56246, 15 Sep.

———. 2012. *Azerbaijan Partnership Programme Snapshot*. www.worldbank.org/content/dam/Worldbank/document/Azerbaijan. Snapshot.pdf.

7 Turkey and Azerbaijan
One religion – two states?

Sofie Bedford

As a result of Soviet anti-religious campaigns, the Azerbaijani Moslems were at the time of independence to a large extent not very knowledgeable about their Islamic faith. Because of this, foreign religious influences played an important part in the country's post-Soviet religious revival. Due to its predominantly Moslem demography and geographic location, missionaries from neighbouring Iran and Turkey, as well as some of the Gulf countries, arrived in the country en masse in the early days of the 1990s. This foreign religious influence and new approaches to religion increasingly became seen as something that could harm the unique nature of "Azerbaijani Islam" that was perceived as distinctively intra- and interreligiously tolerant, non-aggressive and apolitical. While the authorities portrayed brands of Islam from North Caucasus, Iran and Saudi Arabia as dangerous, the work of Turkish Islamic groups for a long time was seen as less threatening and, as such, faced fewer restrictions. Considering that Turkish groups in general are advocates of the Sunni branch of Islam, while the majority of the Azerbaijani Moslems traditionally adhere to the Twelver Shia School, this appears counterintuitive.

This chapter is set to provide a more thorough understanding of what made "Turkish Islam" the preferred choice for the political leaders of independent Azerbaijan as well as highlight and attempt to explain the fact that this amicable reception of Turkish religious representatives seems gradually to be coming to an end. It is argued that even though the religious aspect has never been the most significant in Turkish-Azerbaijani relations, the dynamics within the religious terrain underlying the interaction between the two states can be viewed as a function of the "politicization" of the issue. Put differently, because the embrace of Turkish Islam on the elite level came as a political decision, transformation of and change in the political parameters underlying bilateral relations – both intra-state parameters *within* Turkey and Azerbaijan respectively and, to some extent, the nature of political dynamics *between* the two states – prompted change in the official status of Turkish Islam in Azerbaijan.

The first section of this chapter contextualises Islam in Azerbaijan within various historical epochs to highlight the processes by which the notion of a "unique Azerbaijani Islam" developed. The second section discusses the Turkish input into Azerbaijan's post-independence religious revival and how its success was facilitated by a high degree of religious-political convergence between the two states, much related to the political idea of a local lenient version of religion that needed protection. The third – and final – section examines the reasons behind the weakened position of the agents of Turkish Islam in Azerbaijan.[1]

Historical context as a key determinant in Azerbaijan's embrace of Turkish Islam

Sunni–Shia pragmatism in historical perspective

The religious setting in Azerbaijan is often described as rather particular in the respect that it is one of only four countries in the world with a Shia majority. The reality of this situation, however, is less black and white. The Shia majority has never been overwhelming. According to most estimates, about 65 percent of the population are assumed to be Shia and 35 percent Sunnis (e.g. Yunusov 2004). To be sure, these are "traditional" proportions, and it appears that the share of Sunnis has gradually increased over the last ten to fifteen years. One recent publication, for example, suggests a 45–55 percent ratio (Balci and Goyushov 2013). Most sociological surveys to this end are over ten years old and, as Wiktor-Mach (2012) notes, while drawing an interesting picture, fail to provide steadfast figures. In these surveys, about 10 percent of all believers (of all faiths) acknowledged they were Sunnis and about 30 percent Shia. The rest, excluding members of other religions, said they were "Moslems" (Wiktor-Mach 2012). This outcome may point to the lack of knowledge about the specificities of Islam among Azerbaijanis for whom being Moslem has evolved to be part of national identity, rather than associated with a belief system. It also reflects a desire to avoid the issue, which in the Azerbaijani context comes across as very controversial.

A historical outlook also shows the relationship between the two branches as a dynamic process where ideological differences over time grew increasingly less volatile. Consequently, in Azerbaijan of the 1990s, relations that the two strands of Islam enjoyed were rather pragmatic, a reality that could explain the amicable reception of proponents of Turkish Islam. Still, as I discuss below, it is also true that in recent years the dynamics between Sunnis and Shias among the newly emerged young practicing Moslems has significantly changed.

Indeed, Azerbaijan has since the late fourteenth century been a scene of prevailing competition between Sunni and Shia ruling empires. The process of Islamisation in the region began when the area was incorporated into the Islamic Caliphate in the mid-seventh century. This was not an easy process, and it took almost two hundred years for Islam to become the dominant religion (Balci and Goyushov 2013). At that point, Sunni Islam in its Hanafi and Shafii versions was prevalent and it was only later, under the rule of the Turkic Qara Qoyunlu (1380–1468) and Safavi (1501–1732) dynasties, that Twelver Shi'ism gradually became the leading religious branch of Islam in Azerbaijan (Aliyeva 2013a; Balci and Goyushov 2013; Sattarov 2009). Still, until the 1860s, the number of Sunni and Shia followers was almost even in the area (Swietochowski 1995).

Divergent religious affiliations have traditionally followed a geographical logic, such that Sunni Islam is dominant among Lazgis and Avars in the country's north and west, which border the Russian Caucasus, while the central, eastern and southern parts (bordering Iran), as well as Baku and the Absheron peninsula, are traditionally home to Shia communities (Abbasov 2001).

Some research points to a special type of overlapping relationship that followers of the two branches of Islam in Azerbaijan developed as a result of their long coexistence and interaction. Abbasov (2001) notes that "for all their fighting against each other while supporting Iran and Turkey respectively in the constantly ongoing wars on the territory of the Caucasus, Shias and Sunnis also managed to live peacefully side by side. In Azerbaijan, an original Moslem tradition developed Shia-Sunni 'ecumenism.'" Along these lines, Goyushov and Askerov (2010) write that "many Sunnis shared Shi[a] traditions and made pilgrimages to the holy places of the Shi[as]. Some of the Azerbaijani Sunnis proudly bear Shi[a] titles as *mashhadi* and *karbala'i*" (195). The blurred division between Sunnis and Shias was strengthened throughout the course of history. As is illustrated below, the idea of tolerance between these two groups as something characterising the uniqueness of Islam in the Azerbaijani context was first established by Azerbaijani intellectuals in the Russian empire, then further reinforced as a result of Soviet religious policies and finally inherited by the political leaders of independent Azerbaijan. Hence, it is in the light of the religious landscape being dominated by this rather specific nonsectarian mainstream narrative that the success of the Turkish religious representatives arriving in post-Soviet Azerbaijan should be understood.

Turkicisation, Islam and Europeanisation

After the incorporation of the area into the Russian empire in the early nineteenth century, the Russian rulers initially tried to use the split between Shias and Sunnis to consolidate their power. In conflicts with the Ottoman empire, the Russians insisted that Shias should side with them against the Turkish and North Caucasus Sunnis (Strømmen 1999). As Russian rule gradually grew established in the region and as attempts to convert the Moslem territories to Christianity were largely unsuccessful, the Russian rulers focused on creating a "loyal empire and an Islam that was under their control" (Abbasov 2001, 284). To achieve this, "a system of religious administration for Moslems" was created, through which Moslem spiritual leaders became incorporated into Russian governmental structures. On assuming their duties, higher-ranking Moslem officials had to swear an oath of loyalty to the emperor and, as a reward, were given certain privileges, similar to those of Russian nobility (Campbell 2006). In 1872, two so-called religious directorates were set up, one for Sunnis and one for Shias, the latter with responsibility for the Transcaucasus. This Russian bureaucratisation of the religious leadership gradually isolated both the Sunni and Shia Moslems of Azerbaijan from the rest of the Islamic world (Aliyeva 2013b). It was difficult for the Tsarists to find religious leaders that were obedient and trustworthy as well as skilled. As a result, the knowledge level of the clergy fell and the "provincialism of Azerbaijani Islam increased." According to Abbasov (2001), "the tsarist government was able to realise their goals and create a layer of obedient clergy that did not enjoy sufficient authority among the people, that was not capable of achieving consolidation or play any active role in the anti-colonial struggle" (285).

At the same time, the arrival of the Russian empire brought modern intellectual trends and unleashed a secularisation process in the region (Balci 2004). This paved the way for the development of the so-called Azerbaijani intelligentsia that, influenced by European nationalist movements, promoted a nationalism that did include Islam but merely as a cultural marker (Balci and Goyushov 2013). The efforts of the intelligentsia were consolidated in the Musavat (Equality) Party founded in 1911; and the high point of the nation-building process was the proclamation of the first parliamentary democracy in the Moslem world in 1918 – the short-lived Democratic Republic of Azerbaijan. The ideological basis behind the politics of the Musavat Party – Turkicisation (Nationalisation), Islam and Europeanisation – was, Alieva (2013) writes, "a unique attempt to synthesize the three cultural components of identity and political life of Azerbaijanis, which previously seemed incompatible" (108). Under the banner of modernism and secularism, the new government banned *sharia* courts (Goyushov and Askerov 2010). Their goal was to create a united, integrated, and educated Azerbaijani nation (Swietochowski 1995). As part of the integration process and an attempt to secure religious unity, much effort went into lessening the split between the Shias and the Sunnis. In 1918, for example, the Administration of Moslems of the Caucasus was moved from Tbilisi to Baku and transformed into one single unit headed by two chairmen – one Sunni and one Shia (Alieva and Ayyub 2010; Yunusov 2004).

The secular independent republic lasted only two years before it was overthrown by the Bolsheviks in 1920, but it left behind an important legacy in both the political and religious spheres. During Soviet times, the narrative of Islam by the pre-Soviet Azerbaijani intellectuals as only a cultural component of national identity was strengthened as this approach in many ways fit the Soviet policy towards religion squarely well. At the same time, a notion that if not controlled, Islam could turn out to be potentially explosive for the political status quo took root among the political leadership. As we will see later, both of these perceptions have strongly influenced the attitudes and policies towards religion in post-Soviet Azerbaijan.

Soviet anti-religious policy and the stagnation of Islam

Soviet officials disliked religion for two major reasons. First, religious tradition was seen as representing something backward, a reminder of the rural pre-modern state that the Moslem republics were supposed to have left behind when they became part of the Soviet Union (Omel'chenko and Sabirova 2003). Second and perhaps even more importantly, they feared the mobilising potential of religion as a likely competitor to official Soviet ideology. In order to prevent dangerous supranational ideas (such as pan-Turkism, pan-Persianism and pan-Islamism) from spreading and potentially contributing to shattering the USSR, official rhetoric asserted that it was necessary to "resolve the religious question" (Filimonov 1983, 6). Nevertheless, the Soviet policy towards Islam was ambivalent and hesitant; and, while assertive in some periods, it was very lax in others.

It is difficult to say exactly how successful or unsuccessful the Soviet antireligious campaign really was. Some effects were directly visible, such as that concerning the traditional female head covering, which, save for a few exceptions, was totally abolished. Others were harder to spot, but still noticeable, such as the undermining of religious institutions and weakening of the *ulama*. In 1944, four Moslem Spiritual Boards (*Dukhovnoye Upravlenye Musulman*), also referred to as *muftiat*, were established as official Moslem power structures consisting of religious leaders (muftis) willing to support Soviet policies and serve as mediators between the Moslem population and the authorities (an idea based on the Moslem Administrations in the Russian empire referred to above) (Polonskaya and Malashenko 1994). They were not well received by the population, who saw these religious leaders as part of the Soviet leadership. Given that only a small number of students were allowed to finish their religious education abroad in the so-called officially friendly states, such as Egypt, Libya, Syria, Jordan, Saudi Arabia and Turkey, the religious knowledge of the so-called religious leaders was also in many cases lacking. Shia-dominated Iran was not on the list of accepted countries, which is why the present head of the Azerbaijani Moslem Board (who has held this position since 1980) has never studied abroad (Roy 2000). To a large extent, many people became totally illiterate in terms of knowledge of religious rites and Islam in general. At the two official Islamic institutes in the Soviet Union, the Mir-i-Arab madrasa in Bukhara and the Imam Ismail Al-Bukhari institute in Tashkent, the handing down of knowledge was largely oral, which often resulted in a loss of the original meaning of various features. Moreover, Islam became synonymous with customs rather than textual interpretations. This, Khalid (2007) writes, contributed to a stagnation of Islam in the Soviet period. Most Azerbaijanis did not even know a single *sura* from the Qur'an, did not perform *namaz* and did not fast during Ramadan (Goyushov and Askerov 2010).

Among other interesting implications of the Soviet anti-Islam policy in Azerbaijan was that, as it did not differentiate between Sunnis and Shias, it further contributed to the smoothening out of differences between the two doctrines (Balci 2004). Repression forced Shia and Sunni religious leaders to put their differences aside. According to Balci and Goyushov (2013), "across the whole of Azerbaijan, Sunni preachers appealed to their followers to actively support Shias during yearly Muharram commemorations and Shia mosques banned anti-Sunnite sermons offending the first three caliphs, which previously had been common in local Shi[a] practice."[2] Altogether, as noted by Goyushov (2008), as an outcome of the pre-Soviet efforts by the Azerbaijani intelligentsia on one hand and the lack of religious education and repression during Soviet times on the other, "mainstream Azeris until recently had little connection to the age-old Sunni-Shi[a] rivalry, and viewed the simple public pronunciation of the words 'Shi[a]' and 'Sunni' at least as impolite." In the promotion of a "unique Azerbaijani Islam," the fact that tolerance always existed between the two groups is a key notion. Hence, many mosques in the country still claim to cater to the needs of both groups. According to Abbasov (2001, 283), "as a rule, the mosques of North Azerbaijan are not divided on religious trends, serving both Shi[a] and Sunni, the same Mullah can serve both sides" (also see Dragadze 1994).[3]

Yet another outcome of policies during Soviet times was a strengthening of the Azerbaijani "Moslem identity" that was founded in the pre-Bolshevik era. To minimise the threat from competing supranationalities, Stalin promoted the idea of a titular nationality (*nazhionalnost'*), defined as an ethnic community with a separate language, cultural customs and traditions, all of which had to have a corresponding national political entity (Roy 2000). To facilitate this, customs and traditions played an important role. To a large extent, Islam was able to preserve itself in terms of traditions and customs as it came to be understood as an inseparable part of the cultural heritage of certain nations. Many of the traditions that did live on during the Soviet period lost their original content as knowledge about their source waned. As a result, when the Soviet Union fell, many of those Azerbaijanis who self-identified as Moslem saw Islam as only a signifier of their ethnic or national identity and had no real understanding of conceptual differences between the Shia and Sunni branches, which helped to positively reinforce what became the official "tolerance narrative" in post-Soviet Azerbaijan. Aliyeva (2013b) summarises this narrative very well when she describes the Azerbaijani Islam that was the outcome of these historical turns as "vernacular." It represents, she writes, "a genuine and devout faith of the population . . . a mix of indigenous culture with the authentic teachings of Islam" and "a non-political and non-aggressive form of Islam [that] has the ability to adapt to secular society" (145). Her description also highlights another characteristic of this narrative that became the backbone of independent Azerbaijan's policy towards religion – the perception that this vernacular is vulnerable to threats from abroad. "As a result of various factors," she writes, "vernacular Islam is going through the process of being crushed" (145). However, as will be illustrated below, given the many common cultural and political denominators between Turkey and Azerbaijan, the Turkish religious influence was not seen as threatening by Azerbaijani political elites. Hence, instead of being neutralised, the activities of Turkish religious representatives were facilitated and even promoted by the authorities as a counterbalance to other foreign actors whose presence in society was not appreciated.

Azerbaijan's religious revival and an embrace of Turkish Islam

An externally conditioned religious revival

During *perestroika* and following independence, Azerbaijan experienced something that has often been described as a religious "boom" as religion reemerged on the public scene. The few mosques that existed in Soviet times suddenly turned into thousands, other places of worship were restored, many religious organisations registered and the opportunity to study religion in the country as well as to travel to religious universities abroad was established. A more accurate description of these developments, however, is probably that Azerbaijani society was returning to a normal level of religiosity compared with the unnatural condition during Soviet rule (Cornell 2006). The fall of communism prompted a search for identity in which religion played a natural role. Many started praying, fasting, making the Hajj pilgrimage and attending mosques, because they could and because they wanted to reconnect with values and roots perceived as lost. One problem was that due to the marginalisation of Islamic leaders and lack of qualitative religious education during Soviet times, national preachers and clerics could not satisfy the Azerbaijani public's need for Islamic knowledge. The highest Moslem authority, the Caucasus Moslem Board, the direct successor of the Stalinist Muslim Board of Transcaucasus, was (and still is) suffering from a notoriously bad reputation. Many, believers and non-believers alike, are especially skeptical towards the head of the Board, Sheikh-ül-Islam Hajji Allahshukur Pashazade, elected to this position while the Board was still under Soviet control. Not only does Sheikh-ül-Islam not actually belong to the official Shia hierarchy or possess an appropriate religious title, his organisation is also haunted by a rumor of having been spies during communist times, an accusation which has resulted in a loss of respect from the general public (Kotecha 2006).

The Moslem Board promoted the existence of a "special national Azerbaijani brand of Islam" that was non-political and non-radical as well as featuring a unique peaceful coexistence between Shias and Sunnis (Motika 2001). The bad reputation of the Board notwithstanding, this inkling was in general positively received and has over the years turned into the backbone of the government's religious policy. Well-known national orientalists did initially play a role in the religious revival process, translating the Qur'an and other major religious texts into Azerbaijani and providing general education on religious themes, but on the whole foreign influences were much more influential and noticeable (Goyushov 2008). In its initial stages, the foreign input was very openly provided, including very hands-on help to restore religious life in the country by establishing, and sometimes even constructing, a great number of mosques and madrasas as well as disseminating religious knowledge through literature, teaching and preaching. Among foreign agents of Islam in Azerbaijan, Iranians, various representatives of the Arab world and Turks proved the most active.

Among the Iranians who actively engaged in the religious revival in Azerbaijan, some were actively promoting Khomeinism (the official religious ideology of the Islamic Republic of Iran), others were pursuing independent religious agendas. Both groups concentrated their activities mainly within the southern regions of Azerbaijan bordering Iran; the Nakhchivan Autonomous Republic bordering Iran; and several villages on the Absheron peninsula where Shia Islam has traditionally been influential. Iranian preachers and organisations established more than 150 madrasas in different parts of the country (Cornell 2006; Goyushov 2008).

In the mid-1990s, following the Karabakh war, a number of humanitarian organisations from Saudi Arabia and Kuwait arrived in Azerbaijan bringing food and medical aid for refugees and internally displaced people. They also provided religious education, imams and infrastructure. The Kuwaiti Society for the Revival of Islamic Heritage, for example, financed the construction of what became the center of Salafism in Azerbaijan, the Abu Bakr mosque, and renovated sixty-two other mosques in Azerbaijan (International Crisis Group 2008). Salafism, guided by a purist, orthodox, ultra-conservative view of Sunni Islam, became popular in the traditionally Sunni northern parts of Azerbaijan and in big cities, such as Baku and Sumgait (Goyushov 2008).

Key agents of Turkish Islam in post-Soviet Azerbaijan

The third group of foreign influences came from Turkey. Turkish religious assistance was provided through two main channels. The first was governmental, with Turkey's Ministry of Religious Affairs (*Diyanet Isleri Baskanligi*, generally referred to as the Diyanet) as the leading actor. The Diyanet had already had a history of providing religious services to Turkish expatriates across Europe through Turkish embassies and consulates abroad, and in 1992 they – in collaboration with the Azerbaijani Ministry of Education – helped establish the Department of Religion at Baku State University, modeled on the faculty of theology at Turkey's University of Marmara, and a secondary school associated with it. The Diyanet, moreover, financed the construction of eight mosques across the country (three in Baku and one each in Gusar, Agdash, Nakhchivan, Yevlakh and Mehtiabad), as well as provided hundreds of Azerbaijani students grants to study theology in Turkey and train to serve as Islamic leaders at home upon return (Balci 2004). The distribution of Islam-related literature printed in Turkey and translated into Azerbaijani was yet another way of Turkish religious support. The center for the pro-Turkish religious communities became the Shahidlar mosque (the Martyr's Mosque) and the Ilahiyat mosque attached to Baku State University's Department of Religion. In these mosques, prayers were conducted by Turkish religious facilitators and, in the case of the Shahidlar mosque, by the Diyanet representative (Goyushov and Askerov 2010). On special occasions, such as for Ramadan, imams from Turkey arrived to conduct prayer in cooperation with local religious leaders. For a long time, the Diyanet supervised the operation of both the Department of Religion and the Turkish mosques in coordination with the Azerbaijan State Committee for Work with Religious Organisations, but gradually both the supervision and operation has been solemnly taken over by the Azerbaijani state.

In parallel to the state-sponsored activities, some Turkish non-governmental organisations have, directly and indirectly, been active in the religious sphere of Azerbaijan – noticeably various groups inspired by the religious figure of Said Nursi (1870–1960), founder of the most powerful text-based faith movement in Turkey (Yavuz 1999). One group of non-governmental actors was represented by the "Nurcu classicists," whose goal is to spread the modern revivalist Islamic ideas of Nursi through the study of his core work, *Risale-i Nur* (The Epistle of Light), an exegesis of the Qur'an that "explores Islamic spirituality" (Balci 2013, 71). The Nurcu classicists do not see themselves as part of any clearly defined official religious movement. They seek to raise religious consciousness through education and reason and, as in Turkey, organised their education activity in Azerbaijan in reading circles known as *dershane* and based on discussion of *Risale-i Nur*. These circles are organised by Turkish expatriates, including businessmen and students, in the framework of private and informal networks (Aliyev 2012). In Turkey, the Nurcus have institutionalised themselves by buying homes or apartment floors, which they use as a venue to assemble for reading and discussing Nursi's writings, as well as a dormitory for university students (Yavuz 1999).

Some Naqshbandi Sufi orders were also among the Turkish religious representatives in Azerbaijan, notably those of the religious leaders Osman Nuri Topbaş and Suleyman Tunahan (Balci 2014). As a matter of fact, one of the only Turkish organisations with an openly religious profile was the Azerbaijani Youth Aid Foundation, created by the former. This foundation has been assisting Nagorno-Karabakh internally displaced persons and contributed to the construction of the Zakatala branch of Baku Islamic University and Mosque (International Crisis Group 2008). This group has also been organising English, computing and Quranic reading courses, provided by teachers, increasingly Azerbaijanis, who graduated from studies in Turkey (Balci 2013).

However, first to arrive and, according to some, the most influential Turkish group in Azerbaijan was represented by the followers of Fethullah Gülen, also known as the Hizmet movement. This group is headed by a contemporary spiritual leader, Fethullah Gülen. While in both the public and official narrative in Azerbaijan the terms *nurcular* and *fethullahci* are often used interchangeably, it is important to distinguish between these two groups. Even though Fethullah Gülen is inspired by the teachings of Said Nursi and has been called "Nursi's most influential disciple," he has distanced himself and his movement from the classical Nursi teachings. His movement has been called "neo-Nurcu" and is mostly known as a faith-based international educational network that has been highly influential in Turkey but is very active in the wider Turkic world as well. However, as Yavuz (1999) notes, "despite claims of a central organization and a strict hierarchy, [the different branches of the movement] are rather loose networks of like-minded Turks, whose similar ideas are a result of their internalization of the writings of Said Nursi" (598). Just as in most other countries where it operates, the Gülen movement in Azerbaijan was particularly active in the fields of media, trade and education. Through intimate cooperation with different Turkish businesses in the region, representatives of this movement have been running high schools and other secular education centers in the country since 1992 when they first arrived in Nakhchivan, Azerbaijan's non-contiguous autonomous republic. The schools and university preparatory courses were run under the umbrella of a company called Cag Ogretim, and according to some estimates, in 2013 the movement ran twelve high schools, one university (Qafqaz University) and at least thirteen *Araz* courses (courses for the preparation of students for university accession exams) in Azerbaijan (Balci 2013).

What differentiated the activities of the Gülen movement from other foreign religious movements that arrived in Azerbaijan after independence, including the

Nurcu classicists, is that its representatives did not openly promote religious ideas. All educational programs were completely secular. Voluntary religious courses, which had originally been available, were removed (on the request of the Azerbaijani government). This notwithstanding, many were of the opinion that the movement was nonetheless quietly spreading a Turkish brand of Sunni Islam through the educational system, as well as via newspapers and TV and radio stations that they operated in Azerbaijan. According to some, the religious message is never overt but systematically implied in the model of social moral behavior displayed and promoted by teachers, tutors and administrative staff. Moreover, despite the fact that the religious literature was not used at the schools, it was easily available in bookshops and in the stands around certain mosques (Balci 2004).

Turkey as the preferred choice

The foreign influences on the religious revival soon became seen as threatening by the government in independent Azerbaijan, which started a process of regaining control over religious life. As an attempt to curb the activities of foreign missionaries, the parliament adopted an amendment to the Law of the Republic of Azerbaijan on Freedom of Religious Belief in 1996 banning the activities of "foreigners and persons without citizenship" from conducting "religious propaganda." Moreover, relations that were subordinating Azerbaijanis to foreign Moslem religious organisations were prohibited, which meant that all Muslim groups had to submit to the spiritual authority of the Caucasus Moslem Board. The newly established State Committee for Work with Religious Organisations was put in charge of providing official registration for religious communities, supervising religious education and scrutinising imported religious literature with the underlying purpose of preventing "foreign" Islam from spreading to Azerbaijan. The idea of protecting a unique national Azerbaijani Islam from foreign radical religious influence was at the heart of this new policy direction.

Much of the crackdown on foreign influences targeted the Khomeini Iranian missionaries. Numerous Iranian madrasas were closed in the surroundings of Baku and in the south, and many Iranian imams were forced to leave the country. According to the prevailing narrative, the unique religious traditions in Azerbaijan are softer than in Iran and, because of this, the country is very sensitive about the influx of aggressive Iranian revolutionaries. It also seems that the publicly political agenda, and the attempts to reinforce the Sunni–Shia separation, of these early preachers failed to generate positive feedback with Azerbaijani society at large (Goyushov 2008), perhaps partly given the overall public mistrust of Iran formed by years of anti-Iranian propaganda by the Soviet media (Motika 2001). As Kotecha (2006) notes, "[m]ullahs don't have a good reputation since Soviet times. Iranian 'mullahs' are often the butt of jokes and not well respected either in popular culture and it is often through them that Iran propagates its agenda" (31).

In the same line of reasoning, most organisations from the Gulf countries had to discontinue their work, often amidst accusations of being Wahhabis. Already during Soviet times, mysterious Wahhabis became the symbol of fear of "radicalism" and a catch-all phrase to describe unwanted religious activity originating abroad (Roy 2000). The label is today used frequently across the post-Soviet space interchangeably with expressions like fundamentalism, extremism, and terrorism (always with negative connotations). Undeniably, the conservative, purist version of Islam promoted by the representatives from the Gulf states was rather different from the "traditional" approach to Islam in Azerbaijan and hence appeared provocative and suspect to many. Nevertheless, even though feared by the authorities, this branch of Islam enjoyed much popularity, especially among the young segments of the population that viewed Salafi Islam as a break with "Soviet style religion" and a more genuine approach to worship (Bedford 2009). It is remarkable that the governmental "threat of radicalism" discourse resonates so well also in academic and news articles even from outside the country. Many analysts have been struggling with the question of whether Islamic radicalism will, or could, spread to Azerbaijan (e.g. Cornell 2006; Fuller 2002; Mirzayev 2013; Nedea et al. 2012; Wilhelmsen 2009). Furthermore, there is a tendency among some of the religious communities to use this jargon. In this case, it is used to blame "others" for radicalism in an attempt to distance their own communities from this type of activity.

In the light of this very clear policy to neutralise foreign influences, it is remarkable that Turkish religious movements managed to go largely unharmed by the initial wave of increased pressure and scrutiny (Goyushov 2008). While the activities of the Iranians and Arabs were suspended, the late President Heidar Aliyev, instead, encouraged Turkish activities as a counterweight to "radical Sunnism" (Cornell 2006; Yunusov 2012). Thanks to this preferential treatment, the Gülen movement was allowed to expand and prosper (Aliyev 2012).[4] There appear to have been both political and cultural reasons that underlay the preference for Turkish religious influence. The way "Turkish Islam," whether promoted by the Turkish state or by non-governmental actors, was presented and perceived as a "non-radical," "non-political" expression of religion was more compatible with the historically conditioned Azerbaijani version of Islam than the approaches of Iranian Shias or Salafi Sunnis. As such, the way the Turkish state had handled the issue of religion by seeking to keep it out of politics was attractive to post-Soviet Azerbaijan's secular elites. Finally, the cultural and linguistic closeness between the Azerbaijani and Turkish nations made Turkish Islam easily acceptable to many in the population.

Religious, cultural and political compatibility

Guided by the political motto "one nation – two states," public relations between Turkey and Azerbaijan have been based, since the early 1990s, on their common Turkishness and their linguistic and cultural ties. The fact that the majority of Turks are Sunni Moslems while the vast majority of Azerbaijanis are allegedly

Shia has not affected this feeling of communality (İşeri and Çelik 2013). According to Goyushov (2008), as a result of efforts by Turkish religious organisations, "several thousand young urban Azer[baijan]is of Shia origin began adopting Sunnism in the mid-1990s." Religious literature, teaching and preaching in Turkish was easy to understand for the Azerbaijanis because of similarities between the languages. The image of Turkey as a successful democracy integrated with the West and the way Islam was promoted in the Turkish-run mosques also made religious activities pursued by Turkey attractive to certain parts of the population (Balci and Goyushov 2013). The situation in Iran, to the contrary, is often portrayed as juxtaposed to democracy and modernity. The threat posed by Iranian clergy who would like to turn Azerbaijan into an Islamic state is regularly used to justify state control of religion. In the words of one representative of the SCWRO, "Azerbaijan does not want to turn into Iran. Now you can walk here in your own clothes and do what you want. Have you been to Iran? If you go there, you will see the difference. And then you will understand."[5]

This quote points to two key features – tolerance and secularism – of the state-promoted mainstream discourse on religion in Azerbaijan, both products of the country's pre-independence history, as this chapter has detailed above, which can explain why Turkish religious movements were deemed less harmful than other foreign actors. According to the official discourse, Azerbaijan is a multi-religious, uniquely tolerant country. Geographically located at what can be seen as the religious crossroads between Christianity and Islam, the Azerbaijani government prides itself on the country's "tradition of dialogue, reconciliation, and mutual understanding among the religions" (Orudjev 2011, 93). The need for the state to control religious activities is therefore deemed crucial; it ensures the right balance among different religious groups. Along the same lines of reasoning, secular and religious authorities argue that the precondition for sustaining the special kind of tolerance that exists between Azerbaijan's Shia majority and Sunni minority is a strong government, capable of controlling religious life and preventing controversies from turning into open conflicts. As the former head of the SCWRO, Rafik Aliyev, explains, "previously, Moslems were Sunni and Shia who lived in peace and many of them didn't know to what current they belonged. Now there are ten Moslem currents in Azerbaijan. . . . The committee is working with them: we do our best to maintain public order and ensure the observance of tolerance principles. Yet we enjoy some harmony. But nobody can guarantee the reign of everlasting harmony and that the state won't have to take measures to restore the order, as it used to do it before."[6] Turkish religious influence was supposed to support government efforts to keep this balance, since, according to Rafik Aliyev, "Turkish Islam is the only branch of Islam that is compatible with a secular model of the Azerbaijani state" (Yunusov 2012).

The political leaders of independent Azerbaijan promoted the moral values of Islam as an important part of the national ideology and a part of the new identity at the same time as they upheld the idea of sacredness of a secular state (e.g. Aliyev 2004). This development was similar to that in many other post-Soviet republics. The separation of politics and religion has been a cornerstone in the state's policy. Article 5 of the Law of the Republic of Azerbaijan on Freedom of Religious Belief states, "religious associations shall not partake in the activity of political parties and help them financially."[7] In the same spirit, article 85 of the Constitution states that "religious men" might not be elected deputies of the Milli Majlis (Parliament) of the Azerbaijan Republic.[8] In this regard, Turkey's secular societal model created by Mustafa Kemal Ataturk has been a role model to most Azerbaijani leaders. At the same time, Turkey was not an atheist state and did not interfere in private religious matters as long as they stayed private. This was important for Azerbaijan efforts to distance itself from the anti-religious policies of the Soviet Union (Cornell 2011). In the words of former president Heydar Aliyev, "Mustafa Kemal Ataturk's greatness is that he has lived under the influence of Islam and established a new state, i.e., a worldly state where Islam was dominant. [. . .] This is Mustafa Kemal Ataturk's genius and he has demonstrated to all Islamic worlds that without abolishing Islam and considering this religion as moral values of people we may establish a worldly state" (Nazarli 2004).

The Turkish official narrative is similar to the Azerbaijani discourse in the way that it describes a unique Turkish Islam as liberal minded, tolerant, flexible, pragmatic (non-dogmatic), but still pious. Historically peaceful coexistence with, and protection of, a non-Moslem population is believed to have laid the foundation for this unique open-minded Turkey-specific form of Islam (Aras and Caha 2000; Özdalga 2006). According to this narrative, Turkish Islam is also seen as a safeguard against radical Islamism, political Islam and fundamentalism that is deemed "unfamiliar or alien to Turkish culture" (Özdalga 2006). In general, such a depiction resonates very well with both the perceived image of an ideal tolerant and soft "Azerbaijani Islam" and the idea that representatives of "Turkish Islam" can lead by good example. The role of the Diyanet is perceived as crucial in this respect, as it controls all the mosques in the country, all sermons and publications to ensure a non-political Islam. In the aftermath of the 9/11 events, this approach not only became attractive to the Azerbaijani government, but, as Korkut notes, "almost all parties (Western countries, some Moslem countries in Eurasia, and the Diyanet itself) began to consider the Diyanet system as a model of religion-state relations in Eurasia" (Korkut 2010, 117–139).

Not only the Turkish Islam promoted by the Diyanet, but also that brought by the non-governmental religious actors was very compatible with the way post-Soviet authorities envisioned Azerbaijani Islam. The Nurcus advocate a moderate "educated Islam" with a view to "protect[ing] the people from unbelief, and those in the madrasas from fanaticism." Like the state actors, the Nurcus aim to separate religion and politics, seeing Islam primarily as a private or communal matter (Yavuz 1999, 593). The movement of Fethullah Gülen has been described as neo-Nurcu, and Gülen and his followers have successfully tried to combine Islam and Kemalism by producing a religious-political movement favoring "modernism, Turkish nationalism, tolerance, and democracy without sacrificing religious precepts" (Aras and Caha 2000). It promotes an Islamicised Turkish nationalism, a "Turkish Moslemhood." As Özdalga (2006) explains it, "it would, according to Gulen, be against the spirit of the [Qur'an] to contend that 'Islam' differs from nation to nation, or from one ethnic group to the other, but Moslemhood, the way of living Islam in a specific cultural context, may very well do" (561). In the movement's internal activities, discipline is important. In their schools, the curricula focus on science and technology, rather than faith. Spiritual, moral and behavioral values, such as tolerance, respect and openness, are instead mainstreamed throughout the education (Yavuz 1999). In Azerbaijan, where many among the population have felt disappointed with how social and moral issues are addressed in the post-Soviet context, this aspect of the schools' work has been much appreciated (Goksel 2011). In the movement's external relations, "dialogue" is an important feature, and in the words of Park (2007), "in its sponsorship and support for interfaith and intercivilisational dialogue, the Gülen movement seeks both to counter the impact of the more violent fundamentalist strains in modern Islam and to undermine wherever it can Huntington's 'Clash of Civilizations' thesis" (56).

In sum, the majority of the religious input from Turkey brought a "moderate Sunni form of Islam and has learned to compromise with a secular State," two features that both the Azerbaijani government and the Azerbaijani public treasured (Balci and Goyushov 2013). Sermons conducted by Turkish imams in the "Turkish mosques" were based on the Hanafi school of Sunni Islam and carefully focused on moral and ethical issues, avoiding politics (Cornell 2011). The fact that both governmental and non-governmental Turkish religious activities were conducted mainly in accordance with the Azerbaijani government's laws and other requirements rendered them perceived as less harmful than others. Moreover, not only has the Gülen movement never challenged the state authorities; to the contrary, it has been known to utilise its international networks to help promote the messages of the Azerbaijani government, especially with regard to the Karabakh issue (Goksel 2011). Just like any other school in Azerbaijan, the walls of the Gülen schools are decorated with posters, portraits and quotations of the Azerbaijani president expressing the willingness of the management to embrace the local political situation (Balci 2013). It is particularly noticeable that until just recently, Gülen schools in Azerbaijan enjoyed the support of the authorities, facing no official barriers to their activities. In addition to the factors detailed above, there are several other reasons for this. Given the movement's rather extensive business interests in the country (Aliyev 2012), some mention the movement's overall positive contribution to the latter's economic life. Others point to the educational benefits. Graduates from the school network are generally very well educated relative to their peers, as they are provided with modern quality education that might not always be available in Azerbaijani state schools, often haunted by corruption and still struggling to adjust to the post-Soviet situation (Balci 2013; Yunusov 2012).

Turkey leaving Azerbaijan's religious scene

Turkish mission complete or mission impossible?

Still, gradually the representatives of Turkish Islam seem to be losing their privileged position in Azerbaijan. As for the activities of the Diyanet, the management of all Turkish mosques as well as the Department of Religion at Baku State University and the secondary school affiliated with it have been transferred to the Azerbaijani state. Moreover, following a 2010 amendment to the law on religion proclaiming that only citizens educated within the country can conduct Islamic religious rituals and ceremonies, as well as prohibiting the exchange of clerics, Turkish imams no longer work in Azerbaijan. The Diyanet representative in Azerbaijan describes this development as a natural step in Azerbaijani–Turkish religious relations. According to him, Turkey helped establish religious structures in Azerbaijan after independence when this assistance was needed. Now that the mission is completed and there are already local religious cadres educated in Turkey or at home, it is time for the Turks to step back.[9] Yet, the 2009 closure of two high-profile Turkish mosques seemed to indicate that this development could be part of a different process. The Ilahiyat mosque attached to the Department of Religion was closed amidst accusations of functioning illegally without the proper state registration, but has since reopened. The Shahidlar mosque, mentioned above, was supposed to be temporarily closed for repairs, but stays shut after five years (Muradova 2009; RFE/RL 2009). While some see the closure of these mosques as a retaliation for the Turkish government's attempts to normalise relations with Armenia in 2008–2010 (İşeri and Çelik 2013), the Diyanet representative says the mosque was closed due to the fact that the large number of visitors disturbed the traffic flow in the area. Given its location at the heart of the government district in Baku, near the presidential administration offices, this was seen as problematic.[10] As a matter of fact, it seems likely that the number of visitors to the already popular Shahidlar mosque increased sharply in 2008/2009 following the closure of what at the time was the most popular Sunni mosque in Baku – the Abu Bakr mosque. A grenade attack on the Abu Bakr mosque ostensibly carried out by members of a militant Dagestani group in August 2008 left two worshippers dead and more than a dozen wounded, including the imam. After this event, the mosque was closed down during the ongoing investigation and never opened back up. Consequently, there is at the moment a noticeable lack of places of worship for Sunni Moslems in Baku. The Azerbaijani government is said to currently be building a new mosque to compensate for the closure of the Shahidlar. The Azerbaijani–Turkish Friendship mosque is to be located in the Tenth Microrayon district and will, when finished, be the largest mosque in Azerbaijan.[11]

Officially, there is no animosity between Turkey and Azerbaijan as far as religious relations are concerned. One representative of the SCWRO says that since 2012, the Committee has had great relations with the Diyanet. "In February [2014], we held a commemoration event of the Khojaly tragedy in several mosques in Turkey and we had an initiative called the 'Karabakh Azan.' It is the first and last azan that was recited in Karabakh before the people left Karabakh. We restored this azan and it was played in several mosques in Turkey. This was done in cooperation with the Diyanet. They agreed to play this azan despite the fact that, according to the Hanafi School of Islam, azan should only be recited live, not on a recording, but as a courtesy to the partnership and brotherhood between our two nations and particularly between our two organisations they agreed to play it in the mosques."[12]

Be that as it may, the situation for the non-governmental Turkish religious (and educational) movements has still deteriorated. Many were surprised to hear Sheikh-ül-Islam, the head of the Caucasus Moslem Board, in 2007 for the first time equate the Nurcus with the feared Wahhabis in terms of radical influence (International Crisis Group 2008). Seven years later he still vows to "mercilessly fight with those who stand against the [Azerbaijani] statehood, whether they are Wahhabis or Nurcus" (APA 2014b). From being largely ignored, the Nurcus increasingly became a target for a government crackdown on "radicalism," accused of "causing religious schisms, spreading Nursism and illegitimate activities" (Yunusov 2012). A number of Nurcu Qur'an classes have been closed down, and there are frequent raids of apartments where the followers gather for their reading circles, resulting in heavy fines and arrests (Corley 2014). The main book of the Nurcu movement, *Risale-i Nur*, was officially banned in Azerbaijan at the end of 2012 (APA 2014a).

The Gülen movement at road's end in Azerbaijan?

Perhaps because it was not openly pursuing religious activities in Azerbaijan, the Gülen movement managed to stay mostly unaffected by any restrictions imposed on the religious sphere in Azerbaijan. Although as a political conflict surfaced in Turkey in December 2013 between Prime Minister Erdogan and Fethullah Gülen, this reverberated in Azerbaijan as well and appears to be effectively putting an end to the movement's success story there.[13] In March 2014, all the movement's educational facilities in Azerbaijan were taken over by SOCAR, which since 2011 has run a network of schools with the purported aim of improving Azerbaijani educational standards (Sultanova 2014). In June, there came the announcement that all of the movement's educational activities except the Qafqaz University were to be closed due to "additional costs, financial and management issues" (Daily Sabah 2014). Following a visit by Prime Minister Erdogan to Azerbaijan in early April 2014, where he reportedly handed over a list of Azerbaijanis considered to be Gülen supporters (Sultanova 2014), speculations about a witch-hunt on "Gülenists" inside the Azerbaijani government structures started flourishing (e.g. Ismayilova 2014). These were reinforced by the sudden dismissal of certain important political figures reputedly on this list, including the head of division in the President's Office Elnur Aslanov and SCWRO chairman Elshad Isgandarov. Additionally, newspapers claim a number of Turkish nationals, all supposedly senior members of the movement in Azerbaijan, including the Qafqaz University's rector, were deported back to

Turkey – for the alleged reason that their visas had expired (World Bulletin 2014). While some call the infamous list a red herring, most observers trace the ultimate crackdown on the activities of the Gülen movement to the internal power struggle in Turkey.[14] One representative of the SCWRO confirms this by noting that "the issue is salient now because of the internal politics in Turkey. If there was no tension in Turkey between the government and Gülen movement, nothing would have happened in Azerbaijan. It is a spillover issue."[15]

It does appear that, if anything, the Gülen movement is seen as a political, rather than a religious, threat. "Even if we politically analyse things in Turkey, the Gülen movement was never a radical Islamist movement – they are a political movement trying to get power, but not radical Islamist. They are well educated, well dressed – not at all the same type as bearded Wahhabis," the SCWRO representative says, and continues, "the issue with radicalism does not come from Turkish groups, at least not the official religious groups from Turkey. The issue comes from Salafi/Wahhabi groups, which are funded and financed from completely different sources."[16] Still, in general, some caution is advised in this respect. Due to the sensitivity of this topic, a lack of trustworthy government information and the secrecy that has always surrounded the activities of the Gülen movement in Azerbaijan (Aliyev 2012; Balci 2013), it is hard, not to say impossible, to obtain completely objective information. Very few facts are known, for example, about why the above-mentioned political figures were dismissed from their positions. Consequently, much of the discussion on this topic is based on speculation that in due course risks being taken for the truth.

Sunnis and Shias – tolerance lost?

Another aspect that possibly affects the attitude towards Turkish religious representatives in Azerbaijan is a growing awareness about Islam. While previously there was a certain degree of mutual tolerance between Sunnis and Shias in Azerbaijan, much as a result of a lack of insight into the differences between the branches of Islam, the situation is now more in flux. Especially the young are becoming more knowledgeable, which also means that the differences between various ways of worshipping are much more of an issue than it was before. It is likely that in such an environment it is less easy for the state and others to promote one specific branch of Islam as preferable to others without being contradicted. In some of the popular Shia and Sunni mosque communities in Baku, it is obvious that the members of the respective groups consider their way of believing right and others wrong (Bedford 2009). Some incidents of what could be interpreted as sectarian violence between Salafis and Shias in 2014 demonstrated that perhaps the idea of interreligious tolerance is not as widespread in society as the government might hope (Contact.az 2014). There has also been, and this is important in the Turkish context, considerable animosity between more conservative adherents of the Sunni branch (Salafis) and the moderates. Balci and Goyushov (2013) note that "in all the former Soviet Union the [S]alafism is a sort of 5th madhab because of its antagonism with the moderate [H]anafite Islam, which is on good terms with the State and its official Islam." However, the closure of the main Hanafi mosque (Shahidlar) as well as the main Salafi mosque seems to have brought the Sunni communities closer together on some level. At least in Baku, representatives of both groups are more or less forced to pray together in the two Sunni mosques that remain open. In this context, it is also interesting to note that the Shia majority appears not at all to be set in stone. As mentioned earlier, while many Azerbaijanis who were Shia by "birth" "converted" to Sunnism, very few, if any, have gone the other way (Goyushov 2008). Unofficial estimates even put the Sunni–Shia ratio among the believers in recent years close to 50–50. According to the SCWRO, as a result of Sunnis being more active than Shias, there are in 2014 overall officially more functioning Sunni mosques than Shia mosques in Azerbaijan.[17]

Fear of opposition and the need for control

While the Gülen situation might be understood as a spillover issue, the crackdown on the classical Nurcus is harder to explain in these terms. Instead, the shrinking space for this particular Turkish movement can be seen to reflect a more general trend in Azerbaijani internal politics. In the aftermath of the 9/11 terror attacks, the so-called colour revolutions in other post-Soviet countries and the "Arab Spring," the focus on control has become even more prominent and visible as the authorities are making already existing regulations stricter and extending their power over different spheres of society. This has resulted in a very uncompromising approach towards any community, group or individual that is seen as "oppositional." In the sphere of religion, this applies to those seen as threatening the intrareligious and interreligious tolerance approach. Guided by a discourse rejecting change in the sphere of religion, this has translated into increased restrictions for believers, making it increasingly more difficult for a person to be a good Moslem and a good citizen at the same time. The re-registration process for religious communities is gradually rendered more difficult, and a 2013 amendment to the law on religion imposed the most comprehensive restrictions so far on the sales of religious materials. Religious books, video- and audiotapes and discs can now be sold only if they carry a special marking ensuring that they are allowed for sale in the country. Moreover, the selling of religious materials is limited to a few specially designated stores (RFE/RL 2013).

In the light of this, some also interpret the closure of the Shahidlar Mosque as in line with these efforts to ensure strict control over religious life in the country. As one believer who used to frequent the mosque crudely remarks, "it was not a surprise when we were told that the Shahidlar mosque was closed for repair. Knowing the realities of our country, we were sure that it was going to be a 'major' repair. And unfortunately we were right."[18]

Conclusion

Since the outset of independence, the secular Turkish republic founded by Ataturk became the state role model for Azerbaijan, and Turkish Islam, perceived as non-political, was the preferred religious choice of the authorities. Consequently, allowing Turkish religious movements representing Sunni Islam to operate relatively freely in allegedly predominantly Shia Azerbaijan was a conscious political strategy. Due to the traditionally lenient relationship between Sunni and Shia Islam in Azerbaijan, these movements were not only generally accepted, but also, at least in the case of the Gülen movement, very successful. The linguistic and cultural communalities between the two peoples helped facilitate this progress as well. After some time, representatives of Turkish Islam started to lose their privileged position and some, like the Nurcu classicists, instead became the target of government attempts to dispose of radical elements on the religious scene. Some see the retraction of religious Turkish groups as a logical consequence of the local Moslem communities growing more competent. At the same time, the development seems to reflect certain changes in internal politics in Azerbaijan and Turkey respectively – in the former connected to a move to increase control over religious elements, and in the latter linked to a power struggle between Prime Minister Erdogan and Fethullah Gülen. Some also believe that the Turkish government's temporary policy of improving its relations with Armenia, much loathed by the Azerbaijani authorities, resulted in retaliation expressed in the refutation of some of the privileged conditions Turkish religious representatives previously enjoyed. In this sense, it is interesting to note that while the religious aspect has never been very important by itself in the bilateral government-to-government relationship between Azerbaijan and Turkey, religious issues are very sensitive to changes in the political arena. To end on a slightly cynical note, given that these two countries so adamantly struggle to keep religion out of the political arena, the ease with which questions about religious movements become politicised is certainly interesting.

Notes

1. The author would very much like to thank the editor, Murad Ismayilov, for his valuable comments on the draft of this chapter as well as those other analysts who so kindly contributed to improving the text.
2. However, as Balci and Goyushov (2013) also note, some authors, to the contrary, claim that the Bolsheviks tried to use the Sunni–Shia differences among Azerbaijanis in their antireligious policy. According to these claims, in July 1923, the Azerbaijan Cheka prepared the *Plan of Fragmenting Moslem Religion in the Azerbaijan SSR* (based on the GPU secret police order No. 6).
3. Interestingly enough, I appear to have visited the same mosque as Dragadze, but ten or so years later, still hearing the same thing.
4. Goyushov (2008) notes, however, that a number of Turkish-run Qur'an classes and several madrasas were closed following the 1996 law changes, so Turkish religious messengers were not completely unharmed.
5. Representative of the SCWRO, Baku, 22 April 2004.

6 Interview with Rafik Aliyev, Chairman State Committee for Work with Religious Associations, Baku, 28 May 2005.
7 The Law of the Republic of Azerbaijan "On Freedom of Religious Belief," Chapter 1, Article 5.
8 Constitution of the Republic of Azerbaijan, Section 3, Chapter 5, Article 85.
9 Interview with Sadik Eroslan, Diyanet representative in Baku, May 2014.
10 Interview with Sadik Eroslan, Diyanet representative in Baku, May 2014.
11 Interview with Sadik Eroslan, Diyanet representative in Baku, May 2014. Even though it was initially suggested that this was intended as exclusively a Sunni mosque, there have now been rumors that this might not be the case.
12 Interview at SCWRO, Baku, May 2014.
13 For a good overview of this, see Bayram Balci (2014), "What Future for the Fethullah Gülen Movement in Central Asia and the Caucasus?" *Central Asia–Caucasus Analyst*, 7 February.
14 This is the author's conclusion after a number of interviews with researchers, government employees, experts and others in Baku, May 2014.
15 Interview at SCWRO, Baku, May 2014.
16 Interview at SCWRO, Baku, May 2014.
17 Interview at SCWRO, Baku, May 2014.
18 Conversation with a Sunni Moslem from Baku, June 2014.

References

Abbasov, Ali. 2001. Islam v Sovremennom Azerbaidzhane: Obraziy i Realiy. (In Russian.) In: D. E. Furman, ed. *Azerbaydzhan i Rossiya: Obshestvo i Gosudarstvo*, 280–310. Moscow: Letnii Sad.
Alieva, Leila. 2013. The Characteristics of Political Parties and Elections in Post-Soviet Azerbaijan. In: Leila Alieva, ed. *The Soviet Legacy 22 Years On: Reversed or Reinforced?*, 103–123. Baku: Center for National and International Studies.
Alieva, Leila and Vurgun Ayyub, eds. 2010. *Views on the History of Democracy Development in Azerbaijan and Turkey*. Baku: Center for National and International Studies.
Aliyev, Fuad. 2012. The Gülen Movement in Azerbaijan. *Journal of Current Trends in Islamic Ideology* 14, 27 Dec. www.hudson.org/research/9864-the-gulen-movement-in-azerbaijan.
Aliyev, Rafik. 2004. *State and Religion*. Baku: Abilov, Zelyanov & Sons.
Aliyeva, Lala. 2013a. Shia Islam in Azerbaijan: Historical Approach and Modernity. *Proceedings of the 1st International Global Virtual Conference Workshop*, 8–12 Apr. www.gvconference.com/proceedings/GVW_2013.pdf.
———. 2013b. Vernacular Islam in Azerbaijan. *Humanities and Social Sciences Review* 2:3, 145–151.APA. 2014a. 'Risale-i Nur' Banned in Azerbaijan since End of 2012. *APA News Agency*, 21 Apr. http://en.apa.az/news/210148.
———. 2014b. We Will Mercilessly Fight with Those Who Stand Against the Statehood. *APA News Agency*, 13 May. http://en.apa.az/xeber_allahshukur_pashazadeh____we_ will_mercile_211192.html.
Aras, Bulent and Omer Caha. 2000. Fethullah Gulen and His Liberal 'Turkish Islam' Movement. *Middle East* 4:4, 31–42.
Balci, Bayram. 2004. Between Sunnism and Shiism: Islam in Post-Soviet Azerbaijan. *Central Asian Survey* 23:2, 205–217.
———. 2013. Between Secular Education and Islamic Philosophy: The Approach and Achievements of Fethullah Gülen's Followers in Azerbaijan. *Caucasus Survey* 1:1, Oct., 107–116.

———. 2014. Turkey's Religious Outreach in Central Asia and the Caucasus. *Current Trends in Islamist Ideology* 16, Mar.
Balci, Bayram and Altay Goyushov. 2013. Changing Islam in Post-Soviet Azerbaijan and Its Impact on the Sunni-Shia Cleavage. In: Brigitte Maréchal and Sami Zemni, eds. *The Dynamics of Sunni-Shia Relationships: Doctrine, Transnationalism, Intellectuals and the Media*. London: Hurst & Co Publishers Ltd., 193–214.
Bedford, Sofie. 2009. *Islamic Activism in Azerbaijan. Repression and Mobilization in a Post-Soviet Context*. Stockholm: Dep. of Political Science, Stockholm University.
Campbell, Elena I. 2006. The Autocracy and the Muslim Clergy in the Russian Empire (1850s–1917). *Russian Studies in History* 44:2, 8–29.
Contact.az. 2014. Wahhabis Attacked Believers in Mushfigabad. 7 Jul. www.contact.az/docs/2014/Social/070700083502en.htm#.U7sNvhZpa5w.
Corley, Felix. 2014. Azerbaijan: Beating to Extract 'Evidence'. *Forum 18 News Service*, 8 May.
Cornell, Svante E. 2011. *Azerbaijan since Independence*. Armonk, NY: M.E. Sharpe.
———. 2006. The Politicization of Islam in Azerbaijan. *Silk Road Paper*, Oct. Central Asia-Caucasus Institute & Silk Road Studies Program.
Daily Sabah. 2014. Azerbaijan Closes Schools Affiliated with the Gulen Movement. 18 Jun. www.dailysabah.com/asia/2014/06/18/azerbaijan-closes-schools-affiliated-with-the-gulen-movement.
Dragadze, Tamara. 1994. Islam in Azerbaijan: The Position of Women. In: Camilla Fawzi El-Solh and Judy Mabro, eds. *Muslim Women's Choices. Religious Belief and Social Reality*, 128–152. Providence, RI: Berg.
Filimonov, E. G. 1983. *Islam v SSSR. Osobennosti Protsessa Sekuliarizatsii v Respublikakh Sovetskogo Vostoka*. Moscow: Mysl.
Fuller, Liz. 2002. Could 'Alternative' Islam Become a Force in Azerbaijani Politics? *RFE/RL Newsline* 6:50, 15 Mar.
Goksel, Nigar. 2011. Religiously-Inspired Bonding: Changing Soft Power Elements in Turkey's Relations with Azerbaijan. *Religion and Conflict* 4:8, 320–336.
Goyushov, Altay. 2008. Islamic Revival in Azerbaijan. *Current Trends in Islamist Ideology* 7, 66–81.
Goyushov, Altay and Elchin Askerov. 2010. Islam and Islamic Education in Soviet and Independent Azerbaijan. In: Michael Kemper, Raoul Motika, and Stefan Reichmuth, eds. *Islamic Education in the Soviet Union and Its Successor States*, 168–222. London: Routledge.
International Crisis Group. 2008. Azerbaijan: Independent Islam and the State. *ICG Europe Report* 191, 25 Mar.
Ismayilova, Khadija. 2014. Azerbaijan: Media and Regulators a Family Affair. *OCCRP*, 24 Jun. https://reportingproject.net/occrp/index.php/en/ccwatch/cc-watch-indepth/2494-azerbaijan-media-and-regulators-a-family-affair.
İşeri, Emre and Nihat Çelik. 2013. Turkish Nation-State Identity and Foreign Policy on Armenia: The Roles of Sèvresphobia and 'Brotherly' Azerbaijan. *Turkish Review* 3, 274–281.
Khalid, Adeeb. 2007. *Islam after Communism. Religion and Politics in Central Asia*. Berkeley & Los Angeles: University of California Press.
Korkut, Şenol. 2010. The Diyanet of Turkey and Its Activities in Eurasia after the Cold War. *Acta Slavica Iaponica* 28, 117–139.
Kotecha, Hema. 2006. *Islamic and Ethnic Identities in Azerbaijan: Emerging Trends and Tensions*. Baku: OSCE Office.

Mirzayev, Rasim. 2013. Islamists in Azerbaijan: How Dangerous Are They? *Euxeinos* 9.
Motika, Raoul. 2001. Islam in Post-Soviet Azerbaijan. *Archive de Sciences Sociales des Religions* 115, 111–124.
Muradova, Mina. 2009. Azerbaijan: Mosques Close in Baku, "Capital of Islamic Culture." *Eurasianet*, 26 May. www.eurasianet.org/departments/insightb/articles/eav052709b.shtml.
Nazarli, Safarli. 2004. *Heydar Aliyev about Ataturk*. Baku: AzAtaM (translated from Azerbaijani into English by Ilaha Abdullayeva).
Nedea, B., S. Jafarov, and O. Mamadov. 2012. Radical Islam in Azerbaijan. In: O. Popescu, B. Nedea, and I. Chifu, eds. *Religion and Conflict, Radicalization and Violence in the Wider Black Sea Region*. Bucarest: Editura Ispri.
Omel'chenko, Elena and Sabirova Gusel. 2003. Islam and the Search for Identity. In: Hilary Pilkington and Galina Yemelianova, eds. *Islam in Post-Soviet Russia. Public and Private Faces*. London & New York: RoutledgeCurzon.
Orudjev, Hijat. 2011. Background, Problems and Prospects of Inter-Religious Dialogue in Azerbaijan. In: D. Spivak and S. Shankman, eds. *World Religions in the Context of the Contemporary Culture: New Perspectives of Dialogue and Mutual Understanding in the Russian Federation and Eastern Europe, in Central Asia and the Caucasus*, 87–96. St. Petersburg: St. Petersburg Branch of the Russian Institute for Cultural Research / Russian Baltic Information Center "Blitz."
Özdalga, Elisabeth. 2006. The Hidden Arab: A Critical Reading of the Notion of 'Turkish Islam'. *Middle Eastern Studies* 42:4, 551–570.
Park, Bill. 2007. The Fethullah Gülen Movement as a Transnational Phenomenon. *International Conference Proceedings. Muslim World in Transition: Contributions of the Gülen Movement*. London: Leeds Metropolitan Press.
Polonskaya, Ludmila and Alexei Malashenko. 1994. *Islam in Central Asia*. Reading: Ithaca Press.
RFE/RL. 2009. Turkish Mosque in Baku Closed for Repairs. *Radio Free Europe/Radio Liberty*, 28 Apr. www.rferl.org/content/Turkish_Mosque_In_Baku_Closed_For_Repairs/1617374.html.
———. 2013. Azerbaijani Parliament Limits Sales of Religious Materials. *Radio Free Europe/Radio Liberty*, 22 Feb. www.rferl.org/content/azerbaijan-limits-religious-materials/24909902.html.
Roy, Olivier. 2000. *The New Central Asia: The Creation of Nations*. New York: New York University Press.
Sattarov, Rufat. 2009. *Islam, State, and Society in Independent Azerbaijan: Between Historical Legacy and Post-Soviet Reality*. Wiesbaden: Reichert.
Strømmen, Kari Eken. 1999. Tyrker, Muslim og Sovjetborger. Utvikling av Nasjonal Identitet i Aserbajdsjan under Sovjetregimet. *NUPI Research Reports*. Norwegian Institute of International Affairs.
Sultanova, Shahla. 2014. Azerbaijan Backing Turkey's Crackdown on Gülen Movement. *Eurasianet*, 15 Apr. www.eurasianet.org/node/68274.
Swietochowski, Tadeusz. 1995. *Russia and Azerbaijan: A Borderland in Transition*. New York: Columbia University Press.
Wiktor-Mach, Dobroslawa. 2012. Measuring Muslims: The Problems of Religiosity and Intra-Religious Diversity. In: Luigi Berzano and Ole Riis eds. *Annual Review of the Sociology of Religion, Volume 3: New Methods on the Sociology of Religion*, 207–228. Leiden & Boston: Brill.

Wilhelmsen, Julie. 2009. Islamism in Azerbaijan: How Potent? *Studies in Conflict & Terrorism* 32:8, 726–742.
World Bulletin. 2014. Azerbaijan Deports 8 Affiliates of Fetullah Gulen. *World Bulletin* 23, Apr. www.worldbulletin.net/news/134491/azerbaijan-deports-8-affiliates-of-fethullah-gulen.
Yavuz, M. Hakan. 1999. Towards an Islamic Liberalism?: The Nurcu Movement and Fethullah Gülen. *The Middle East Journal* 53:4, Autumn, 584–605.
Yunusov, Arif. 2004. *Islam v Azerbaydzyane*. Baku: Zaman.
———. 2012. *Islamskaya Palitra Azerbaidzhana*. (In Russian.) Baku: Institute for Peace and Democracy.

8 Conclusion
Azerbaijan, Turkey and the future of Eurasia

Norman A. Graham

In late April 2015, I had the good fortune to participate as a panelist at the Third Global Baku Forum on "Building Trust in the Emerging/New World Order" sponsored by the Azerbaijani government through the Nizami Ganjavi International Center. The opening address by President Ilham Aliyev stressed Azerbaijan as the place where civilisations met historically, serving essentially as a cultural and political bridge for the West and the Moslem world. He then went on to describe the "remarkable" years of Azerbaijan's transformation, blessed with substantial fossil energy resources and supportive neighbors, including Turkey. He stressed the importance of efforts to improve education and of industrial diversification but also described the delicate position in which his country found itself. Some of this relates to the need to continue supplying energy to European markets, without further alienating Russia. Noting the progress made on the Southern Gas corridor, the South Caucasian pipeline and the Trans-Anatolian pipeline, he expressed some satisfaction and long-term optimism. National security cannot now be separated from energy security in his view.

But some of the "delicacy" stems from the ecological and political challenges that can be traced to the Soviet period and the early independence years and the conflict over Nagorno-Karabakh with Armenia. The president stressed the dilemmas entailed with the need to rely on international law and ineffectual global security institutions at a time when respect for both was at an unprecedented low point. Reforms should never stop, in his view, and there are important advantages that flow from freedom.

Later during the forum, Abdullah Gul, president of Turkey from 2007 to 2014, added his support for Azerbaijan's ambitions and work towards meeting these challenges. He stressed the need to be true to articulated values and to avoid the apparent tendency to operate with a double standard, as in the conflict over Nagorno-Karabakh.

Much of the rest of the forum focused on Russia and Ukraine, featuring three of the four previous presidents of Ukraine (in startling unanimity in condemning Russia, despite past rivalry and differences in their postures towards their eastern neighbor), current or former presidents or prime ministers from Poland, Bulgaria, Czech Republic, Greece, Italy, Georgia, Slovenia, Estonia, Latvia, Lithuania, Macedonia and Malta, among others. Russia was represented (publicly) only by

Alexander Likholtal, president of the Green Cross International in Moscow. He argued that changes in the world order made the Ukraine crisis possible. The Russian annexation of Crimea was not the actual "change point" in the post–Cold War international system; one needs to see the big drivers for this situation and especially the wasted opportunities that were available with the collapse of the Soviet Union.

The final major focus of the forum was on the need to respond to radicalised religious and ethnic movements and the attendant challenges to Europe and Eurasia, including the abuse of subject populations and the resulting push of mass migration. The threat of ISIL/ISIS was discussed at great length, as was the prospect for ameliorating religious and sectarian conflict more generally.

If we review briefly the arguments made in Chapters 2–8 in this volume, one can find some illumination of many of the themes covered in the Third Baku Forum. This may go some distance to addressing the future of Azerbaijan, Turkey and Eurasia in the present challenging international environment.

Azerbaijan's relations with Turkey and beyond: path dependency and emerging geopolitics

In Chapter 2, Elnur Soltanov describes in detail the "romanticised relationship" between Azerbaijan and Turkey, evident immediately after the collapse of the USSR but soured shortly thereafter in large measure due to the conflict with Armenia over Nagorno-Karabakh and Azerbaijan's disappointment with Turkish policy and the lack of support for a just settlement. He skillfully discusses the balancing of idealism with reality after reviewing the key contextual factors that intervene in or otherwise mediate the relationship. Perhaps most noteworthy among these is Turkey's reluctance to side too closely with Azerbaijan on matters that would alienate Russia. This seems to be an impediment too solid to remove even today with the widespread condemnation of Russia's recent policy and actions towards Ukraine, particularly as long as US–Turkish relations remain tense.

This is problematic for Azerbaijan, since, as Soltanov notes: "in the beginning, the Azerbaijani elite was more concerned about making Azerbaijani independence irreversible than Karabakh per se. For them, the larger, by far the more important issue was about preventing Russia from coming back." Indeed, this may seem even more concerning since the Russian annexation of Crimea, as was evident in the statements of so many regional leaders presenting at the Third Baku Forum.

Still, Turkey performed a critical role in the drive for Azerbaijan's economic independence by signing on to the BTC pipeline project when both Russia and Iran opposed it. And while Soltanov describes the complexity of this undertaking and some ambiguity over the relative economic benefits of it for each side, he points to the importance of the personal relations and skill evident in the handling of the relationship by Aliyev and Demirel and the long-term complementarity of key interests.

Misunderstandings remain in the discourse, especially in Azerbaijani nationalism on the one hand and the AKP posture towards Russia and the West on the other. But there are pluses in the relationship that may prevail, especially given the role Azerbaijan plays in Turkish energy security. Soltanov's reference to Raymond Vernon's "obsolescing bargain" thesis is quite apt, however. In his words:

> The difficulties in the current gas deals are partly the result of this understanding that Azerbaijan is already over-dependent on Turkey and Turkey remains to be the best option for its next pipeline. The fact that Turkey started to talk about opening the borders to Armenia after these projects were completed through Turkey raises eyebrows too. Azerbaijan deserves to be treated better than what OBT theory suggests. If not, then it should play hardball; Turkey does not hold the key to the gates of Europe – the Black Sea is another one.
>
> (p.49)

The energy dimension in the relationship remains critical but may be less so if the low global oil prices of 2014 and 2015 do not rebound in the common cyclical fashion we have come to expect. There seems to be some reason for an exception in the growing "fracking revolution" and the unusually sustained drive for alternative energy technology that seem newly evident.

In Chapter 3, Emre Erşen confronts the critical geopolitics of Turkish and Azerbaijani conceptions of Eurasia. With some emphasis on the "Turkic-world-centered tradition," Erşen examines the posture of Turkish policy to attempt to integrate the Turkic successor states to the former Soviet Union. Is this an ideological commitment? Can Azerbaijan serve as a bridge in this effort? Is the Turkic view of Eurasia doomed to run up against Putinist conceptions of Eurasia that may lead to serious conflict, especially in the wake of the Russian annexation of Crimea? Is there a role for the West to play in limiting Russian dominance, or are the lingering effects of the impetus for the "anti-imperialist political dialogue" between Ataturk and Lenin still at play? Erşen discusses the Asian-centered geopolitical tradition in some depth, while noting that "not everyone in Turkey believes that Asia and Europe should be understood in binary terms as two opposite civilizational alternatives" (p.63).

Finally, Erşen examines a Moslem-world-centered geopolitical tradition, pointing to the arguments made initially by Ahmet Davutoglu in *Strategic Depth: Turkey's International Position*, but also making reference to the heritage of the Ottoman empire. Is Azerbaijan a crucial ingredient in this Turkish conception, given its general disposition towards secularism, deriving somewhat from the Soviet experience but also due to its wariness about political Islam and the threat of radicalism in the region. Or is Turkey the central element and true bridge? What is the most viable strategy for Azerbaijan to pursue given these uncertainties and pressures? Erşen concludes that Azerbaijan can only play "a role of a supporting actor – rather than a protagonist – in a neoimperialist strategy, which defines Turkey as Eurasia's real center" (p.67). What remains to be addressed, perhaps, is Russia's role in this potential geopolitical conflict.

In Chapter 4, Michael Hikari Cecire discusses the "emerging evidence of trilateralism between Turkey, Georgia, and Azerbaijan," formalised with the Trabzon Declaration of June 2012, but also reflected in a series of collaborative projects for strategic trade and transportation. The Turkish-Azerbaijani partnership is central but, according to Cecire, allows the possibility of a Turkey partnership with Georgia. After a long history of enmity, this partnership does seem real now and is complemented by a strengthening of relations between Georgia and Azerbaijan.

Indeed, Mikheil Saakashvili, president of Georgia in 2004–13, made a strong presentation at the Third Baku Forum, which stressed the importance of Azerbaijan to the region, particularly now given the impact of the Russian posture in Crimea and Ukraine and the growing destabilisation of Syria and Iraq. He stressed that for the time being (until expected large liquefied natural gas exports from the US come online), Azerbaijan is the only reliable source of natural gas for Europe. The partnership among Azerbaijan, Georgia and Turkey is thus a stabilising influence. How to strengthen this without provoking an even more aggressive Russian response, in light of Putin's conception of responsibility for the "near abroad," is an important aspect of Cecire's concern.

One key element of a "self-sustaining trilateralism" among these three states is the economic integration that has begun to grow beyond their pipeline "tethering" to a common energy source. This is separate from existing and prospective integration with the European Union or, in the case of Azerbaijan, the Eurasian Economic Community pushed by Russia, and may be more intense than either existing institution. Cecire points to the BTK railway as a recent example of practical integration and notes that Turkey and Azerbaijan are Georgia's top two trade partners.

Frustrated in its inability to support Georgia during its conflict with Russia in 2008 and since, Turkey proposed the CSCP. Georgia, however, continues to look towards a Euro-Atlantic relationship for its long-term security. Azerbaijan is understandably cautious about this strategy, having been warned explicitly by visiting Russian dignitaries against a campaign to join the West. Indeed, the action by the "Caspian Five" (Russia, Azerbaijan, Iran, Kazakhstan and Turkmenistan) in September 2014 to agree to exclude foreign military forces from the region would seem to support a return to Russian dominance.

Turkey, after a period of AKP moves to assert some independence from NATO and indeed the EU, reestablished its Western ties somewhat in late July 2015 with a decision to permit the use of Turkish air bases, like Incerlik, by US forces for more efficient air strikes on ISIS in Syria. The connection of this action to the electoral concerns of President Erdogan and his renewed attention to the Kurdish separatist movement in Turkey is the subject of considerable press and political speculation.

Some normalisation in Russia's relationship with Georgia occurred after Bidzina Ivanishvili's Georgian Dream coalition surprisingly won parliamentary elections and the Georgian Dream nominee for president, Giorgi Margvelashvili, eventually replaced Saakashvili as president in 2013, but the Russian annexation of Crimea and support for separatist forces in eastern Ukraine have raised new alarm. Saakashvili stressed the need to support Kiev against Russian pressure at the Third Baku Forum, characterising the events of 2014–15 as a second step (after the 2008 Russian conflict with Georgia) in a larger campaign by Russia to reassert Russian influence or control in the Soviet successor states. He was named chair of a Ukraine International Reform Council and subsequently was appointed governor of Odessa. In these roles, he stressed the "four D's" of the reform package he had employed rather successfully in Georgia:

> Debureaucratisation – the need to take decisions more quickly
> Deoligarchisation – the man behind the scenes deciding must be removed
> Deregulation – so as not to hamper private initiative
> Decentralisation – can't know everything and act effectively centrally

Saakashvili is of course out of favor with the current Georgian Dream government. Indeed, he was reportedly the subject of a request during the Third Baku Forum from the Georgian government to Azerbaijan for arrest and return to Tbilisi for trial. Nonetheless, he was able to board the plane from Baku to Frankfurt after the forum with no interference.

Cecire stresses the clear perception among the trilateral partners that Russia has the power to play a "spoiler" role in the region, potentially disrupting the non-Russian energy corridor to Europe that has developed, but he also underscores the importance of the effort to prevent a return to Russian dominance. Avoiding direct and flagrant competition and a public declaration to join the West, which would back the Russians into a political corner, remains an important goal, particularly in Baku. To this end, Cecire notes:

> Trilateralism remains almost entirely interests-based and, beyond bilateral ties between Azerbaijan and Turkey, is not burdened with any overwhelming sense of sentiment... [but] Russia's residual presence in the region is also a potential obstacle, given Moscow's potential suspicions of regional balancing.
>
> (p.85)

Economic relations and the search for prosperity in Eurasia

With Chapter 5, we begin a discussion of the economic dimension of Azerbaijan's relationship with Turkey and beyond. Azerbaijan became an important destination for Turkish FDI, as part of Turkey's initial interest in establishing a Turkic Eurasian economic community, and Turkey also became an important destination for Azerbaijani FDI. Both economies, however, suffer from a number of weaknesses. Both are in need of an injection of foreign capital and technology. Both seem committed to industrial diversification and innovation but have been unable to take off and develop competitive high technology sectors. Fortunately for Azerbaijan, Turkish foreign economic policy has become centered on the Caucasus, down from the larger Central Eurasia ambitions. Azerbaijan then emerges as the centerpiece of this effort. The promise of the 2010 Turkey–Azerbaijan High Level Strategic Cooperation Council has yet to be fully realised, but the intent to establish a special economic relationship is clear.

Elkin Nurmammadov examines this economic relationship from the Azerbaijani side. His specific focus is on the gap between actual and potential levels of bilateral economic relations. If there is a clear gap, what explains it? A comparative analysis is employed to determine whether the Turkey–Azerbaijan relationship is what one would expect given similar ties with Georgia and Kazakhstan for Turkey and with Russia for Azerbaijan. Does energy trade and FDI "crowd out" other sectors? Apparently not, according to Nurmammadov. What about the impact of political factors? Again, the impact is modest, and in some cases positive. More important is the lack of formal agreements, disparities in levels of economic and institutional development and inadequate infrastructure and human capital in Azerbaijan.

Nurmammadov concludes that there is a significant gap and recommends that Azerbaijan join the WTO as soon as possible and that there should be considerable Azerbaijani investment in infrastructure and human capital development. On the bilateral side, he suggests an immediate bilateral free trade agreement and joint ventures to invest in third countries.

In Chapter 6, Pinar Bedirhanoğlu examines state–business relations in Azerbaijan. Working with interviews conducted with Turkish business executives and association leaders, the focus is on how business practices and corruption issues are viewed from the Turkish perspective. Clearly, the situation has evolved from the chaotic early days after independence when Turkish businesses were largely alone in the Azerbaijani marketplace. The regulatory environment has improved substantially, but there is a "duality in the business climate – formal improvements in regulations on the one hand and discretionary interventions therein by informal power structures, on the other" (p.118). The logic of the concept of *hörmet* is explained carefully in this connection, particularly as it relates to common Western conceptions of rule of law. Bedirhanoğlu finds that large Turkish companies are hesitant to make risky investments in this climate. Cultural and socio-political features of the Azerbaijani state–business relationship are clearly challenging for business leaders.

This raises a series of larger questions about the prospects for economic development and true broad-based prosperity in post-communist Eurasia, as well as in Turkey. The key here, not surprisingly, may well be the proper role for the state to play in the economy, particularly in a region commonly identified increasingly as characterised by persistent authoritarianism or fragile democratisation. One of the strengths of the AKP-led governments in Turkey has been a successful program of economic liberalisation, begun in part to support possible full membership in the European Union.

Islam in Turkey, Central Eurasia and Europe

In Chapter 7, Sofie Bedford explores the religious linkages between Azerbaijan and Turkey. This is a complicated relationship that has important implications for the larger region. What has been the impact of "Turkish Islam" and the tradition of secularism promoted by Ataturk on the Azerbaijani experience? Does this mesh well with the sensibilities and facts on the ground in Azerbaijan and the lingering impact of the Soviet posture on religion in "its" Moslem territories? There is an obvious connection with the "Turkic World" ambitions of Turkish political leaders after the collapse of the Soviet Union, but there are also interesting issues to explore stemming from the rise of the AKP administration in Turkey, led by Prime Minister, now President, Recep Erdogan. Partly this derives indirectly from the recent political struggle between Erdogan and Fethullah Gülen, inspirational and financial figure behind the Gulen, or Hizmet, Movement, which has its own history of involvement in Azerbaijan. Bedford captures this in some detail, noting:

> What differentiated the activities of the Gulen movement from other foreign religious movements that arrived in Azerbaijan after independence, including the 'Nurcu classicists,' is that its representatives did not openly promote religious ideas. All educational programs were completely secular.
>
> (pp.135–6)

However, some Azerbaijanis (and others coming into contact with the movement in Europe, Eurasia and even North America) may have harboured suspicions on this score (see Hendrick 2013; Turam 2006), and the Azerbaijani government's posture has been cautious at times, given its general reluctance to submit to foreign influence. "Turkish Islam" was seen as non-radical, unlike the Wahhabis or more recently the followers of ISIS/ISIL. Is there a long-term compromise with the concept of a secular state? Can Sunnis and Shias coexist? The potential normalisation of relations between the West and Iran adds interest to this question.

Reconciliation is not easy, particularly when there is little hope for a better life. The importance of economic development and employment opportunity is hard to underestimate in both Azerbaijan and Turkey if the "Arab Spring" teaches us anything. Radical Islam is nurtured where hundreds of thousands of unemployed youth have no other promising outlet and have access to guns.

This raises the question of the prospect for resolving the conflicts and resulting migration pressure so evident in Syria, Iraq, Turkey and North Africa. Turkey is in many respects a key to this challenge, serving as both an initial safe haven for large numbers of refugees as well as a transit point for traffic to Greece and southeastern Europe and from Europe to Syria for ISIS/ISIL volunteers. Washington and some important capitals in Europe still see Turkey as the bridge between the "Christian West" and the Muslim world. Stresses on this relationship abound, as fears of the success of ISIS/ISIL continues on the ground and the

Conclusion 157

press of refugees from the conflict centers increases daily. The dormant conflict between the Turkish government and the PKK separatist movement threatens to resume the ferocious levels of the past, as Erdogan joins the anti-ISIS/ISIL coalition more actively but also threatens the important contribution made initially by Kurdish fighters by its simultaneous moves on PKK supporters. This "bridge" may indeed lead to nowhere the West really wants to go, except to the extent that the connections to Azerbaijan and Central Eurasia remain important. What then determines the prospect here?

Prospects for broad-based economic prosperity in Turkey, Azerbaijan and Central Eurasia

The energy and broader trade network that has emerged between Europe and Central Eurasia, with Turkey and Azerbaijan at its heart, is a clear source of economic benefit for all concerned, as discussed in previous chapters. It also continues to support the prospect for national political independence for Azerbaijan, Kazakhstan and other post-Soviet states in Central Eurasia. But the true test of sustainable and broad economic prosperity must extend beyond the production and marketing of fossil fuels. This takes us to the question of how to extend economic development beyond the carbon fuel sector – indeed how to avoid the oil/natural resource curse? There is no space here for a full examination of this question in this volume, but a few comments on how this relates to the future of Turkey and Azerbaijan, potentially, and their relationship with the broader region and indeed the world economy seem in order. The oil curse phenomenon in Central Eurasia has been explored in some depth by Luong and Weinthal (2010), but the dynamics of the challenging process of industrial diversification are not well understood or studied thoroughly as yet.

First, how sustainable is the Azerbaijan political economy as now configured? This obviously raises immediate questions of the size of oil and gas reserves, the volatility of oil pricing and the security of transportation networks – all of which are potentially constrained in the Azerbaijani case. There is no immediate crisis in any area as yet, but estimates of reserves suggest that key deposits may be exhausted in a decade or so; many analysts suggest that oil prices may remain well under $100 a barrel for some time, as global production continues to increase when new technology is applied (hydraulic fracturing in the US and Europe) and political decisions make continued production levels high (in Saudi Arabia) and expand it elsewhere (to Iran); and the possibility of transportation network disruptions in Georgia (by Russia) and Turkey (by the PKK) is not out of the question.

With these potential constraints in mind, the incentive to look for economic development and prosperity from other sectors is high. Azerbaijan has marshaled resources from previous energy exports for investments to this end (in contrast to many kleptocratic systems that simply steal the profits or make wasteful or otherwise unproductive expenditures). A preliminary review of these investments indicates considerable infrastructure development, improvements in K-2 and higher education institutions and ancillary enterprise development in the energy sector, but little exemplary economic development in non-energy sectors. There is high-level public and private commitment to diversify the industrial and commercial base in Azerbaijan, but like many oil- and/or gas-rich countries – especially those with authoritarian regimes – the result is modest at best. Certainly, there is no evidence of an economic take-off in manufacturing, high technology innovation and commercialisation, agricultural productivity or even indigenous service industries. What explains this?

The first part of the answer to this challenging question is that there is something critical missing in all post-Soviet states that have not liberalised economically and politically. As Linda Weiss (1998) reminds us, state-led industrialisation can work under certain circumstances (e.g. in Germany, Japan, Korea), but more often than not it seems that states make poor investment decisions and waste resources on industrial and commercial dead ends. This is particularly true if the system is beset with corruption, as is the tradition in most of Eurasia (see Henry Hale's [2014] analysis and Karen Dawisha's [2014] elaborate focus on the Russian kleptocratic tendency).

Lillia Shevtsova (2010) discusses some elements of this failure to liberalise economically with respect to Russia. She notes the impact of the West's involvement in the Balkan crisis, the bombing of Belgrade, recognition of Kosovo's independence and the American invasion in Iraq as impetus for the "patriotic consolidation" which derailed liberalisation and modernisation reforms. In her words:

> Putin and Medvedev couldn't offer the elite and Russian society a modernization agenda that could realistically become the foundation for a constructive consolidation. . . . [I]f the West did not exist as a scapegoat, the regime would have to invent it. . . . How can we hope for modernization if investors are too afraid to invest in a country where the prime minister can crash the market with just a few words spoken in public? How can there be modernization if there are no rules?
>
> (pp. 134–135)

Speaking directly to a Russian audience, she asks:

> Where is the actual program of this modernization? Where is Putin's plan, which was in the [United Russia] party's election platform? And generally, how can you modernize a country and defeat corruption while rejecting political competition, rule of law, and independent institutions? If there is a recipe for this innovation, it would be good to show it at last.
>
> (*Vedomosti*, 23 October 2008)

And quotes Bobo Lo:

> The global financial crisis, for all its disruptive impact, has had three salutary consequences. The first is to take much of the heat out of tensions between

Moscow and Washington. The second is to explode the myth of Russian invincibility (epitomized in the triumphalist slogan, 'Russia is back'). The third, and most important, is to emphasize the extent to which we are all interdependent. These realities allow us to hope for a more constructive relationship between Russia and the West, one based on positive-sum modernization rather than a mutually debilitating *realpolitik*.

She counters: "It may happen only if the Russian elite stops faking modernization and does it for real, and the West decides to support it" (Shevtsova 2010, 94).

The heat in Russia's relationship with the West is obviously back now (since the annexation of Crimea), as is reinforcement of the decline in the myth of Russian invincibility. Russia is not back, given the sustained decline in oil prices and the apparent impact of sanctions. Shevtsova's notion of fake modernisation includes a fake or at least halting effort to modernise its university and technology development system. Promised new investment was curtailed or withdrawn as the amount of money available after endemic graft and payoffs was much reduced in a world of low oil prices. This appears to be in contrast to more sustained higher education modernisation expenditures and efforts in Kazakhstan and Azerbaijan, where important university and technological research investment proceeds, despite less income from oil and gas.

There were various attempts by the US, Germany and France (especially by Sarkozy in 2009) to offer partnership for modernisation, but as Shevtsova argues:

> They were bound to fail. The Kremlin sees modernization as a tool to strengthen the status quo, so it expects the West to infuse Russia with money and technology without any conditions or talk of values. But how could one expect any high-tech modernization program to succeed if the Russian leadership is not ready to allow competition or to guarantee property rights, or if it intends the state to keep a tight grip on "innovations"? . . . [The EU] must try to persuade the Russian leadership that their concept of modernization is a non-starter.
> (Shevtsova 2010, 222)

Arkady Moses (2008) believed that the global financial crisis forced a change in the calculus of relations between Europe and Russia:

> With the crisis, the word "energy" is no longer magical. As demand declined [in Europe], the panic over Europe's dependence on Russian supply began to vanish, to be replaced by an understanding of the mutual dependence of Russia and Europe. . . . Russia's potential return to the international loan market or even a simple listing of Russian corporate debts reminds the West that it has instruments of influence on Russia.

Russia did make some investments aimed directly at enhancing its participation in high technology industries. For example there was the ill-fated plan for

Miracle/Innovation City – Russia's Silicon Valley. In February 2010, Vladislav Surkov announced the plan to build an "innovative city" concentrating 30,000 to 40,000 of the brightest and most talented people from all corners of the world in a new high technology center. According to Surkov, by 2015, this Miracle City would generate up to $7 billion of annual income. Vladimir Ryzhkov countered: "The real attraction of the Kremlin's Innovation City lies not in what it will accomplish for innovation but in how it will line the pockets of Russia's corrupt officials" (Moscow Times 2010).

This kind of effort at industrial diversification and economic liberalisation was promoted by President Medvedev, as he made clear in his article entitled "Go Russia!", which appeared 10 September 2009. Shevtsova quotes Vladimir Putin's response to the failure of Innovation City, as he put himself in charge of the Russian government's high-tech commission: "Two years and billions of dollars have been spent to promote innovation and no results. It's my turn to get things done!" (Shevtsova 2010, 324–325). (See the assessment by Appell [2015] for details on the shortcomings.)

Loren Graham, perhaps the foremost Western authority on Russian and Soviet science and technology successes and failures, puts his finger on the nub of the problem facing Russia and other post-Soviet states that restrict freedom. Graham (2013) reports on the partnership of his university, the Massachusetts Institute of Technology (MIT), with Russia to establish the Skolkovo Institute of Science and Technology in Skolkovo Oblast on the outskirts of Moscow. A project begun in 2011 and estimated to involve payment of at least $300 million to MIT, it was slated to graduate its first students in 2015.

Graham also analyses RUSNANO, a foundation established by the Russian government at President Dmitry Medvedev's urging and patterned somewhat after the US National Nanotechnology Initiative. The aim of RUSNANO was to fund nanotechnology business ventures, and many have been supported since the first round of applications in 2011–12. The level of investment made in these two ventures is impressive, but Graham points out some flaws in both the "SkolTech" and RUSNANO efforts. Quite simply, the technological research promotion and entrepreneurial training are not accompanied by a larger political and economic environment that supports freedom of idea exchange and productive commercial development investment. In his words:

> The stated goal of the Russian government's spending so much money on Skolkovo is to elevate the Russian economy from one dependent largely on extractive industries to one boosted by knowledge, by high technology. . . . [S]o much of the success of commercial technology depends on factors outside the laboratory (politics, social barriers, investment climate, corruption, etc.) a micro-technical center like Skolkovo, however talented its researchers and students, is likely to have limited commercial success in Russian society at large. . . . The greatest flaw of the Skolkovo and Rusnano projects is that both are attempts to improve technology

without basically changing the society in which technology must develop. This is the same defect that has plagued modernization efforts in Russia for three hundred years.

(Graham 2013, 158–159)

This digression into some of the features of the Russian failed (so far) industrial and technological diversification effort is offered here for two reasons. First, it may be seen as a contrast to the more successful efforts under way in the last ten to fifteen years in Turkey, as an economic liberalisation strategy was pursued, along with strategic investments in universities and university–industrial collaboration. TUBITAK, the Scientific and Technological Research Council of Turkey, encourages research partnerships with a wide range of grant programs, including the relatively new Mevlana program to promote faculty and student exchanges and research collaboration with North American and Asian universities. This is an ancillary effort to the European Union's Erasmus Program, of which Turkey has made good use from its Association Agreement with the EU, still working through the "accession" process of its long-time candidacy for full membership. Major Turkish universities like METU, ITU, Gazi University, Istanbul University, Koc University, Sabanci University, Haciteppi University, Seljuk University, Ankara University and Ege University have developed high-quality science and ABET-accredited engineering degree programs and "technoparks" for incubating new companies and promoting industrial partnerships. Turkey's industrial and technological sectors have not fully matured, but in contrast to Russia, Turkey makes and grows things that other countries want to buy – beyond oil, gas and timber (and weapons).

Second, although the government has pursued some elements of economic liberalism, as discussed in previous chapters, Azerbaijan is in some danger of falling into the Russian trap of authoritarianism, crony capitalism, and restrictions on economic choice. One can see broad-based impacts of the fossil fuel wealth in social programs and infrastructure development. The focus on educational reform and modernisation seems sincere and stable, despite the effect of low energy prices. Industrial and technological partnerships with Turkish and Western companies are priority goals for the government, but the regulatory environment and ease of doing business ratings are not yet promising.

Moreover, the Caspian Five agreement of 2014, which seems to draw Azerbaijan back into the Russian orbit more seriously, should be worrisome for Azerbaijanis, Turks and Europeans. Perhaps this is a necessary step to relieve pressure from Russia in the post-Maidan environment, but it reinforces the apparent ambivalence that is increasingly evident in Washington and European capitals, given reluctance to confront Russia directly, and the post-Afghanistan hangover. If Azerbaijan also appears ambivalent to a close relationship with the West, whether it be economically or politically, the options for industrial diversification may be limited. An Association Agreement with the EU, and a Mevlana-like effort to promote university linkages and industrial partnerships beyond

Europe would be valuable steps to take instead. An investment fund readily available to independent entrepreneurs with innovative product development plans would be important. For its part, the EU should find ways of engaging the Eurasian Economic Community so as not to repeat the blunder of forcing potential members or associates to choose between the options in an either/or dynamic (Maresceau 2015).

Theories of small-power foreign policy may have something to contribute to "rational" decision making in this situation (see Zierler 2015). As stressed by many speakers at the Third Global Baku Forum on Building Trust in the Emerging/ New World Order, small states face a serious predicament in the present global "order." They remain highly vulnerable to their dependence on international law while missing global and regional governance with serious enforcement capability. There is a tightrope to walk in decisions about whether to join European and Transatlantic concern about the new aggressive role of Russia in the post-Soviet/ post– Warsaw Pact space. Is it possible to capitalise on this concern in some way without being dragged into conflict or, perhaps more likely, losing autonomy or even independence? Former Georgian president Saakashvili points to Azerbaijan as a bulwark against radicalism in the region. But can it continue to be so under the careful watch of the Putin regime and without more emphasis on the value of freedom for economic development?

Breaking or reducing the imperatives of the network of "patronal politics," so evident in the region according to Henry Hale (2014), may be the key step for broad-based diversification and prosperity. Many in the West assumed that Russians (and Azerbaijanis, Kazakhs, Uzbeks, etc.) would welcome and continue to fight for freedom after the collapse of the Soviet Union. Indeed, some naively believed that Russia would want to join the West as a normal democratic and liberal economic member. There clearly were some missed opportunities and perhaps some humiliating decisions by arrogant and short-sighted Western leaders, but the naiveté that discounted the pull of Russian nationalism (and fear of encirclement) and the tradition of authoritarianism (see, for example, Gel'man [2015] and Hedlund [2005]) must be added to the calculus.

References

Appell, James. 2015. The Short Life and Speedy Death of Russia's Silicon Valley. *Foreign Policy*, 6 May.

Dawisha, Karen. 2014. *Putin's Kleptocracy: Who Owns Russia?* New York: Simon & Schuster.

Gel'man, Vladimir. 2015. *Authoritarian Russia: Analyzing Post-Soviet Regime Changes*. Pittsburgh: University of Pittsburgh Press.

Graham, Loren. 2013. *Lonely Ideas: Can Russia Compete?* Cambridge, MA: MIT Press.

Hale, Henry. 2014. *Patronal Politics: Eurasian Regime Dynamics in Comparative Perspective*. Cambridge: Cambridge University Press.

Hedlund, Stefan. 2005. *Russian Path Dependence: A People with a Troubled History*. London & New York: Routledge.

Hendrick, Joshua D. 2013. *Gulen: The Ambiguous Politics of Market Islam*. New York: New York University Press.

Luong, Pauline Jones and Erika Weinthal. 2010. *Oil Is Not a Curse: Ownership Structure and Institutions in Soviet Successor States*. Cambridge, UK: Cambridge University Press.

Maresceau, Marc. 2015. *Building Trust in the Emerging/New World Order*. Discussion at the Third Global Baku Forum, 28–30 Apr.

Moscow Times. 2010. Build Innovation City and They Won't Come. 25 Feb.

Moses, Arkady. 2008. Byez Samodovol'stva i Strakha. (In Russian.) *Gazeta.ru*, 12 Nov. www.gazeta.ru/comments/2008/11/11_x_2879867.shtml.

Shevtsova, Lillia. 2010. *Lonely Power: Why Russia Has Failed to Become the West and the West Is Weary of Russia*. Washington, DC: Carnegie Endowment for International Peace.

Turam, Berna. 2006. *Between Islam and the State: The Politics of Engagement*. Redwood City, CA: Stanford University Press.

Weiss, Linda. 1998. *The Myth of the Powerless State*. Ithaca, NY: Cornell University Press.

Zierler, Matthew. 2015. *Foreign Policy Goals, Multilateralism, and the Role of International Governmental Organizations for Small States*. Paper presented to the Annual Convention of the International Studies Association, New Orleans, Feb.

Index

Note: Page numbers with *t* indicate tables.

Abbasov, Ali 129, 130, 132
Abu Bakr mosque 134, 141
Administration of Moslems of the Caucasus 130
Ağaoğlu, Ahmet 25, 59
AKP *see* Justice and Development Party, AKP (Adalet ve Kalkınma Partisi)
Ali Bey, Hüseyinzade 59
Alieva, Leila 130
Aliyev, Heydar 12–13, 22, 41, 54, 115, 137
Aliyev, Ilham 150
Aliyev, Rafik 138
Aliyeva, Lala 132
Ankara, Turkey *see* Azerbaijan/Turkey relations; Turkey
Arab Spring 144
Armenia: AKP phenomenon and 33–5, 37–8, 44; closure of Turkish borders to 30–1, 45; Iran's support for, in Nagorno-Karabakh conflict 4–5; liberation movement in 22; Turkey's support for, in Nagorno-Karabakh conflict 6, 7, 10; Turkish-Azerbaijani relations and 27–30, 41–2; Turkish normalisation of bilateral relations with 101–2; Zero Problems policies and 74, 75
ASAM *see* Eurasia Strategic Research Center (ASAM)
Ash, Timothy Garton 56
Asia-centered geopolitical tradition 60–4
Askerov, Elchin 129
Aslanov, Elnur 142
Asya-Avrupa 58
Ataturk, Mustafa Kemal 4; Bolshevik Russia relations of 25–6, 28–9, 45; Çeçen and 62–3; Ilhan and 62; 'modernisation' project 8; political dialogue with Lenin 61; as role model 139; Turkish nationalism of 22, 26, 35
ATIB *see* Azerbaijan-Turkey Business Association (ATIB)
Avrasya Bir Foundation 58
Avrasya Dosyası (TİKA bulletin) 58
Avrasya Etüdleri (TİKA journal) 58
Ayhaber 58
Azerbaijan: AKP governance and 36; bilateral trade volume with Turkey 90*t*; changing conditions for doing business in 115–18; cons of relations with Turkey 46; cultural traditions of 39; *Doing Business* rankings for, 2010-11 105*t*; exports to Turkey, composition of 95*t*; imports of 94*t*; Logistics Performance Index 106, 106*t*; nationalism in 43–4; non-oil exports of 94*t*; PKK as terrorist group and 42; political Islam in 35–6; Popular Front government of 29; postcolonial/post-Soviet identity for 1–2; pros of good relations with Turkey 45–6; religion and (*see* religion, Turkey and Azerbaijan); rule of law prospects in 122–3; state-business relations in, through *hörmet* 119–22, 155 (*see also* Turkish businesspeople in Azerbaijan); struggle for recognition 7–8; trade with Turkey and Russia 91*t*; trading across border rankings, 2011 106*t*; Turkey's non-oil FDI in 98*t*; Turkey's trade share in 93*t*; Turkish businesspeople in (*see* Turkish businesspeople in Azerbaijan); Turkish exports to, composition of 96*t*; Turkish language in 40; World Economic Forum Competitiveness Report 2011 108*t*; as world's top

Index

regulatory reformer 115; XI Red Army invasion of 29, 45
Azerbaijani Business Association 99
Azerbaijani intelligentsia 130
Azerbaijani Islam 127, 132
Azerbaijani Moslems: identity, strengthening of 132; Islamic faith and 127; Sunni-Shia pragmatism and 128–9
Azerbaijani Youth Aid Foundation 135
Azerbaijan-Turkey Business Association (ATIB) 113
Azerbaijan-Turkey economic transactions 88–112, 154–5; bilateral agreement shortcomings hypotheses of 102–3; crowding out hypotheses of 99–100; economic development hypotheses of 103–4, 104*t*; FDI flows and 96–9; inadequate human capital/infrastructure hypotheses of 107–9; institutional development hypotheses of 104–7; introduction to 88–9; political issue dominance hypotheses of 100–2; potential level of 89–92; recommendations for bridging gap in 109–11; statistical data for 111–12; trade flows and 92–6
Azerbaijan/Turkey relations 1–13, 151–4; AKP role in 33–8; determinants of (*see* determinants of Turkish-Azerbaijani relations); energy politics and 10–12; Georgia role in 3–4; interstate interaction and 12–13; Iran and 4–5; Israel and 6–7; overview of 1–3; pros and cons of good 45–8; United States and 7–10; the West and 7–10
Azersun 118

Bahçeli, Devlet 62
Baku, Azerbaijan *see* Azerbaijan; Azerbaijan/Turkey relations
Baku-Ceyhan oil pipeline 22
Baku-Erzurum gas pipeline 22
Baku-Tbilisi-Akhalkalaki-Kars railway project 22, 72, 78–79
Balci, Bayram 131, 143–4
Baran, Zeyno 46
Barmek 118
Big Asia Union 63
bilateral agreement shortcomings hypotheses 102–3
bilateral to trilateral alignment 73–7; Turkey-Azerbaijan relations and 74–6; Turkey-Georgia ties and 76–7
Black Sea Economic Cooperation 58, 60

BOTAS 33
Bozdaglioglu, Yucel 22
'the Bridge of Hope' 2
Brzezinski, Zbigniew 55
"Building Trust in the Emerging/New World Order" (Third Global Baku Forum) 150–1
Bulaç, Ali 65

Caglayan, Zafer 88, 103
Cag Ogretim 135
Caspian Five 153, 161
Caucasus Moslem Board 133, 136, 142
Caucasus Research Resource Centers 76–7
Caucasus Stability and Cooperation Platform (CSCP) 80
Çeçen, Anıl 62–3
Cem, Ismail 63–4
Cold War, Turkey and 2
Cornell, Svante 35, 47, 116
corruption, in Azerbaijan 114–15, 119–22
Council of Europe 122
critical geopolitics: defined 55; objective of 55; Turkish Eurasianism and 55–7
crowding out hypotheses 99–100
CSCP *see* Caucasus Stability and Cooperation Platform (CSCP)

Davutoğlu, Ahmet 64, 65, 66, 73, 152
Dawisha, Karen 158
Debureaucratisation, of four D's reform package 154
Decentralisation, of four D's reform package 154
Demirel, Suleiman 12–13, 35, 41, 58, 64
Democratic Left Party 35
Deoligarchisation, of four D's reform package 154
Deregulation, of four D's reform package 154
de-romanticisation process 38–41; described 23; Turkish-Azerbaijani relations and 38–41
dershane 135
determinants of Turkish-Azerbaijani relations 21–50; AKP factor and 33–8; border closures and 30–1; BTC pipeline and 31–3; de-romanticisation process and 38–41; historical context of 24–6; introduction to 21–4; nationalism and 43–4; negative perceptions due to misperceptions 41–4; Obama factor as 44; pros and cons of relations 45–8;

Index 167

Russo-Turkish relations and 24; Soviet collapse and 27–30; visa-free regime and 43; the West role in 44–5
DHT Metal 118
Diyalog Avrasya 65
Diyanet 134, 139, 141–2
Dugin, Alexander 57

Eastern Europe/Central Asia: Logistics Performance Index 106t; trading across border rankings, 2011 106t
economic development hypotheses 103–4
economic factors, of self-sustaining trilateralism 78–9
economic relations, defined 88–9
efficiency seeking economic motive 96, 97
Elchibey, Ebulfez 4, 22, 27, 28, 29, 38, 46, 115–16
energy politics, Azerbaijan/Turkey relations and 10–12
Erdoğan, Recep Tayyip 41, 44, 66, 73, 76, 142, 145, 153, 156
Erşen, Emre 54–67, 152
Eurasia, Azerbaijan in Turkish views on 54–67, 152; Asia-centered geopolitical tradition and 60–4; critical geopolitics and 55–7; introduction to 54–5; Moslem-world-centered geopolitical tradition and 64–6; Turkic-world-centered geopolitical tradition and 57–60
Eurasian Project 64
Eurasia Strategic Research Center (ASAM) 58–9
Euro-Atlantic integration and trilateralism case study 81–3
European Union 122–3; Erasmus Program 161

FDI flows, Azerbaijan-Turkey 96–9
FDI-specific motives, described 97
formal geopolitics 55, 56
Freedom of Religious Belief amendment 136–7, 139

geopolitical factors, of self-sustaining trilateralism 79–81
geopolitical traditions 56; Asia-centered 60–4; Moslem-world-centered 64–6; in Turkey 56–7; Turkic-world-centered 57–60; in United Kingdom (UK) 56; in United States (US) 56
Georgia: Azerbaijan/Turkey relations and 3–4; bilateral to trilateral alignment and 76–7; bilateral trade volume with Turkey 90t; *Doing Business* rankings for, 2010-11 105t; Logistics Performance Index 106t
Georgian Dream coalition 77, 83, 153–4
Goyushov, Altay 129, 131, 138, 143–4
Graham, Loren 160–1
gravity equation 92–3
Green Cross International 151
Gül, Abdullah 79, 118, 150
Gülen, Fethullah 65, 135, 139, 140, 142, 145, 156
Gülen movement 35, 135–6, 137, 139–40, 142–3

Hajji Allahshukur Pashazade, Sheikh-ül-Islam 133, 142
Hale, Henry 158, 162
Haushofer, Karl 55
Heydar Aliyev Fund 120–1
Hizmet movement 135
hörmet: defined 119; legitimisation of 120–1; state-business relations in Azerbaijan and 119–22, 155; Turkish businesspeople explanation of 120
Huseynzade, Ali Bey 25

Ilhan, Attila 62, 64
Ilhan, Suat 60
inadequate human capital/infrastructure hypotheses 107–9
institutional development hypotheses 104–7
institutional motives, defined 97
International Association of Azerbaijani 113
International Finance Corporation 115
interstate interaction process, Azerbaijan/Turkey relations and 12–13
Iran, Azerbaijan/Turkey relations and 4–5
Isgandarov, Elshad 142
Islam: Europeanisation and 129–30; Soviet anti-religious policy and stagnation of 130–2; Sunni branch of 127; Twelver Shia School of 127
Islamic conservatives, in Turkey 35
Israel, Azerbaijan/Turkey relations and 6–7
Ivanishvili, Bidzina 153

Justice and Development Party, AKP (Adalet ve Kalkınma Partisi) 33–8

Karagül, Ibrahim 65

Index

Kardas, Saban 102
Kars-Akhalkalaki-Tbilisi-Baku railway 78–9
"Kemalist Eurasianism" 62
Khalid, Adeeb 131
Kılınç, Tuncer 61
Koç Holding 118
Kotecha, Hema 136
Külebi, Ali 60
Kurdish Worker's Party (PKK) 42
Kuwaiti Society for the Revival of Islamic Heritage 134

Likholtal, Alexander 151
Logistics Performance Index (LPI) 106
Luong, Pauline Jones 157

Mackinder, Halford J. 55, 59
Mahan, Alfred T. 55
Mammadyarov, Elmar 7
Mansimov, Mubariz 47
Margvelashvili, Giorgi 153
market seeking economic motive 96, 97
Massachusetts Institute of Technology (MIT) 160
Mavi Marmara (aid boat) 6, 7
Mead, Walter Russell 56
Medvedev, Dmitry 160
Miracle/Innovation City 160
Moses, Arkady 159
Moslem Spiritual Boards 131
Moslem-world-centered geopolitical tradition 64–6
Motherland Party 35
muftiat 131
Musavat (Equality) Party 130
Mustafayev, Shahin 88
Mutallibov, Ayaz 115

Nagorno-Karabakh conflict 2, 5, 22, 23, 27, 29–30, 43, 48, 74, 102, 108, 150, 151
Nationalist Movement Party 35
NATO Partnership for Peace 123
nazhionalnost 132
"the neoliberal discourse on corruption" 114
neo-Nurcu movement 135, 139
Nizami Ganjavi International Center 150
Nurcu classicists 134–5, 136
Nursi, Said 134, 135

objective hypotheses 89
obsolescing bargaining theory 49, 152

OECD *see* Organisation for Economic Co-operation and Development (OECD)
"one nation, two states" slogan 54, 60, 74, 137
Organisation for Economic Co-operation and Development (OECD) 103; Anti-Corruption Network for Transition Economies 123; trading across border rankings, 2011 106*t*
Ó Tuathail, Gearóid 55, 56, 57
Özal, Turgut 58
Özcan, Ahmet 65
Özdağ, Muzaffer 59, 60
Özdağ, Ümit 59
Özdalga, Elisabeth 140

Park, Bill 140
Pasha, Nuri 28
perestroika 132–3
Perinçek, Doğu 61, 63
Perinçek, Mehmet 61–2
Petkim 99
PKK *see* Kurdish Worker's Party (PKK)
political issue dominance hypotheses 100–2
Polyakov, Evgeny 102
Popular Front 115, 116
popular geopolitics 55, 56
potential level, of economic relations 89–92; defined 89–90; quantifying 90
practical geopolitics 55, 56

religion, Turkey and Azerbaijan 127–45, 156–7; Azerbaijani religious revival and 132–4; cultural and political compatibility and 137–40; Freedom of Religious Belief amendment and 136–7; Gülen movement and 142–3; Islam awareness and 143–4; opposition fears for 144; overview of 127–8; Russian empire incorporation and 129–30; Soviet anti-religious policy and 130–2; Sunni-Shia pragmatism and 128–9; Turkish Islam in post-Soviet Azerbaijan and 134–6; Turkish Islam representatives in Azerbaijan and 141–2
Republican People's Party 35
resource seeking economic motive 96–7
Reyhan, Hakan 61
Risale-i Nur (Nursi) 134, 135, 142
romantic relations, components of 38
rule of law prospects in Azerbaijan 122–3
RUSNANO 160

Russia Logistics Performance Index 106*t*
Russo-Turkish relations 24
Ryzhkov, Vladimir 160

Saakashvili, Mikheil 153–4
Sabancı Holding 118
Scientific and Technological Research Council of Turkey (TUBITAK) 161
SCWRO *see* State Committee for Work with Religious Organisations (SCWRO)
"secular center-right," in Turkey 35
self-sustaining trilateralism 77–84; challenges to 83–4; economic factors of 78–9; Euro-Atlantic integration case study 81–3; geopolitical factors of 79–81; key element of 153
Shah Deniz II agreement 11–12
Sheikh-ül-Islam 133, 142
Shevtsova, Lillia 158–9
Shia-Sunni ecumenism 129
Skolkovo Institute of Science and Technology 160–1
Smith, Graham 56
SOCAR *see* State Oil Company of the Azerbaijan Republic (SOCAR)
South Caucasus trilateralism 72–85, 153; bilateral to trilateral alignment 73–7; overview of 72–3; self-sustaining 77–84
Soviet collapse, Turkish-Azerbaijani relations and 27–30
Stalinist Muslim Board of Transcaucasus 133
State Committee for Work with Religious Organisations (SCWRO) 136, 142–3, 144
State Oil Company of the Azerbaijan Republic (SOCAR) 98–9, 142
STEAS 99
Stratejik Derinlik Türkiye'nin Uluslararası Konumu (Davutoğlu) 64, 73, 152
subjective hypotheses 89
Sultan-Galiev, Mirsaid 62
Sunni-Shia pragmatism 128–9
Surkov, Vladislav 160

TİKA *see* Turkish Agency for Technical and Economic Cooperation (TİKA)
Tinbergen, Jan 92
Topbaş, Osman Nuri 135
Trabzon 3 72, 84
Trabzon Declaration 4, 72, 80, 153
Trans-Adriatic interconnecting pipeline (TAP) 75

trilateral alignment, bilateral to 73–7; Turkey-Azerbaijan relations and 74–6; Turkey-Georgia ties and 76–7
trilateralism 72, 153; *see also* South Caucasus trilateralism; challenges to 83–4; self-sustaining (*see* self-sustaining trilateralism)
TRT Avaz 65
TRT-Int Avrasya (TV channel) 58
True Path Party 35
TUBITAK *see* Scientific and Technological Research Council of Turkey (TUBITAK)
Tunahan, Suleyman 135
Türkeş, Alparslan 58
Turkestan Confederation 59
Turkey: Azerbaijan energy deals with 31–2; Azerbaijani exports to, composition of 95*t*; bilateral trade volume with Azerbaijan and Georgia 90*t*; border closure cost to 30–2; BTC pipeline and 31–3; cons of good relations with Azerbaijan 48; *Doing Business* rankings for, 2010-11 105*t*; EU membership and 9, 22–3; Europeanisation in 36; exports to Azerbaijan, composition of 96*t*; liberalised ideological shift in 36–7; Logistics Performance Index 106*t*; Ministry of Religious Affairs 134; nationalism in 43–4; non-oil FDI in Azerbaijan 98*t*; political groups in 35; post-Cold War identity for 1–2; pros of good relations with Azerbaijan 46–8; religion and (*see* religion, Turkey and Azerbaijan); Shah Deniz I gas deal and 32–3; share in Azerbaijan's trade 93*t*; struggle for Western recognition 8–9; trade with Azerbaijan and Kazakhstan 92*t*; trading across border rankings, 2011 106*t*; World Economic Forum Competitiveness Report 2011 108*t*
Turkey-Azerbaijan High Level Strategic Cooperation Council 155
Turkey/Azerbaijan relations *see* Azerbaijan/ Turkey relations
Turkicisation (Nationalisation), Islam and 129–30
Turkic-world-centered geopolitical tradition 57–60; geographical definitions of Eurasia in 59; Turkishness and 59
Turkish Agency for Technical and Economic Cooperation (TİKA) 58, 65

Turkish Business Association in Azerbaijan 97
Turkish businesspeople in Azerbaijan 113–23, 155; changing conditions for 115–18; corruption and 114–15; *hörmet* and 119–22; introduction to 113–15; rule of law prospects for 122–3
Turkish Energy Market Regulatory Authority 99
Turkish Eurasianism 55, 57; *see also* Eurasia, Azerbaijan in Turkish views on; critical geopolitics and 55–7
Turkish Industrialists and Businessmen (TUSIAB) 113, 116
Turkish Islamic groups 127, 156; Azerbaijani religious revival and 132–4; cultural and political compatibility of 137–40; in post-Soviet Azerbaijan, key agents of 134–6
Turkish Statistical Institute 90
Türk Yurdu 58
TUSIAB *see* Turkish Industrialists and Businessmen (TUSIAB)

Ukraine International Reform Council, four D's of 154
Ulusal (journal) 61
umma 35

Unified Turkestan 59
United Kingdom (UK), geopolitical traditions in 56
United States (US): Azerbaijan/Turkey relations and 7–10; geopolitical traditions in 56; National Nanotechnology Initiative 160

Vernon, Raymond 49, 152

Weinthal, Erika 157
Weiss, Linda 158
Welfare Party 35
the West: Azerbaijan/Turkey relations and 7–10, 44–5; genocide recognition and 44
"Westernised elite," in Turkey 35
Wiktor-Mach, Dobroslawa 128
World Bank 108, 115

Yarın (journal) 64, 65
Yavuz, M. Hakan 135
Yeni Avrasya 58
Yeniçeri, Özcan 60

Zero Problems with Neighbors policy 73–4
Zeybek, Namık Kemal 59